"Karen Speerstra tackles the ineffable in her wonderful book, weaving her lifetime of experiences and insights together with prehistory, science, art, religion, and much more. She is just the trusted author to share depths and wisdom with skill, erudition, and heart."

—Lillian Habinowski, artist

"This book explores and reports through a very deep, thorough, and thoughtfully documented journey Karen Speerstra's research and interpretation of color and how it impacts our total existence from birth to death and beyond. Color to me is the silent equivalent of music, the mysterious magic that totally surrounds and penetrates our being. Speerstra's book covers so much territory so well that it is something one will want to read again and again and again."

—Karen Petersen, sculptor and painter

"A fearlessly personal account of a lifetime spent in the emotional pull of color.

As a painter, and a teacher, I find this book especially memorable in that it brought to my ears the voices of historically "known" scientists, philosophers, mystics, and artists, all giving their 'firsthand' accounts of personal experiences and thoughts about light and color. Delightful to read as well are the first-person 'voices' of the colors themselves.

This is both a reference book for further investigations into this hugely fascinating subject and a reminder to me, as an artist, to be fully mindful of my love for and daily use of the always mysterious gifts of sunlight and color."

—Bunny Harvey, painter and Director, Studio Art, Wellesley College

"The invitation to let our imaginations blossom with Speerstra's meditative exercises and Julia Blackbourn's luminous watercolors will change the way you see the world. I've read many books on color, but none of them leaps into the ecstatic realm as this one does. Like a prism revealing the rainbow waiting in white light, this magical book opens our eyes to the hidden dimensions of color waiting to amaze us."

—Sharon Bauer, psychotherapist and artist

"I have long felt the power of color in a muted, general sense, but now the doors have been opened—I will not be able to look at flowers, fields, or my own paints without allowing them to touch me on a deeper level."

—Katie Runde, artist

"Karen Speerstra leads the reader on an expansive but playful journey of Planet Earth and beyond through the investigation of color. A full spectrum of color's connection with philosophers, inventors, scientists, artists, healers, writers, and poets becomes food for the soul."

—Sherry Rhynard, stress management and health coach

"*Color: The Language of Light* could also be called *An Ode to Color and Light*. I particularly love how Speerstra weaves her personal stories about relatives and friends who influenced and supported her creativity and spirit throughout her life."

—Anne Gilman, author and artist

"When Speerstra becomes someone else and speaks in narrative, she does some direct channeling. I am still hearing her words in my head. How wonderful!"

—Ellen Allen, color production editor, designer, and artist

"After reading *Color*, I will never look at a sunset the same way again."

—Penny Hauser, author and psychiatric nurse

"Speerstra is able to write about spiritual concepts that we can all understand, digging deep inside us, and pulling out what we felt we knew but couldn't express — certainly not the way she does."

—Debra Marckres, librarian

COLOR

THE LANGUAGE *of* LIGHT

KAREN SPEERSTRA

Published by DIVINE ARTS
DivineArtsMedia.com

An imprint of Michael Wiese Productions
12400 Ventura Blvd. # 1111
Studio City, CA 91604
(818) 379-8799, (818) 986-3408 (Fax)
www.mwp.com

Cover design by Johnny Ink www.johnnyink.com
Copyediting by Gary Sunshine
Book layout by Gina Mansfield Design

Printed by McNaughton & Gunn, Inc., Saline, Michigan
Manufactured in the United States of America

Library of Congress Cataloging-in-Publication Data

Speerstra, Karen.
 Color : the language of light : how color feeds the soul / Karen Speerstra.
    pages cm

 ISBN 978-1-61125-018-3 (pbk.)
 1. Light--Religious aspects. 2. Color--Miscellanea. 3. Colors--Religious aspects. I.
Title.
 BL265.L5S66 2013
 203'.7--dc23
                              2013015289

Printed on Recycled Stock

DEDICATION
AND
ACKNOWLEDGMENTS

Introduction:
to Ellen A., Sharon B., Jan F., Carol F., Annie G., Mary Ann G., Jonna G., Penny H., Betty L., and Judy W., all friends who from the beginning, walked this colorful journey with me.

Chapter 1:
to Nate, whose birth story and subsequent life stories continue to bring humor, light, and color into my life.

Chapter 2:
to Josie, whose rainbow presence brightens the world.

Chapter 3:
to Joel and Laura, artists both, who helped me stumble and catch my breath and were there to inspire (and edit) the work.

Chapter 4:
to Traci, who as a chemist has actually created color and whose clear and grounded insights anchor my perceptions.

Chapter 5:
to John, my loving spiritual mentor and guide.

Meditative Palette:
to Julia, whose creative ventures have brought so much joy into my life.

Index:
to Carol, who is my dear Sophia Sister and a professional indexer.

Thank you, all.

TABLE OF CONTENTS

INTRODUCTION

"Color is the language of light;
it adorns the earth with beauty.
Through color light brings its passion,
kindness and imagination to all things:
pink to granite, green to leaves,
blue to ocean, yellow to dawn."

John O'Donohue, *Beauty*

What did Jesus really mean two thousand years ago when he told a small group of ordinary people sitting around him on a remote Middle Eastern hillside: "You are the light of the world"? What did those fisherfolk know of physics? What do I, for that matter? Or you? Or even physicists, come to think of it, because our scientific understandings of color and light change over time and color theories shift as surely as moonbeams. But if, as this book claims, color is the language of light, and we are light, then you and I — and those scraggly Galileans lounging in the grass as described in the fifth chapter of the book of Matthew — embody all the *color* that fills this world.

Colors tap down deep into the very roots of our archetypes — of who we are — and offer truths that need no persuasion to be real. Colors pull the heart along a rainbow path familiar to anyone who has ever stood in dripping sunshine and looked up.

I walk my Vermont pathways and marvel at tiny neon-orange mushrooms — electric-orange aliens perched on a stretch of moss. I'm in awe of metallic-green wings of insects and the deep pinks leading to black seeds hidden in peony petals. I count the shades of gray in the sky. But what if, in addition to *taking color in*, we also *give color off*? What if we are transformed from color observers to color emitters?

While writing *Sophia: the Feminine Face of God*, I read a great deal about one of the nineteenth-century Russian Sophiologists, Vladimir Sergeevich Solovyov. From his poetry and essays I realize that color and light are integral to the understanding of the Divine Feminine Force that inhabits and colors our lives. This understanding can bridge all sorts of dualisms (men vs. women, liberal vs. conservative, light vs. dark) to create rainbow-circled "wholes." Yet even in unity, each colorful soul maintains its unique distinction. We, too, remain who we are, but by melding of "opposites" into one, we discover that we are so much more than we once thought we were. And, best of all, we're free to color outside the lines! The Bible calls this feminine divine figure Lady Wisdom — "a reflection of eternal light... fairer than the sun."

When she was a little girl, Mary Catherine Bateson, daughter of Margaret Mead and Gregory Bateson, loved to make up stories. One fairy tale she told her mother was about a sad and very dreary kingdom that had no color. Everything was the same. Only the princess could see color and differences but by showing others how to see as she did, she brought new life (and diversity) to the kingdom.

Color sucks our feet up and out from our muddy tracks and places them on sure footing. But this path is like no other. It's like walking on a crusty rainbow or dancing inside a flashing kaleidoscope. We twist the kaleidoscope just a teeny bit—not adding any more colored bits to the mix, but simply shifting it—and a whole new mandala appears. We live in a multi-hued "world soul." A world fully penetrated by Her light rays. She brings new life to our kingdom.

But it's not enough just to *reflect* on Her beauty, Her colors. We actually *reflect them.* How? By loving. Loving others, loving our world, and most importantly, by truly loving ourselves. Even when we feel goofy gray and sad-sack brown. Even when we face that "Dark [colorless] Night of the Soul," as John of the Cross, the sixteenth-century Spanish mystic described it, She sends Her colors into our minds, into our bodies, and most importantly of all, into our soul-spirits.

Contemplating writing a book on color, I closed my eyes and stretched out on the bed one morning in direct eastern sunshine and saw squares of the most intense reds I'd ever seen. They were far from solid, but broken into wavy reflective pieces of the sun. I wasn't experiencing those sharp shards of intense colors that sometimes preview a migraine. Instead, I was wrapped in gentle yet commanding reds. At first it seemed somebody had glued a carefully stitched quilt to my retinas. The color-pieces were constructed in such a way that no bit of it was boringly the exact same color. It was all a shimmering, strong *red* but each textured piece a bit different—some surfaces looked rough, some smooth, some lines were a bit wider than others, some squares had red circles in them and the pieces were not perfectly or geometrically-rigidly formed. I saw brilliant apple reds, crimsons, and clarets, vermillions and maroons. Some pieces seemed to be smaller rectangles than others but together they formed a perfectly woven, shimmering tapestry. It saddened me to realize that if I blinked it would all disappear and I had no way to scan it and print it out. As I was held captive by these vivid and varying red colors, my inner self just said, "Ohhhhh." I didn't want them to go away, but of course they did. I shook my head, got up, crossed the hallway to my office, and scribbled down a draft table of contents for a book on "color."

As soon as I began typing, my confidence was shaken. I wasn't a color expert. What could I possibly add? But the sunshine-retina inner experience of that morning-red called me to want to try to figure out how colors and the many ways we experience them help to form our spiritual selves. Artists and clothing manufacturers, color theorists, interior decorators and landscape architects already know a great deal about color — but do they address *our inner selves*? Chromotherapy tackles color and healing. But how does Sophia experience color? How do I? How do colors feed and shape my soul? That's the question that continued to flicker as the word became pages and the pages became chapters.

When Jesus spoke to his disciples gathered on the hilltop, he said you're not just light. You're also salt. When I think of light and salt, I think of light as coming from the sun and salt coming from the earth. My husband and I recently crowded into an antique lift and decended a shaft deep into the Wieliczka historic salt mine deep in Poland's Carpathian mountains. Salt has been mined here for seven hundred years. Methane gas, fires, water, tunnel collapses — over the years, miners found it very dangerous work. Chapels for miners, marked by religious salt sculptures they have created, dot the passageways through two hundred miles of underground chambers. Breathing in the "gray gold," my lungs were bathed in the mine's refreshing, healing, sweet, salty air. Breathing salt air, as anyone who has spent time near the ocean knows, is a rare and healing gift.

We are surrounded, up and down, with color from light as well as the "salty" earthy colors we get from chemicals, minerals, resins, insects, and plants.

The Buddhist Dogen said, "Handle even a single leaf of green in such a way that it manifests the body of the Buddha." Every leaf! Every color! Together we can learn to read the language of light.

Chapter One

OUT OF THE NIGHT, VISIBLE COLOR

Prelude

Its iridescent wings beat rapidly as if it knew I planned to catch it and keep it in my carefully washed Bonne Maman strawberry jam jar. I balanced the red and white gingham-patterned lid with one hand, planning to quickly screw it on, thus trapping my "beauty." I had never seen such a rainbow-hued wingspan before. Its silver-tipped wings shed tiny metallic diamond-shaped flakes along with sprays of color every time it beat its wings, more frequently as it sensed my intent.

It wasn't a dragonfly. Nor was it a butterfly. Instead, it was a magical cross between the two. It fought for its life, this creature from nowhere I'd ever been, from no textbook I'd ever read. Then suddenly I was struck by a horrifying thought. If I lock it up, I will likely destroy it.

Just then, it escaped. Flying away, it looked back at me with large, black, compassionate eyes as if to say, "Did you think you could capture color in a jar?" And I awoke.

In the Beginning

> *"Darkness, become a light-possessing darkness."*

> A Maori chant

He was born shortly after four on a Sunday morning—matins hour, the darkest time of the night. My doctor plunked all eight-and-a-half pounds of our younger son onto my stomach and I gasped at the heft of this precious being.

He looked up at me and squinted his big blue eyes as if to say, "What's all this light?" I looked back down at him and mumbled, "What's all this gray-greenish-whitish stuff covering your body?" It was the first time I'd ever seen a newborn. I had squeamishly vacated my body during the birth of our first son, but for this one, I was determined to be awake.

I learned later this was normal. *Vernix caseosa* wraps most full-term babies at birth. It means "cheesy" and it helped him to slip out, kept him warm, and may have provided a little antibacterial barrier.

As an embryo he had only experienced a deep blue. "This color is not even and dull, it is full of the radii and patterns of the veins, nerves and tissue density. It is subject also to changes of external light, day and night, and is affected further by electric light and the colors which are worn by the mother during pregnancy."[1]

So our "cheesy" son, Nate, left the soft watery upside-down darkness of my womb in order to explore a new world of creation. He came forth, as all good Scandinavian children do, from "Ginnungagap, The Mighty Yawning Gap" where all life begins. Heaviness hardened but, as the early poets tell us, that "Yawning Void was lighted by sparks and glowing masses."[2]

At some point he must have begun to ask: What is this light? And how did it get here? He studied English in college and no doubt ran across Milton's description of light as "the prime work of God." And Shelley's "the white radiance of eternity."

Light-Birthing Stories

The command of Genesis "Let there be light!" was so strong, according to the Hebrew tradition, that Adam could see from one end of the universe to the other. This primordial light is sometimes called a "Hidden Light." Howard Schwartz, professor of English at the University of Missouri, describes it as coming forth from the place in the universe where the Temple in Jerusalem would one day stand. Some say it came when "God wrapped himself in a prayer

---

[1] Theo Gimbel, *Healing Through Colour* (London: The C.F. Daniel Company, Limited, 1980), 64.

[2] Snorri Sturlson, *The Prose Edda* (The American-Scandinavian Foundation, London: Humphrey Milford Oxford University Press, 1916), 17.

shawl of light." Where did it go? Perhaps it's hidden in the stories of the Torah. Others say it's not hidden at all, but only the righteous can see it.[3]

Our Divine Creator may have said, "Let there be time and space!" "Let there be a universe filled with possibility." "Let there be a womblike environment for all things to grow." *But first, the Creator said, "Let there be light."* Why? Because our Creator wanted to have us help with the creating of something in His/Her image. We come from light and color. And we will return to light and color. Physicists tell us everything, every atom that forms what we see around us, inside us, and within everything on earth, and in fact, in all the planets we can number, once came from the stars. Every breath we take is "star-breath." Kenneth F. Weaver, a science writer who died at 94 in 2010, once put it like this: "It may come as a shock to learn that nearly all the atoms in your body and in the earth were once part of a star that exploded and disintegrated, and that probably those same atoms were once the debris of still an earlier star."[4]

People from around our globe tell various stories of how we were collectively birthed into light on that "first day." The ancient Mayas-Quiché say in their sacred book, the *Popol Vuh*, that "The Heart of Heavens" was the "track of lightning," the "flash that wounds." Australian aborigines explain it like this: "In the Beginning the Earth was an infinite and murky plain, separated from the sky and from the great salt sea and smothered in a shadowy twilight. There were neither Sun nor moon nor Stars... On the morning of the First Day, the Sun felt the urge to be born... The Sun burst through the surface, flooding the land with golden light, warming the hollows under which each Ancestor lay sleeping... "[5]

The Maoris' oral culture from New Zealand tells how Ranginui, the sky father, and Papatuanuku, the earth mother, came together and birthed seventy children. They were so close, however, that their embrace kept the light out so all their kids had to live in a world of darkness. Finally, a long, rhythmic, Maori creation chant tell us, the children managed to separate their parents from their embrace and then light streamed into the world.

---

[3] Howard Schwartz, "On the First Day," *Parabola* Vol. 26, No. 2, May 2001, 16.

[4] Quoted in *The Rainbow Book* edited by F. Lanier Graham (New York: Vintage Books, 1979), 103.

[5] Bruce Chatwin, *The Songlines* (New York, Penguin Books, 1987), 72.

From the conception the increase,
From the increase the thought,
From the thought the remembrance,
From the remembrance the consciousness.
From consciousness the desire...[6]

From nothing our planet received the begetting. It all came, Japanese traditions explain, from a place beyond. "Before the heavens and the earth came into existence, all was a chaos, unimaginably limitless and without definite shape or form. Eon followed eon: then, lo! out of this boundless, shapeless mass something light and transparent rose up and formed the heaven. This was the Plain of High Heaven."[7]

The Kono people of New Guinea tell the story of how the tou-tou bird sang its first notes and that brought light. The Yoruba people of Nigeria sing of Olorun, a great being in the sky who sparked gases into an explosion and from this fireball came earth's light. And the Mossi people of Africa say everything originally came from truth. Interestingly enough, the ancient Greeks also used the same word for "light" as for "truth."

Scientists tell us blue-green algae and bacteria lived on our planet for two billion years — all alone. From these first colors sprouted all life.

Peel Away the Night

> "Seeing into darkness is clarity...
> This is called practicing eternity."
>
> Lao Tzu

When our older son, Joel, was in first grade he announced one day: "You have to peel away the night to find the day."

It's frightening for children — and indeed for most of us — to think of

---

[6] David Adams Leeming, *Creation Myths of the World: an encyclopedia*, Volume 1, Second edition (Santa Barbara, CA: ABC-CLIO, LLC, 2010), 184.
[7] From the Kojiki, the "Record of Ancient Things," Japan's oldest chronicle compiled 500-700 CE by O. No Ysumaro.

not being able to peel away the dark. My colleague-writer at Divine Arts, Kiara Windrider, who speaks knowledgeably about earth cycles and global shifts, talks about the likelihood that we could one day soon face three days of no light, no sun. Darkness.

Don Alejandro, a Mayan Elder, spoke to him of thirteen prophecies, twelve of which have already come to pass. The thirteenth is yet to come: three days of darkness. When I read this, I think, "And three days of no color! How will we survive?" Here are Don Alejandro's own words: "When you find yourself in these three days of darkness, go inside your homes, close the doors and start to celebrate. These are the times you have been waiting for."[8]

When our boys were young, Madeleine L'Engle was a constant nighttime companion. We read together *A Swiftly Tilting Planet*: "Light and darkness dancing together, born together, born of each other, neither preceding, neither following, both fully being in joyful rhythm." L'Engle's story goes on to describe how this dazzling light was swallowed up by a star and the glory of the harmony was broken by "screeching, by hissing, by laughter which held no merriment but was hideous, horrendous cacophony." Who wants that? Is it our job, too, to help bring the light back? Yes! I've come to the conclusion, the most important thing we can do is to make the dark more conscious, as Carl Jung put it. To call things by their right and real names. And to acknowledge the shadows.

All creation comes out of nothing, the theologian Matthew Fox reminds us. "There is a necessary link between darkness, nothingness and creativity. All creation is birthing something where previously there was nothing. Darkness is the origin of everything that is born — stars born in the darkness of space, our ideas and images born in the darkness of the brain, children born from the darkness of their mothers' wombs, movements of liberation born from the darkness of slavery and pain."[9]

For the Dogon people in Africa, night is the beginning. Full of possibility. Night is a combination of white, red, and black and embodies all the primordial

[8] Kiara Windrider, *Year Zero* (Studio City, CA: Divine Arts/Michael Wiese Productions, 2011), 100.

[9] Matthew Fox, *Original Blessing* (Santa Fe. NM: Bear & Company, 1983), 175.

elements and the spirit of divinity. Air is identified with white; earth and water with black; fire with red. These three colors were the ones also used by our earlier cave-painting ancestors in Europe. The early Australian aborigines had only these color names, as well. And they are the three colors most associated with early goddess figures around the globe. In a perverse move, no doubt seeking to establish ancient roots, Hitler chose those very three to color his swastikas.

Winter solstice marks the time when we lie down to sleep each night assured the next day will be a few minutes longer. Around 3500 B.C.E., Celts in Ireland marked this returning light at their "cave of the sun" by constructing an earth chamber we now call New Grange in County Meath, twenty-five miles north of Dublin. It was once covered with thousands of white quartz stones. Even with most of the white stones gone, it's still an impressive World Heritage Site with its intricate carvings and aisles of stone. Our ancient relatives in Ireland were at ease with the darker "underworld." For three mornings in late December the sun streams through a square window and illuminates a triple spiral on the far wall. This experience was once described by a visitor, George Russell: "A light began to glow and pervade the cave, and to obliterate the stone walls and the antique hieroglyphs written thereon, and to melt the earthen floor into itself like a fiery sun suddenly uprisen within the world, and there was everywhere a wandering ecstasy of sound: light and sounds were one; light had a voice, and the music hung glittering in the air..."[10]

Over the years, many mystics have embraced the dark. Juan de Yepes, for one. He lived in Spain in the sixteenth century, the son of poor silk weavers. Now we call him St. John of the Cross. He left home at fourteen to serve the poor and severely ill and eventually became a priest. After meeting Teresa of Avila, he helped found her Carmelite Order. For refusing to return to Medina and choosing instead to remain with Teresa's nuns, he was imprisoned for nine months in a cell six feet by ten feet and beaten three times a week by the monks who imprisoned him. In the dark and cold, he was "visited" by angels. One night he escaped with his poetry under his arm. In *Dark Night of the Soul*, he

---

[10] W. Y. Evas-Wentz, *The Fairy-Faith in Celtic Countries* (Bucks: Colin Smythe, 1977).

describes how the soul must empty itself in order to be filled with God. He called this "soul-purging." We emerge from the Dark and are filled with flaming light and love. He quotes Job who said, "In the night my mouth is pierced with sorrows and they that feed upon me sleep not." John of the Cross struggled in "dark contemplations" with doubts and misgivings, but he repeats again and again the words "on a dark night, kindled in love with yearnings, I went forth..." He described the illuminations we experience on earth as the "lightnings of God... produced by this Divine contemplation in the faculties of the soul."[11] The soul, he said, puts on three colors: the white tunic of faith, a green livery for hope and security, and a splendid over-garment of purple for charity. He died at forty-nine, after writing the words, "In the happy night. In secret, when none saw me, nor I beheld aught, without light or guide, save that which burned in my heart."[12]

People who suffer clinical depression know how light eclipses them and they often see only in shades of gray. Parker Palmer, the prolific writer, teacher, and activist for justice, describes his own descent into Dante's "dark woods" in *Let Your Life Speak: Listening for the Voice of Vocation*. Palmer did not respond to depression with passivity or resignation but rather as an explorer. He felt he was moving into a field where one's deepest self seems alien. This mystery, he said, demands that we reject simplistic answers, both "religious" and "scientific." " The deeper we go into the heart's darkness or its light, the closer we get to the ultimate mystery of God."

Depression is a void, an empty place... "the ultimate state of disconnection" as Palmer put it. It deprives one of that relatedness that is the lifeline of every living being. But from the dark void, as many creation stories describe it, out of the chaos, comes life. All of our colorful creativity, it seems, stems from this dark place.

Light Streams In

People began to seriously study light in the seventeenth and eighteenth

---

[11] St. John of the Cross, *Dark Night of the Soul* (New York: Image Books, Doubleday, 1959), 163.
[12] Ibid., 192.

centuries. You will recognize many names of these "light researchers": Galileo, Kepler, Descartes, Boyle, Leeuwenhoek, Roemer, Huygens, and Newton. Artists and photographers tried to control and capture the movement of light rays and map its colors. Visionaries and poets wrote about light and color. "Seeing the light" became a way of finding truth. The great English painter James Mallord William Turner studied light science and color theory and put it to work. He called his paintings his "color beginnings." In his brilliant chrome yellows, organic oranges, and cloudy whites, he connected color to our deep spiritual feelings. When he died, the last words on his lips were: "The sun is God."

Edwin Babbitt, who wrote a book called *The Principles of Light and Color*, said light reveals the glories of the external world. "It is quite time that the wonderful world of light and color which is invisible to the ordinary eye, and which is capable of being demonstrated by spectrum analysis and otherwise should be made known, especially as so many mysteries of nature and human life are cleared up thereby, and such marvelous powers of vital and mental control are revealed."[13] He believed color provides a storehouse of power capable of revitalizing us, healing and delighting us.

I've noticed when I visit Santa Fe, people talk about the light a lot — probably because there's so much of it there! A photographer I once spoke with worked at night using technologies born of military spying. He explained to me the theory of "visual" versus "haptic" sight. Haptic comes from the Greek word *haptos* meaning "hands on." You "see" with your body. He said, "We're all a bit of both."

Helen Keller must have been more "haptic" than most people. She scolded us sighted ones a bit. "The panorama of color and action which fills the world is taken for granted... it is a great pity that in the world of light, the gift of sight is used only as a mere convenience." Keep your face to the sunshine, she advised, and then "joy in all things shall be reflected."[14]

The Gospel writer Matthew tells us, "The eye is the lamp of the body. So, if your eye is healthy, your whole body will be full of light, but if your eye is

---

[13] Edwin D. Babbitt, *The Principles of Light and Color* (Babbitt and Co., 1878, University Books, edited and annotated by Faber Birren, 1967), Preface, xviii.

[14] Helen Keller, *Don't Miss the Miracle*, a poem written by Keller from her essay, "If I Had Three Days to See," (*Atlantic Monthly*, January, 1933.)

unhealthy, your whole body will be full of darkness. If then the light in you is darkness, how great is the darkness!"[15]

In our Episcopalian *Book of Common Prayer*, we have a hymn called *Phos hilaron* or "O Gracious Light," which is based on early Jewish prayers.

> O gracious Light,
> pure brightness of the everliving Father in heaven,
> O Jesus Christ, holy and blessed!
> Now as we come to the setting of the sun,
> and our eyes behold the vesper light,
> we sing your praises, O God: Father, Son and Holy Spirit.
> You are worthy at all times to be praised by happy voices,
> O Son of God, O Giver of Life,
> and to be glorified through all the worlds.[16]

Glorified through all the worlds! Not just this one, but *all the light worlds. All the color worlds.*

Sun Mystery schools existed throughout medieval Europe. Christ was called *Sol Invictus*. And his mother, Mary, was called "starlight": *Stella Maris*. Ancient mysteries tell us that beyond our sun lies another sun. A spiritual sun. People have been known to meditate on the sun until they see the "sun at midnight" or the "sun beyond the sun." Even if we don't mediate like this, we're apt to notice the sun and its magnificent colors at two times during the day: dawn and sunset. We have learned that looking directly into the sun can harm our eyes. However, sun-gazing has been a part of most ancient mysteries and spiritual practices. Even St. Patrick said he'd been saved from Satan by *Helios*. The Sun. The Devil fell upon him "like a rock," he wrote in his *Confession*. He couldn't move. Then, with all his might, he called on the Sun and he was freed from his misery. If you visit the Vatican you can see a mosaic in the chapel cave of St. Columbanus, of monks praying to the sun.

For about six hundred years Christian monks lived on Skellig Michael,

---

[15] Matthew 6:22-23.

[16] *The Book of Common Prayer...according to the use of The Episcopal Church* (Kingsport, TN: Kingsport Press, 1977), 112.

the rock pinnacle that sticks up out of the Atlantic, eight miles off Ireland's Kerry Coast. They braved Viking raids and harsh conditions, collecting dew and rainwater to drink. A half-dozen of their beehive huts are still there. St. Fionan supposedly founded it in the 500s but legends about this mysterious rock indicate it was a sacred spot long before the Christians came. Recognizing the spiritual importance of the sun, it's very likely these monks began the tradition of carving Irish crosses with circles on top, honoring the sun. Monks copied old precious manuscripts that would have been lost to Europe's Dark Ages had not these scribal scholars known that "the White Gospel page turned darkness to light."[17]

Further remnants of how the early Irish valued the sun can be seen in the sixty-five tall round towers still scattered around Ireland, many with conical roofs intact. Some experts believe they may have functioned like antenna to collect subtle magnetic sun radiation. Rubble and dirt fill the bases leading to speculation that the towers were "tuned" like huge organ pipes. The monks who didn't build them, but set up residence near them, benefited from whatever sun vibrations they collected, as did the plants that flourished around them.[18]

The early Egyptians revered sunlight by many names: *Kheperi*, the infant sun of the morning; *Re*, the powerful sun at noon; and *Atum*, the enfeebled but creative sun of the evening. They called it The Great Disk. The Flaming One. Normandi Ellis points out that "Light is the source of life, an electrical impulse and binding force that sizzles and snaps through nature and the human body, through every animal, every chromosome and atom... We are tongues of flame leaping from the One Fire. We are gods in the body of God."[19]

And the Persians, a thousand years earlier than Abraham, learned about light and darkness from their prophet Zarathustra or Zoroaster. Ahura Mazda was the divinity associated with light. Evil, they believed, sprang from Angra Mainyu, who was associated with darkness. On a cosmic plane armies of light warred against armies of darkness. A series of messianic figures would come, he said, to bring people back to oneness. This early Iranian prophet who wore

---

[17] Thomas Cahill, *How the Irish Saved Civilization* (New York: Doubleday, 1995).

[18] Philip Callahan, *Ancient Mysteries, Modern Visions: The Magnetic Life of Agriculture* (Austin, TX: Acres U.S.A., 2001).

[19] Normandi Ellis, *Dreams of Isis* (Wheaton, IL: The Theosophical Publishing House, 1995), 21.

white until he died in about 551 B.C.E. called God "Self-Luminous" and "The King of Light."

We're All Divine Sparks

A few years back, I wrote a book called *Divine Sparks: Collected Wisdom of the Heart*. The title comes from Hildegard of Bingen's belief that we are all sparks of the Divine flame. It's a collection of thousands of quotations about various aspects of our spiritual lives. Inside my copy I have taped the E. E. Cummings poem thanking God for "this most amazing day: for the leaping greenly spirit of trees and a blue true dream of sky… " and whenever I opened that book, and read his poem, I thought: "Someday I'm going to write a book about color." I knew I couldn't ever be as eloquent as Cummings' words, but something inside me kept nagging: "*Write about color!*" So, now, each early morning as I write, I watch my Vermont dawn drizzle grays and pinks across my southern office window and I place words, like shards in a kaleidoscope, in patterned flashes across my computer screen and remember we're all sparks. We're all elusive color shards.

Jane Roberts described the modulating panorama of light this way: "Light has valleys and peaks, but the colors and intensities are never the same. Sometimes light seems to cling to an object, hugging it. Sometimes it scurries around the edges of an object like a tiny insect, glowing, moving so swiftly that you can't really follow it with your eyes."[20]

Like Benjamin Franklin, "I am much in the Dark about Light."[21] And I'm not alone. For centuries, Hebrew scholars have sifted through the Bible for clues to figure out how the author of Genesis could say in those opening verses that there was darkness and then God said, "Let there be light and there was light." But this was before verse 14–16 when the sun and moon and stars were created. So where did that first light come from? Where is it today? Some believe this primordial light was hidden in a stone passed down from Adam,

---

[20] Jane Roberts, *The World View of Paul Cézannne* (New York: Prentice-Hall, 1977), 215.

[21] Benjamin Franklin, (from a letter Franklin sent to Cadwallader Colden April 23, 1752. *The Papers of Benjamin Franklin* Vol. 4, New Haven, 1961), 299.

through succeeding generations. Others think it's hidden in the Torah. It's been with us all the time, many say, just waiting to be seen.

Quaker theology teaches that each of us has a palpable inner light. Worshipers silently wait until "they can hear that place where the light of God shows itself in full agreement."[22] Most mystical traditions refer to the Divine One as the light-consciousness whose absolute nature is joy, peace, and boundless creativity. Light-consciousness, according to all sacred scriptures, loves its creation. The mystical scholar and teacher Andrew Harvey writes about what he's learned from his mentor, Father Bede Griffiths. "Every pebble and fern and fish is a unique creation of the Divine Light, infinitely loved and cherished, and entirely inhabited by the Light."[23]

When Hildegard of Bingen, the twelfth-century Benedictine nun who taught me about "divine sparks," was three years old, a dazzling light appeared in her room and made her shudder. It took years for her to build up enough courage to realize the divine nature of that light and finally write about her experiences. As an adult, she became brave enough to call herself "*a small sound of the trumpet from the Living Light*." When she was forty-two, she wrote: "Heaven was opened and a fiery light of exceeding brilliance came and permeated my whole brain and inflamed my whole heart and my whole breast, not like a burning but like a warming flame, as sun warms anything its rays touch."[24]

It took Hildegard ten years to write her first book, *Scivias*, which is a contraction of the Latin phrase, *Sci vias Domini* or "Know the Ways of the Lord." In it, she describes one of her many visions. She saw a being of light seated on a throne "of wondrous glory, of such brilliance that I could in no way apprehend him clearly... and from that light seated on the throne there extended a great circle of color like the dawn."[25]

Shortly before she died on a bright September afternoon in 1179, two streams of light appeared in the sky and swept across the small bedroom where her frail body lay. Her "trumpet" was silenced but her overtones keep ringing. The light she described still illumines the paths of many who follow her wisdom.

---

[22] Wayne Muller, *How, Then, Shall We Live?* (New York: Bantam Books, 1996), 56.

[23] Andrew Harvey, *The Hope* (Carlsbad, California: Hay House, Inc., 2009), 39.

[24] Hildegard of Bingen, *Scrivas* (New York: Paulist Press, 1990), Preface.

[25] Ibid., 3, 1.

The Daoist sage Lao Zi said, "Use light to develop insight." Ah-ha! Light *enlightens*. When we say "I want to be enlightened," what do we mean? Lit up like a Christmas tree? Washed in Divine Light? Have our inner darkness burned away?

Helen Greaves was a medium who communicated with her dear friend Frances Banks after Frances died.[26] Sister Frances Mary had lived in the Community of the Resurrection in Grahamstown, South Africa. "What's it like where you are now?" she asked after Frances died and Frances replied: "What is left is essentially Light, is Reality, is permanent and is true. I call this my new Body of Light and that, indeed, is what it truly is. A body of Light, not dense and material and dull and heavy as the physical body, not insubstantial, shadowy and unreal as the astral body in which I have been sheltering, but brilliant, encelled [don't you love that word? *Encelled*.] with Light, ethereal in that there is no weight, no dragging down into matter but is enmeshed with color and beauty into form and substance... I still have a mind, I still have a body, but both are inevitably changing and because of that I feel as if I am emerging, like a grub from a chrysalis to a butterfly. Gradually I can function more readily and for deeper periods in my Body of Light... I feel as though I am starting on a Path of Light which leads upwards and onwards into Realms of unimaginable beauty and wonder and of which I have, as yet, but the faintest glimmer of comprehension."

"The Soul," she said, "is Light infused... or infused Light. The shutting away of the Soul is darkness. As the sun is the carrier of light-beams to the earth, so is the Son the Second Manifestation of the Divine Energy of Creative Mind, the transmitter of light-beams to the Soul."[27] This Light Frances talks about, through her friend Helen, penetrates us and becomes Essence within us. It is all color, all harmony, all Light in One. We carry this Light within us. We "wear" this energy moving through space.

An ancient Indian text states: "There is a Light that shines beyond all things on earth. Beyond us all, beyond the heavens, Beyond the highest, the very highest heavens. This is the Light that shines in our hearts."[28]

---

[26] Helen Greaves, *Testimony of Light* (London: Neville Spearman, Ltd, 1977), 124, 125.

[27] Ibid., 83.

[28] *Chandogya Upanishad*, 3.13.7

As our consciousness expands, it seems, we let in more light. The Irish poet John O'Donohue said light unfolds its "scriptures" of color. Light is the "greatest unnoticed force of transfiguration in the world: it literally alters everything it touches and through color dresses nature to delight, befriend, inspire and shelter us... Color is the visual Eucharist of things. In a world without color it would be impossible to imagine beauty; for color and beauty are sisters."[29]

Light blends into each object so completely that as Henry David Thoreau wrote in one of his journals, "we can hardly tell at last what in the dance is leaf and what is light."

C. S. Lewis, as quoted in *The Inklings*, said light is refracted through us and then we, in turn, splinter it from "a single White to many hues, and [it is] endlessly combined in living shapes that move from mind to mind." We're color-generators. Like multistriped whirligigs, we spin light and color to all we meet.

I've read that there is a bit of graffiti inscribed on a Cologne cellar wall where some Jews hid during the Nazi occupation: "I believe in the sun even when it is not shining. I believe in love even when not feeling it. I believe in God even when He is silent."

We live in a graffitied universe; there are "light" messages everywhere. But if we look at this light will we get cataracts on our eyes? Will our skin be so reflective and dazzling from God's radiance, that we'd have to walk around with a veil over our face as Moses did when he came back down from Mount Sinai, just to keep people from freaking out?

What if one day, like Moses, we all actually become *lighter* — and even more colorful? And I don't mean by losing weight by drinking fewer sugary drinks. Or by raising our vibrations and becoming less dense by eating no meat, although that might be a factor. What if we actually become *more light-like*? What if we could even learn to communicate with light? Heal with light? Power all our transportation and our homes with solar? We might rediscover what our ancient ancestors knew about light and color.

---

[29] John O'Donohue, *Beauty, The Invisible Miracle* (New York: Harper Collins, 2004), 82.

A Universe of Light

For several hundred years, we thought light was a wave, but in 1905, Albert Einstein found a little photon — a tiny bundle of light energy that's always in motion. Like billiard balls. But then the physicist Niels Bohr said light is actually like "billiard balls" and "ocean waves" at the same time. It's not *either/or*, but *both/and*. Like a Zen koan. But we experience just one at a time... and we're never sure which it will be. John Wheeler, one of Bohr's students, proposed that in the same way light can be a wave or a particle, our inner realms of consciousness — our minds — are connected to the outer world, the universe.

I look up at the stars and think: that light is so old! It takes years to reach us. And its speed never varies. Einstein went so far as to say we are separated from light by 299, 792,458 meters per second.[30]

Edwin Hubble grew up in rural Missouri in the late 1800s, an avid reader of Jules Verne. He loved watching the stars, too, and eventually he discovered how to measure their brightness. He decided the Milky Way is just one galaxy in a firmament of galaxies and calculated it is 100,000 light years across. He said Andromeda is a million light years away. He helped us understand how it takes sunlight eight minutes to actually reach us. And in 1927 color helped him learn more about our expanding universe. Objects speeding away from us appear redder. He called it the "red shift."

Our universe, physicists tell us, was born 13.7 billion years ago. Stored sunlight here on earth keeps us alive. Every year the sun creates blossoms but the seeds for those blossoms contain last year's sun-forces. Everything builds from what has gone before. In fact, until we find alternatives to fossil fuels, we seem to have no choice other than to keep burning up the ancient sunshine folded into our earth.

Most of us could dredge up what we learned in freshman science and repeat by rote that the sun is a giant natural thermonuclear reactor that converts hydrogen to helium and gives off heat. Every now and then it flares.

But I've come to believe that our sun-star is so much more. It is our very

---

[30] Arthur Zajonc, *Catching the Light: The Entwined Story of Light and Mind* (New York: Bantam Books, 1993), 269.

life. It is liquid gold, perfumed ether. And, in a very mysterious way, we are "like" the sun. Goethe argued that if the eye were not sunlike itself, how could we see the sun? Planets, as they orbit their sun-stars, tug at the star, causing it to wobble. Earth pulls at the sun and the sun slightly wobbles. The more massive the planet and the closer it moves to its sun, the more the star wobbles. Scientists search for these wobbly stars and are discovering more and more solar-planet systems at the rate of about one every two weeks. That's a great deal of light around us!

Sometimes, when I sit on our deck, I think "sun and star" thoughts. Rudolph Steiner said sun forces stream down on us in a wave of intellectual life in service to the Spirit. Christ was a "Sun Being." He came to earth in the body of Jesus and has been connecting us to this Cosmic Intelligence ever since that incredible Golgotha event when, as a man, he died. And then he came back, but in a changed body — one that could walk through walls and teleport. He showed his disciples, and by extension, us, that we too are radiant. We each hold his Divine Christ-Spark within us now.

Steiner spoke of how the sun and the moon's forces can be stored in the earth and then released. In fact, the shining light we generate on earth radiates out into the universe. Our radiance, he said, goes out a ways and then is reflected back to us. The fiery ball we see as the sun is, as initiates have suspected for centuries, actually a reflection of *our* energy.

In *Solar*, Ian McEwan describes sunlight as falling "on us in a constant stream, a sweet rain of sun. A single photon striking a semiconductor releases an electron and so electricity is born, as simple as that, right out of sunbeams... Less than an hour's worth of all the sunlight falling on the earth would satisfy the whole world's needs for a year. A fraction of our hot deserts could power our civilization. No one can own sunlight and no one can prioritize or nationalize it. Soon everyone will harvest it, from rooftops, ship's sails, from kids' backpacks... some of the poorest countries in the world are solar-rich. We could help them by buying their megawatts."[31] What a wonderful alternate vision of the future.

---

[31] Ian McEwan, *Solar* (New York: Random House, 2010), 154.

Edward Tryon of Hunter College said back in 1973, the universe is "something which happens from time to time." But does it "just happen"? David Hume, eighteenth-century Scottish philosopher, said, "God so loved the earth that He put the earth just right from the sun." It's true. The planet Venus, for instance, is far too close. If we lived there, we'd be burned to a crisp. And we're suspended exactly "right" in the Milky Way about two-thirds from the center. Any closer and the radiation would be too intense. It sounds like the "Goldilocks Theory" — this porridge is too hot, this is too cold, but this is just right! None of this is pure happenstance. I like the analogy Hugh Ross, an astronomer, posed. If this universe were purely accidental, he said, it would be like a Boeing 747 aircraft being completely assembled as a result of a tornado striking a junkyard. No, there was and is a plan. And we're right in the middle of it.

The physicist Freeman Dyson said, "It's as if the universe knew we were coming."[32] It makes us wonder if new colors, then, also may "just happen" in this vastness of life. Or are they being planned in a universe hovering directly over our own?

All I really know about black holes is that matter somehow spills into them and they are enormously heavy. John Wheeler of Princeton coined the phrase back in 1967. But what I've recently learned is that inside every collapsed black hole lies the seed to a new expanding universe. Astronomers tell us that 73% of all matter and energy is "dark energy" or Lambda. Gravity was the first to spin off and hop across the universe. In a black hole, matter is torn down to its fundamental state — which, it turns out, is *light*. David Ian Cowan in *Navigating the Collapse of Time* says that right at the edge of the hole is an area called an "event horizon." People have described this as "the point of no return." Gravitational pull causes most of the light to disappear into the hole, but some doesn't. It clings to that event horizon and creates a photon band that radiates out into the rest of the galaxy and this is where the "events" part no doubt comes in. In this galactic light of very high frequency — in the gamma range and beyond — higher octaves of creative light go on to... well, no one

---

[32] Michio Kaku, *Parallel Worlds: A Journey through Creation, Higher Dimensions and the Future of the Cosmos*, (New York: Doubleday, 2005), 248.

knows. But I'm guessing to create new universes as soon as a "Creative Word" is spoken. Something like "Let there be photon light!" All this is fairly new news. We've thought our planet has been feeling the influence of this photon band for about five hundred years. But no one knew this metaphysical, spiritual band of light actually existed until the 1960s. We live in a universe of expanding event horizons.

Christian Doppler experimented with the colors red and blue and applied them to the stars. Higher frequency light is bluer and is approaching the observer; redder stars, of lower frequency, are receding. Color allows astronomers to track our expanding heavens.

This universal light we enjoy comes down and lives in nature. I can think of no better description of how this happens than in Annie Dillard's own "pilgrim" words: "Then one day I was walking along Tinker Creek thinking of nothing at all and I saw the tree with the lights in it. I saw a backyard cedar where the mourning doves roost charged and transfigured, each cell buzzing with flame. I stood on the grass with the lights in it, grass that was wholly fire, utterly focused and utterly dreamed. It was less like seeing than like being for the first time seen, knocked breathless by a powerful glance. The flood of fire abated, but I'm still spending the power..."[33]

To better understand this phenomenon I turn to Teilhard de Chardin's prayerful words: "Far from light emerging gradually out of the womb of our darkness, is the Light, existing before all else was made which, patiently, surely, eliminates our darkness. As for us creatures, of ourselves we are but emptiness and obscurity. But you, my God, are the inmost depths, the stability of that eternal milieu. Without duration or space, in which our cosmos emerges gradually into being and grows gradually to its final completeness, as it loses those boundaries which to our eyes seem so immense. Everything is being; everywhere there is being and nothing but being... Radiant Word..."[34]

It seems creation is back-going as well as on-going. Once we achieve this "light-dom" we will go on as Light-Beings to do further work in some universe

[33] Annie Dillard, *Pilgrim at Tinker Creek* (New York: Bantam Books, 1975), 35.
[34] Pierre Teilhard de Chardin, *Hymn of the Universe* (New York: Harper and Row, 1972), 14-15.

we can only dream of right now. But the more we understand about light and color right now, in this lifetime, the more prepared we will be for that future way of being.

One day, we will see beyond all this into colors more magnificent than we can now even imagine. But until then, we can simply stand in them, absorb them, reflect them as best we are able, and live each day in complete awe of their majesty. And we can thank the dedicated people attributed here, for spending many waking hours pursuing their theories, measurements, and definitions. They've helped us to better understand light as well as the many colorful hues and values, regardless of how we perceive them. What we call colors, how we see them, use them, and reflect on them will follow in subsequent chapters.

Colorful Voices

When I began writing this book, I realized my own feeble voice could never adequately portray the color-wisdom others have spent their entire lives researching and describing. So I decided to bring a few additional voices into our color dialogue and allow them to "speak" to various chapter topics as they wished. I've taken great liberties here, as there is nothing that exists exactly like this in their own real words. Instead, I looked at various things they had written or said and pretended they were speaking directly to us. Please forgive me if it's not exactly the same way you might hear these folks speak. It's what I "heard." Each "Colorful Voice" begins with a short biography so you can more easily position them in time and place.

. . . . .

JOHANNES ITTEN (1888–1967)

Itten was a Swiss expressionist painter, researcher, and color theorist who taught elementary school prior to 1916 before he was invited by Walter Gropius to teach a foundation course in craft through the study of color and form. At the Weimar Bauhaus Academy, he placed emphasis on spiritual openness and peace of mind, using gymnastics and meditation in his courses. He is said to be one of the first people to define and identify strategies for successful color combinations. Josef Albers was one of his students. Gropius' direction for the school differed from Itten's so Itten resigned in 1923 and opened a small art and architecture school in Berlin. The Nazis closed it down in 1933. All of Itten's work explores the use and composition of color.

Color is life. A world without color appears to us as dead. Colors are forces, primordial ideas, the children of light. They seem to me to be radiant energies that can affect me positively or negatively whether I think about them or not. But if I'm not devoted to learning everything I can know about them, I won't be able to unveil their deeper mysteries. If I don't truly love them, they'll hide.

When I think of color, the word that comes to mind is "quality." Ever since I wrote *The Art of Color* in 1961 (and I understand students still find it useful — I am humbled) I've used four ways to investigate the quality of colors: hue, value, intensity, and temperature. Even when I know the "hue" or the name of a color — like red — that doesn't tell me what kind of red. Does it smolder like an ember or blaze like the setting sun? Or look like an apple? So I add "value." How does that red relate to black? To white? Or is it a middle value — somewhere in between? Then I look at "intensity." How pure is that red? How saturated? And finally, there is "temperature." I respond psychologically. Red is "hot." Yellows through red-violets are warm. Yellow-green through green, blue, and violet are cool. Paintings with warmer colors "feel differently" than paintings where the cooler colors dominate.

I had my students collect newspapers, wire mesh, cardboard, wood, feathers, moss — whatever. And they created such colorful art.

Gropius thought I was too eccentric. I suppose my leaving the Bauhaus was mutual. I felt that he seemed more interested in the business of art and couldn't see the validity of how true creativity stems from self-knowledge and wholeness, regardless of what compartmentalized technology and industry thinks. I left, clinging to my convictions. Many of the ways I look at things go way back as far as the Zoroastrians. I smile remembering how I'd shave my head and wear robes. I was a vegetarian all my life. More than anything, I wanted my students to understand that art and color and spiritual growth were all of a part, so I was happy when they caught on to breathing and meditation exercises. And before they could draw circles, I had them move their arms in wide circular motions. They needed to experience what they were to paint. When we analyzed powerful emotional paintings, such as Grünewald's *Crucifixion*, I encouraged them to "become" Mary Magdalene. Many cried. And that was fine! Colors are emotions.

I was very fortunate to associate with great artists and architects teaching at the Bauhaus school. I spent a lot of time trying to come up with a grammar of color. Klee and Kandinsky were of great help in that regard, although Kandinsky saw no need for a theory of colors at all. He said all he wanted to do was render light simply as unfolding energy.

I'd often ask my students: "What happens when one color collides with another?" Some colors look cool and sophisticated with they're alone, but when they're combined... is the clash intentional? Maybe harmony isn't what we once thought. Maybe it's really more about equilibrium. I eventually came to understand, myself, that any color combination that doesn't result in a neutral gray when combined, is disharmonious. Just as all colors appear within black, all colors warm to gray, and create a oneness, a lifelike harmony, within it.

I felt I was a successful teacher when my students began to understand that color is life.

· · · · ·

JOSEF ALBERS (1888-1976)

One of the most influential artist-educators of the twentieth century, Albers studied under Itten and taught handicrafts in the Weimar Bauhaus in Germany during the 1920s, founded by Walter Gropius. In 1933 he and his wife, Annie, a textile artist, came to the United States. He taught at Black Mountain College for sixteen years before joining the Yale University faculty as chairman of the Department of Design. In 1971 Albers was the first living artist ever to be given a solo retrospective at the Metropolitan Museum of Art in New York.

Colors are like actors on a stage. They have faces. They breathe together. They interact. When I place gloomy raw sienna next to another color, it can turn to gold. A weak color is made rich and beautiful by working alongside its neighbor.

I have eighty different kinds of yellow and forty grays and I nest squares of pure unmixed color next to others and I sit back to watch how they behave.

When I began my endless "Homage to the Square" — when was it? 1950? — I was using optical illusions and free-floating squares to talk about relationship. Old Wilhelm von Bezold taught me a lot. I remember he said, "Colors hold moral correlations." It sounds like he got that from Goethe. Red, yellow, and blue are cheerful; black, green, and white, more serious.

My students have always been wonderful people who didn't need "right" answers as much as the "right" questions. It was my old friend Kandinsky who used to say, "It's never about the *what* but always about the *how*." Teaching is never a matter of method, but always of the heart. So we collect paint chips and colored paper or leaves and "paint" with them. If we're lucky, we can see the "how."

I'm amused by people who want to put my work into a neat little box. They use words like *abstract expressionism. Geometric abstraction. The constructivist movement*. Why do they do that? There really are no divisions to art. Fine arts. Functional arts. Crafts. It's all one. It's like music. It's the harmony that's important, not the titles. And like music, it's not the individual tones that make it — it's how they're put together. Individual letters don't make poetry, after all.

I remember some of John Ruskin's words that hold a special place in my heart. "Hundreds of people can talk, for one who can think. But thousands of people can think for one who can see."

Ah, yes. And *seeing* with emotional freedom. That is what every artist craves. Indeed, every person! I know that's what I've been looking for my whole life.

· · · · ·

FABER BIRREN (1900–1988)

Faber Birren graduated from the Chicago Art Academy and spent much of his career in American industry as a color researcher and consultant. He devoted thirty years of his life to researching and creating color standards linked to our perception of and response to color. Besides numerous articles, he authored twenty-five books and deserves the title of foremost color authority of our time. The Faber Birren Collection of Books on Color was his gift to Yale University and is considered the foremost collection of works on color.

How can I talk about color? Even my favorite — maroon. Especially when I think, like the old Zoroastrians, that light comes from a great god — more spiritual than physical. It's almost too big to even discuss.

Nevertheless, I have. And I usually have to begin with Aristotle and sift out from his hundreds of books what he said in *De Coloribus*. He thought all colors came from black and white. And they were connected with air and fire. When black hits sunlight or firelight, it always turns crimson, he thought. But a vivid bright violet is obtained from a blend of feeble sunlight with a thin dusky white. He called color a drug, and when he looked into the sun, he saw a flight of colors. I try it, without blinding myself. I close my eyes. After a bit, I see an afterimage of crimson, purple, then black and then... nothing. Just like Aristotle. I've read that when Goethe tried it, he saw an afterimage of yellow, then purple, then blue.

I learned a lot from Chevreul, the famous French chemist. He continued his work until he was well over a hundred, working primarily with tapestries and carpets. He named colors primaries, secondaries, and intermediate hues — we still use those words. He gave me the idea that complements enhance and offer each other more brilliance than they'd have alone. I suppose it's rather like people.

I take pleasure in thinking back and remembering how I've helped people work with less fatigue in more enjoyable colors in their workplaces. Color can even reduce accidents. The military still uses my color codes.

I came up with a triangle that anybody can draw. It helps me understand all aspects of color in a simple scheme. In the middle of the triangle I write "Tone." On the three triangle points I add the words: "Color," "White," and "Black." Between "Color" and "White" I add "Tint." Between "White" and "Black" I put "Gray." And between "Black" and "Color" I write "Shade." There it is: all colors in a triangular nutshell.

People used to gaze at a rainbow, convinced it held the secrets of the universe in its colors. Now we use a spectroscope. Science has taken the universe down to the most infinitesimal details. But the exact nature of light and color is still an enigma. I continue to live with its mystery.

Chapter Two

BENDING THE RAINBOW

Prelude

Albert Einstein had just flunked math and his parents were trying to talk him into becoming a plumber. One night, he had a dream.

I was sledding down a snow-packed hill with some friends. They slid down, climbed back to the top, and slid down again many times. After many trips, one slide down was different. My sled began to go faster and faster. It sped down the hill so fast that light from ahead spread into rainbow colors. I knew I was going almost as fast as light itself.

In a later interview with Edwin Newman, Einstein said, "My entire scientific career has been a meditation on that dream."

> *"Even the rainbow has a body*
> *made of the drizzling rain,*
> *and is an architecture of glistening atoms*
> *built up, built up*
> *yet you can't lay your hand on it*
> *nay, nor even your mind."*

D. H. Lawrence, "The Rainbow"

The *Arc-en-ciel*

The first movie I ever saw was *The Wizard of Oz*. Color flooded my young consciousness when my parents and I entered that magical land of Oz, but the "real" Kansas at the beginning and at the end when Dorothy wakes up is all in black and white. That seemed jarring to my four-year-old sensibilities. Didn't "real" mean "color?" Oz was obviously more real than Kansas. For months afterwards, I dreamed of yellow brick roads, emerald cities, blue birds and red slippers. Not to mention the horse of a different color. To this day, every time I see halos of color unfold in the rain, I look around for Toto, leprechauns, and pots of gold because I know I'm in magic territory.

In Sunday school, I heard about Noah and his amazing boat large enough to save not only his family but pairs of all those animals. And there they were, all cooped up in a bobbing, smelly wooden barn for a hundred and fifty days. To add to their misery, they had to spend another forty days teetering on some cliff on Mount Ararat while they made sure the land was dry enough to disembark. Finally a voice said, "I have set my bow in the clouds, and it shall be a sign of the covenant between me and the earth."[1] When a bow is carried with its end pointing downward, it indicates peace. Surely to a waterlogged, ark-sogged Noah, the upside-down bow was a welcome sight. The water-war was over. Time to get out of the boat!

Physicists later informed me that when I see these colorful raindrops, I'm looking at dispersive refraction. Large drops make more intense colors; tiny drops form multiple, more frayed arcs. "Color comes from plucking the rainbow."[2] We see rainbows best about a mile away, but we can also spot them in soap bubbles, the spray of the garden hose, or a misty waterfall.

Jack Kerouac called the rainbow a "hoop for the lowly." The Greeks called this bow in the heavens *Iris* who wears gauzy colored veils. She was the daughter of the god of wonder and the west wind.

In the 1600s René Descartes brought reason into the study of rainbows. He said it's too old fashioned to call this colorful phenomenon in the sky *Iris* any longer. We're way beyond that! Now, let's call it *Arc-en-ciel*, an arch in the sky. He tried to duplicate one by putting a glass globe of water in sunlight, and then watched to see what happened when light rays entered it. By carefully measuring

---

[1] Genesis 9:12.

[2] Philip Ball, *Bright Earth: Art and the Invention of Color* (New York: Farrar, Straus and Giroux, 2001), 25.

the angle of refraction, he found the sun must be no higher than fifty-two degrees above the horizon for rainbow colors to appear. Subsequently, people spent their lives isolating, naming, and measuring color light fringes.

Boston is a great walking city and when we lived in Cambridge, I used to find interesting sidewalks everywhere. One day I stopped to watch a pigeon walking beside an oil slick. The sun caught the pigeon's feather in just such a way that gray glistened into teal and pink that washed into several shades of lavender I'd never seen before. I moved my eyes just a bit and there on the oil slick was the exact same color pattern! Nature had duplicated this incidental rainbow and flung it directly at my feet. Had I not looked down at that precise moment, I would have missed this bit of iridescent heaven.

Because rainbows appear, as if out of nowhere, and disappear equally as magically, they transform the world, if only for a couple of seconds. I think of the rainbow that appeared in the sky over Washington, D.C., just as people left the funeral of Tim Russert, a beloved NBC newscaster. Everyone there and those watching on TV saw what John the Biblical writer earlier had called an *emerald bow*.

Goethe's Faust sees a rainbow over a waterfall. "In this way the real mystery of color makes its appearance, which Goethe has expressed in the matchless phrase, 'the fluctuating duration of the colorful arc.' It is the eternal light which reveals its presence in the flux of earthly event."[3] Mephistopheles tries to convince Faust that colors are just fun things to play with — aesthetic tools. But Faust knows color goes much deeper than that. He knows that color colors our souls and allows us to step onto hallowed ground.

Many medieval people believed the rainbow would not appear in the sky for forty years before the end of the world. So when it appeared, they heaved a great sigh of relief. They knew they could count on at least forty more years!

The rainbow is a combination of earth, water, and air so early Christians saw in the rainbow a symbol of the Trinity: Father (gold), Son (red), and the Holy Spirit (green) whom I call Sophia, in one combined spectrum of love. Of course that omits blue — which traditionally is associated with Mary — the Virgin's color.

---

[3] Ernst Benz, "Color in Christian Visionary Experience," *Color Symbolism: Eranos Yearbook*, 1972 (E. J. Brill, 1974), 122.

Lady Rainbow or Ix Chel is known by some Central American women to regulate pregnancies. It may all come from an early Peruvian story of how a young girl's menstrual blood gave birth to the rainbow. Central and South American people have a tradition of standing very still in silence and awe for as long as a rainbow appears.

This arched prism of color hooks heaven to earth in mysterious ways.

The elephant god Ganesh wrapped Maya in a rainbow and she became pregnant with Buddha. Australians called the rainbow a great grandmother serpent. Some northern Australian groups call her a cosmic female who contains within her all of life. In their cosmology, when the rainbow came into the sky, it signified their movement out of a dream time of asexuality into a time of masculine and feminine balance. Rainbow ladders reach the heavens in Native American myths and in southern Alaska the Tinglit people tell of a time when a grandmother spirit rainbow came down from the heavens.

Rainbows are bridges between dimensions. Jung says in *Psychology and Alchemy*, "Only the gods can walk a rainbow bridge in safety... human beings must pass under it." My Norwegian ancestors believed the rainbow, Bifrost, was a bridge that leads from Midgard, earth, to Aasgard, the hereafter. In the Mesopotamian Gilgamesh story, the hero must pass through the rainbow that guards paradise.

The Cahinawa in Peru relate the rainbow to their practice of using *ayahuasca*, which often includes visions of multicolored snakes. The vine from which the brew is made has a serpentine appearance. These jungle vines intertwine in a spiral helix, like DNA of the spiritual realm. When red snakes appear in visions, they can be used for killing and healing, but white snakes are just for healing. Green snakes know all about plants and yellow snakes know everything about rocks and minerals. Blue snakes signify wisdom and intelligence.[4] When angels appear in visions, colors have great significance. Green is the principle of life; blue for zest and energetic strength; yellow for freshness and joy. Fuchsia prevents boredom. Waves of color signify spiritual energy.

---

[4] Pablo Amaringo et al, *The Ayahuasca Visions of Pablo Amaringo* (Rochester, VT: Inner Traditions, 2011), 100.

The Rainbow Colors

Newton saw as many as eleven colors in his prismed arc, and sometimes as few as five, but he settled on seven to coincide with the musical octave. I grew up thinking the rainbow was limited to Newton's ROYGBIV (red, orange, yellow, green, blue, indigo, and violet). I confess I still can't, to this day, find indigo. But when I squint, I see many more than seven. Not as many as Virgil for whom the rainbow "a thousand intermingled colors throws." That's an awesome, albeit hyperbolic, image. However repeated tests over that last 150 years do tell us there are 120 discernable colors in the spectrum.[5]

One of my favorite places to read is the sofa under the south window in my office. When the sun hits the many-faceted Austrian crystal hanging in the window, a rainbow often falls onto my book's page. One day I decided to see, as Goethe did, what it looked like against a black paper instead of my white book pages.

What I saw at the bottom of the bow was a red moving into a deeper and deeper shade of red until it was blue-red, which then begins to match the colors at the top. If you could join the bow into a tube and then slice it like a salami, the color wheel would be a circle. Rudolf Steiner said if the rainbow were a closed circle, we'd see where we humans fit into it. That would be the peach-blossom part that we can't normally see… the subtle blending of red and blue. Magenta. That seems to be the way our five-year-old granddaughter Josie sees it. (Josie's Rainbow, page 145)

Homer described the rainbow as merely "violet-purple." Aristotle, on the other hand, said there were three rainbow colors: crimson, leek-green, and golden yellow. These are the colors, he said, that can't be mixed on a palette. They're too atmospheric. Seneca came along later and added green, blue, and yellow-orange.

Isodore of Seville, a Middle Ages "school book" author, assigned four colors to the rainbow: "it draws its fiery-red color from the heavens, its purple from the waters, its white from air, its dark color from earth."[6]

---

[5] Rolf G. Kuehni, *Color* (New York: John Wiley & Sons, 2005), 53.
[6] Peter Dronke, "Tradition and Innovation," *The Realms of Color: Eranos Yearbook*, 1972 (E. J. Brill, 1974), 70.

One theory I've read, describing our human evolutionary advancement, is that we, as a human species, have been systematically moving through the ROYGBIV rainbow color sequence and we're now in the "V" or violet stage. This is the stage where we recognize the importance of our spiritual lives.

The rainbow was made from what people in the Middle Ages and Renaissance called "apparent colors." Up until then, colors were either simple or mixed. But then somebody raised the question: How could fire, which is red and yellow and orange, be held in black coal? And how could cold snow be white? How could gold look yellow by moonlight but silver in the sun?

It's obvious that colors of the rainbow melt into each other — there are no sharp divisions. No lines between. They blend into one another, "the progression being toward superior fineness, coolness and penetrating power, as we move from the red through orange, yellow, green, blue, indigo and violet and toward superior warmth and animation as we move in the opposite direction."[7]

Stepped Rainbows

A recent visit to the Yucatan Peninsula reminded me again of how drab ancient rocky ruins now seem compared to how colorful they once were. The Classic Maya painted their buildings brilliant reds, blues, greens — fertility, water, life itself. And yellow, of course, for the sun.

Colorful ziggurats once appeared around what is now Iraq and Iran from about 2100 B.C.E. They were Chaldean stepped structures built in seven tiers with a temple on the top. Seven was the number of the planets they were familiar with.

In 1939 the English archeologist Leonard Woolley unearthed one at Ur, which was once a city-state between Baghdad and the Persian Gulf. It is a massive rectangular structure two hundred feet long, one hundred and fifty feet wide, and about seventy feet high. The colors, as in most richly painted ancient monuments and statues, have washed away, but he believed the lowest stage was originally black; the highest, red. Each step represented a key color of a planet that they usually connected with a higher power. The lowest part of the ziggurat tower was

---

[7] Edwin Babbitt, *The Principles of Light and Color* (University Books, 1967), 17.

black for Saturn. Next was orange for Jupiter; third, red for Mars; the fourth, yellow for the sun; the fifth was green and blue for Venus and the sixth step a darker blue for Mercury and the seventh was white for the moon. The Ur ziggurat was originally built for the patron of the city, Nanna, the moon goddess. The temple shrine at the top was covered with blue-glazed bricks and the roof was gilded metal. Earth and heaven were connected by color. Pilgrims would start out in the dark underworld and move up to the habitable earth, and then climb up to the heavens. Each level was eighteen feet high. Saddam Hussein restored the lower facade in the 1980s and during the First Gulf War he parked his fighter planes next to it, believing no one would bomb this World Heritage Site. As it turns out, he was right.

Colors: What Do We Call Them?

"A light was upon it for which his language had no name...
He [Frodo] saw no colour but those he knew,
gold and white and blue and green,
but they were fresh and poignant, as if he had at that
moment first perceived them and
made for them names new and wonderful."

J. R. R. Tolkien, *The Lord of the Rings*

Those of us more comfortable with paradox and both/and rather than either/or language might be able to begin to understand how color can be a single entity and, at the same time, many "things." Plotinus, the Roman third-century philosopher, said color is devoid of parts. Indivisible. We know color flows and dances and seems to have no outer form. Are colors, then, only delineated by the words we use to describe them?

And, of course, the naming of various colors is a matter of cultural usage. The Greeks, for instance, laid out their colors on a scale from light to dark, *brilliance* or *luster* to *dullness*. Yellow was at the brilliant end; red and green in the middle; and blue, a variation of black, on the dark, dull end. Perhaps Homer had a word for blue, but he makes no mention of it in the *Iliad*. We read of "the wine-dark sea," "rosy-fingered dawn" and something yellow as "saffron robed." People don't have red hair — it's "tawny." "Pale" and "wan" might mean yellow and they used many words to indicate shades of gray, which were various species of black. No doubt, the Romans had even more color names since twenty-nine different pigments have been uncovered in Pompeii's ruins.

Our granddaughter sat with me on the deck one July evening as we waited for fireflies to put on their flashy show. She noted how many colors of gray there were in the late evening clouds. She said, "Look, Grandma. The grays are coming together bringing in the night." Homer would have been proud.

Once I believed I lived in a rigid kaleidoscope where colors just automatically clicked into place when somebody else turned the end of the tube. I was just an observer. But I've come to realize *I'm* doing the choosing. I can choose to see through gray to a happier yellow. I can even BE the kaleidoscope — or even the kaleidoscope maker. I'm living in a free-will colorful game where my choices make a difference.

Colors are so hidden within light, that we can see only about one-tenth of all the colors that exist. And even that small percentage amounts to several million different colors our ordinary eyes can see. But there are many more we can't see.

We can "hear" only an abbreviated score of the colorful light-music around us. Or as the poet-priest John O'Donohue put it: "Color is always a dance where the vital partners are invisible."[8]

Colors are pigments — minerals, plants — earthy colors. Colors are also sensations of light. And the colors of nature are "hemoglobin, melanin, carotene, and chlorophyll."[9]

When you hear, "red," what do you see? Josef Albers cautioned that suggesting the same color can provoke innumerable readings. Color is so deceptive that it shifts and what we think we see, we may not really be seeing. He said, "If there

---

[8] John O'Donohue, *Beauty: The Invisible Embrace* (New York: HarperCollins Publishers, 2004), 89.
[9] Helen Varley, *Colour* (Marshall Editions, 1983), 10.

are fifty people listening, it can be expected that there will be fifty reds in their minds. Even when a certain color is specified which all listeners have seen innumerable times — such as the red of the Coca-Cola signs which is the same red all over the country — they will still think of many different reds."[10] Some eyes are better prepared to see color, and others, more receptive. It's hard to remember distinct colors, he points out, because we have poor visual memory — poorer than our auditory memory. Colors are, he said, "a dangerous magic." They aren't faithful to any precise or ideal system. Our granddaughter Josie has different associations with red than I do. Or than her parents have. Or than you may have.

We don't know precisely what to call colors, shades, and tones. Though there are innumerable colors in our daily vocabularies, Albers said there are only about thirty common color names.[11]

Some colorists working for market researchers belong to an elite group of designers and artists in Manhattan called the Color Association of the United States. They were founded in 1915 to give, as their charter says, "global color intelligence across industries." It was aimed initially at textiles, but now they serve seventy-three different industries. Their 1,500 members analyze sales-competitive color data, do market research, and sit around, trying to figure out "what's the hot palette this year?" So when you go through your favorite clothing store and see racks and racks of chartreuse, for instance, you now know whom to blame. Or when you see that an airline has changed the color of its logo, they no doubt got their information from www.colorassociation.com.

Like many women I got caught up in the "color craze" back in the '80s. Victoria Jackson's book *Color Me Beautiful* made a huge hit. She created four palettes (I still have my fabric swatches somewhere — they were intended for you to take with you into stores so you wouldn't be tempted to buy something in "another season" even if the price was right.). I'm a "summer." My hair and skin tones suggest I should avoid wearing *autumn* colors — oranges and reds, or the deep jewel tones of winter that I love so much... and stick to the more pastel, duskier colors.

---

[10] Josef Albers, *Interaction of Color* (New Haven, CT: Yale University Press, Revised Ed. 1975), 1, 3.
[11] Albers, 3.

Paint colors today get named not by their hues but by our own lifestyles. "Tempest," "Turbulence," "Weekend in the Country," "Synergy," "Rejuvenate," "Polished Leather," or Martha Stewart's "Crème Brulée." As of this writing, the Benjamin Moore company offers customers 3,300 colors.

We're told by the U.S. Bureau of Standards that our eyes are capable of recognizing ten million different color surfaces. Unlike Albers, they also say we can name 267 of them. But the amount of choices can be overwhelming.

If you've read any of James Joyce, you'll know how he names colors in his typically stream of consciousness way. "Blueblacksliding constellations" and "seamless rainbowspell." All authors try to find fresh color images. While reading Jonathan Kellerman recently, I noted a few pretty vivid descriptions from *Victims*:

"Aging stucco was the color of freezer-burned chicken."

"The woman's color wasn't anything you'd see outside a morgue."

"skin blanched to a bad shade of gray."

"bright burnt-chocolate eyes."

"The precise green of pimiento olives."

"Hair dyed the color of over-cooked pumpkin."

In *Cold Mountain*, Charles Frazier describes a woman whose "face was white as a stripped tendon." In Chelsea Cain's *The Night Season*, "the sky was the texture and color of freshly poured concrete."

In one of Faye Kellerman's latest books, *Straight into Darkness*, one of her characters has "palettes of red" filling his brain: "red, ruby, crimson, scarlet, carmine, maroon, vermillion... so many varieties of one wavelength... more reds than there were names."

In her book *The Cookbook Collector*, Allegra Goodman described some Goldman Sachs executives in "suits of navy so dark the color could not exist in nature, except possibly in the deepest ocean, where giant squid inked out their predators."

Kate Atkinson, the popular English author who crafts clever, funny novels, spiced one of her descriptions of red in *When Will There Be Good News?* this way. The airline official was "dressed in a uniform that would have allowed her to drown in a vat of Heinz tomato soup without anyone noticing..."

In 1903 Binney and Smith introduced Crayola crayons in that familiar yellow and green flip-top box. Remember how your new box of crayons smelled when you opened it the first day of school? They were all sharp like rows of pointy fence posts. Research tells us red will wear down first. They originally offered eight: black, brown, orange, violet, blue, green, red, and yellow. My first box contained forty-eight with wonderful names such as *Apricot, Gold, Silver, Bittersweet, Spring Green, Thistle, Periwinkle, Brick Red, Magenta, Prussian Blue* (changed to "Midnight Blue" by teacher request during World War I), *Mahogany, Cornflower, Melon, Salmon,* and the ubiquitous *Flesh,* which, thankfully, was changed to *Peach* in 1962 when people gradually became aware that skin tones do vary. Sixteen new colors were added in 1993, all named by consumers: *Asparagus, Denim, Macaroni and Cheese, Tropical Rain Forest.* And twenty-four more were added in 1998, which means Josie can now choose from 120 standard colors bearing names such as: *Inch Worm, Jazzberry Jam, Piggy Pink,* and *Mango Tango.*

Gardening catalogues try to standardize some of their flower names, but "lemon yellow" and "straw" became mixed up with "aconite yellow" and "majolica yellow" and "apricot." And what color is "campanula blue" anyway?

Color names are fluid. And I know from experience that we women recognize names for colors that tend to baffle most men. Ask a man to describe *mauve, taupe,* or *magenta* and see what his reaction is. My husband and I, who currently drive a red Subaru, discuss *reds* a lot. When we see another red car on the road, one of us is apt to say, "I don't like that red. Do you? Too tomatoey." Or "Oooh, that one's like a fire engine." Ours is a deeper, more jewel-tone red. Like a ruby. "Did you know that New Zealand Maoris had a hundred different words for red?" "Hmmm." Either he was too busy driving to comment further, or he wasn't as interested in names of colors as I seem to be.

How do we even begin to talk about color? Mary O'Neill in her wonderful children's book *Hailstones and Halibut Bones: Adventures in Color* comes closest to how I wish I could describe color. "Like acrobats on a high trapeze/The Colors pose and bend their knees/Twist and turn and leap and blend/Into shapes and feelings without end... "

To describe colors we often resort to similes: mustard yellow, emerald green, sky blue. Colors in many African languages, for example, don't carry simple names but are, instead, only rich similes. "Like the bush-buck's hair," "like the egg of a fern-owl," "like the water in which the (specific name) plant has been soaked." Their master dyers knew that strong colors came from the earth: koala nuts and sorghum leaves for red. Or black called *from the water of* (a certain pond.)[12] The Celtic word *glas* refers to the color of a mountain lake: blue and gray. And in Japanese *awo* can mean green, blue, or dark, depending on the context.

We usually think of the primary colors as being red, blue, and yellow and from them come other all other colors. And we can generally agree on what reds and blues are but greens... ah, greens are another story. My husband as a child summed it up well: "It's a mix of bwoo and geen." How right he was. Green can be more yellow or more blue. Take your pick.

In all the twenty-six Mayan languages there are common terms for blues and greens. Artists used turquoise gems, glazes, green jade, blue obsidian... so they had dozens of terms. The Inca had more than twenty different terms for the colors of the dyes they used. Even today Andean shepherds use at least nineteen different terms for colors ranging between "absolute" white and "absolute black."[13]

The Malayo-Polynesian people in the Philippines, for example, have four color terms: dark, light, fresh, and dry. That covers it for them. They don't even have a word for "color."

Azure is a Persian word meaning blue; *indigo* is an abbreviation for "blue Indian dye." Neither the Chinese nor the Japanese have a word for brown. Instead they use descriptors such as "tea-colored" or "fox-colored."

Like the colors in a child's crayon box, names often come from current culture and history. Magenta, for instance, got its name in 1859 when that particular dye was invented. It was named after the Battle of Magenta when French and Sardinians defeated the Austrians in northern Italy.[14]

The people in Angola and Zambia, according to the anthropologist and rituals expert Victor Turner, have no word for green so they called it "water of sweet

[12] Dominque Zahan, "Colour Symbolism in Black Africa," *Color Symbolism* (Eranos Yearbook, 1972), 58.
[13] John Gage, *Color and Meaning: Art Science, and Symbolism*, (Berkeley, CA: University of California Press, 1999), 106-109.
[14] Varley, 50.

potato leaves." And for them blue cloth was black cloth and yellow or orange objects were simply red. There are no words for "blue," for instance, for a tribe in Namibia so when shown eleven green squares and one blue, they could not see the difference. If you don't have a word for it, you can't see it.

Guy Deutcher, an English linguist and author of *Through the Language Glass* and *The Unfolding of Language,* taught his eighteen-month-old daughter all the colors. But as an experiment, neither he nor his wife ever called the sky "blue." Little Alma learned to correctly identify all the colors, including blue, and one day when they were outside, her father pointed to the sky and said, "Alma, what color is that?" She stared and stared and did not answer — she could readily identify blues and greens, but in looking at the sky, she saw nothing to identify. Finally she said, "white." He kept asking about the sky and after a while she said "Blue," "No, white." "No, it's blue." "No, Daddy. The sky is white." This seemed to convince him that recognizing blue is not always so easy.

Two anthropologists, Brent Berlin and Paul Kay, studied cultures and by using Munsell color chips, determined that there are about a half million different colors considered commercially viable. They also determined that there are about eleven color terms found universally. No language has only one color term, but some have only "black" and "white." Then these two researchers went on to figure out if there are three terms, what that color is. It's always red. And if one more is added... and two more added, what are those colors? Here's the standard order of the "add-ons":

Two colors	Next Add:	Next:	Next:	Next:	Next:	Next Four:
Black	*Red*	*Green*	*Yellow*	*Blue*	*Brown**	*Purple*
White		*or*	*and*			*Pink*
		Yellow	*Green*			*Orange*
						Gray

*"Brown" doesn't appear in Melanesia, Welsh, Eskimo and Tamil languages. The Siamese and Lapps call it "black-red."[15]

---

[15] Varley, 50-51.

Later researchers challenged Berlin and Kay's findings believing they did not have first-hand knowledge of the languages they were researching and skewed the experiments by using only a Western point of view.

We tend to lump colors into "primary," "secondary," or "tertiary" depending on where they fall on the color wheel. (Ellen Donaldson Allen's Color Wheel, page 148) Red, blue, and yellow are, we believe, the three primaries from which other colors are mixed. But over time which colors fit those categories has varied. Aristotle, for instance, claimed the primary colors were yellow, white, and black. Pythagoras said there are four: yellow, red, white, and black. Empedocles, the Greek philosopher born in 490 B.C.E. who taught that all matter is made up of four elements (water, earth, fire, and air) spoke of four primary colors: white, black, red, and yellow. Thomas Young, a precocious nineteenth-century man who had read the Bible twice by the age of four, did retina research in London and said there were three primary colors: red, green, and violet. What's "primary" in our minds obviously shifts.

Colors: How Do We See Them?

We see colors everywhere: in music, poetry, in all of nature, the sky, museums, galleries, clothing, flowers, pottery glazes, theater stages, gardens. Still, seeing color is a great paradox. It's easy to see, because it's everywhere, and it's hard to see because it's always moving. Annie Dillard said, "The color-patches of vision part, shift and reform as I move through space and time... what I see before me at any given second is a full field of color-patches scattered just so. The configuration will never be repeated. Living is moving; time is a live creek bearing changing lights."[16]

The sun itself is so brilliant that it overwhelms color vision, making color judgments unreliable, but if the noon sun were dimmed sufficiently, its color would appear a pale greenish yellow.

Because we live pretty far north and in a rural area with low ambient light to distract the night sky, we can, on rare occasions, see northern lights, or the aurora borealis. It's the culmination of power around the north magnetic pole that gives

[16] Annie Dillard, *Pilgrim at Tinker Creek* (New York: Bantam, 1975), 84.

its most brilliant effects in autumn. They start with streamers of bluish white light darting up into the night sky. One August night, Nathan and I watched a polar light show for about twenty glorious minutes. We found ourselves *oohing* and *ahhing* as if we were watching Fourth of July fireworks. The luminous ribbons — some people have called them "merry dancers" — were various shades of green and violet, rose, and even darker purples. I've read that some of these light columns can reach from five to several hundred miles in height. The northern hemisphere has strong currents of electricity flowing northward. Axial motion creates magnetic curves, so it seems the earth is a gigantic battery and every now and then she burps out dancing nightlights.

Colors in a mirror, I've noticed, seem different than colors viewed head on. They are deeper and not quite as sharp. The colors of the mountains I see out my west windows change. Sometimes they are shades of aqua, blue, and turquoise. How can they be blue? I've driven over those mountains so I know they're not blue. They're very green from all the trees and interspersed are distinct patches of grays and browns, with some white rocks every now and then.

At sunset the sun has to pass through our atmosphere sideways, at a slant, and most of the blue and green wavelengths are scattered causing us to see reds and oranges, even neon pinks. Clouds, smoke, and volcanic ash change what we see. Morning light is rosier due to temperature and humidity fluctuations. In 1957 forest fires in Canada increased the particles in the atmosphere, turning the moon faintly but distinctly blue.[17]

We now know that when light shines onto an object, it bounces back at us, is absorbed by the object, or is transmitted through the object. When that happens, it appears colorless. White reflects the most light; ivory and yellows next; dark greens, blues, red, and black absorb light. Snow reflects all color back to us, so it looks white. On the other extreme, a black cloth absorbs all light so it appears to be black. When light falls on a blade of grass, the grass reflects green light better than it reflects any of the other colors in the spectrum. Hence, we see green.

I have brilliant blue lobelia spilling out from my planters by the front steps.

---

[17] Varley, 212.

Without the porch light on, I noticed the other evening that each little flower is totally black. And why is the sky blue? Because when white light encounters oxygen and nitrogen atoms in the earth's atmosphere, it scatters in all directions and all we can see are the high frequencies like violet, indigo, and blue. Or, we could just take Lucy's answer in *Peanuts*. When Linus asks her why the sky is blue, Lucy shouts: "Because it isn't green!!"

Under a blue light with no red rays, a red object would look dull black.

We've all been fooled by colors under artificial lights — some contain more yellow, some more blue — which is why you might want to take that new shirt or sweater out into the sunlight before buying it.

"The difference between brown and yellow, or between maroon and pink, is solely a difference in luminance — that is the position along the black-white axis."[18] The eye sees yellow-green, for instance, as the brightest region of the spectrum in daylight.

What happened when sunlight fell on my Boston pigeon? Or when I see a colorful dragonfly's wing? Where does that teal-green come from? Or the floating rainbows on a soap bubble? They're not pigments; they're interferences of light. Troubled light. Diffracted waves.

Without getting into the whole physics thing about interference and diffraction, let's talk about peacocks. During the 600s, a Byzantine writer posed this question: "How could anyone who sees the peacock not be amazed at the gold interwoven with sapphire, at the purple and emerald green feathers, at the composition of the colors of many patterns, all mingled together but not confused with one another?"[19]

A friend who knew I was writing this book sent me a card with a beautiful peacock and the line by Ralph Waldo Emerson, "Nature always wears the colors of the spirit." Flannery O'Connor herself once said the peacock was a symbol of the "transcendent aspects of Christ because of its resplendent beauty and its absolute inutility."

A real peacock displays about two hundred deep teal and turquoise, blue,

---

[18] Margaret Livingstone, *Vision and Art* (New York: Harry N. Abrams, 2002), 90.

[19] Philip Ball, *Bright Earth* (New York: Farrar, Straus and Giroux, 2001), 30.

indigo. and green feathers. His iridescent colors don't come from pigments that absorb light, but rather from intricate and extremely precise layers of melanin granules in the tiny barbules that make up the feathers. These layers interfere with and scatter the light. They create a thin oily surface color that turns what is normally green into radiant hues, similar to oil on the surface of a water puddle or soap bubble, which changes colors depending upon the angle of our vision. Scientists tell us it is the tiny photonic crystals layered onto that impossibly blue Morpho butterfly that create its magnificence. Colors shimmer in peacocks, hummingbirds, dragonflies, mallards, sea anemones, and shot silk fabric when *we* change *our* positions.

When the Nissan Motor Company realized why Morpho butterflies look blue from those millions of intricately ridged scales that produce the illusion of blue, they created a fluorescent blue car finish with structured "scales" not pigment.[20]

Honeybees zoom to flowers that vibrate to a specific color. I've heard that bees are blind to red, but they can perceive ultraviolet as a color. Ants will carry their larvae out of ultraviolet and into visible red. A yellow-painted trap will attract more Japanese beetles than other colors. Plant research tells us that red neon makes flowers and strawberries flourish and oat seedlings are retarded by blue light.

Tracking and healing dogs can sense body odors and changes in a body's system. Energy affects every cell in our bodies. You and I send out vibrational energies of fear, love, acceptance, and rejection without even realizing it. Sensitive people can pick those up as easily as a honeybee heads for particular flowers. And we know what perfumes and shaving cream scents can do for the libido.

Bower birds of Australia compose attractive patterns with colored pebbles in front of their nests. And if a pebble is removed, it will replace it *with one of the same color*. PBS's *Frontline* aired a special in June 2012 on a Massachusetts artist named Mary Jo McConnell, who has been painting the intricate bowers of these robin-sized birds in the Indonesian cloud forest of West Papua New Guinea. She thinks these elusive birds are artists, the way they work with color and light.

---

[20] Diane Ackerman, *Deep Play* (New York: Random House, 1999), 186.

They always orient their massive woven twig-and-leaf constructions to the east, to catch the morning sun. Beautiful flowers, seeds, pebbles, sometimes a signature feather or a bit of shiny sardine can are all collaged into a striking composition. Each has a distinctive style. Like all artists, she believes, they create for the sheer joy and wonder of creating.

Turtles' color vision is apparently quite keen. Orange, green, and violet tend to be their favorites. And in Holland, farmers sometimes paint stables and cow stalls blue to repel flies. Are you wondering how to repel mosquitoes? Use pink and yellow netting. Research indicates those troubling insects are attracted to dark reds, blues, and browns.

Chameleons, normally green, can turn colors because they have layers of overlapping cells — some with yellow pigment, some with a light-scattering blue capability, and another layer with brown melanin. They can change to match their background. Although I haven't tried this, I've read that if you put a patch over one eye of a chameleon, only half of its body will change color when it crawls over a colored surface. Like those lizards, colors aren't predictable and stable — they morph, they move, and have many meanings.

Cones and Rods

We humans are able to see colors because we have three different kinds of receptors in our brains for color: red, blue, and yellow. Each cone is able to perceive about a hundred shades, and with all three, about a million. Some women, it turns out, have been found to have four receptors. If they have this rare condition, they're called tetrachromats and can see about a hundred million colors. We first learned about tetrachromats in a 1948 paper on color blindness. It describes the work of the Dutch scientist HL de Vries who was studying the eyes of color-blind men. By using various matching tasks, he determined that although the men had two normal cones, they also possessed an additional mutant cone — one far less sensitive to either green or red.[21]

Dogs and most monkeys have two types of cones; butterflies apparently have five. And perhaps most marvelous of all, the shrimp mantis have sixteen!

---

[21] Veronique Greenwood, *Discover* magazine (July-August) http://discovermagazine.com/2012/jul-aug/06-humans-with-super-human-vision.

Imagine the colors this iridescent turquoise twelve-inch-long, and very aggressive, shrimp can see.

Impressionists worked with light and were constantly evaluating its effects on what they saw. Paul Cézanne once said, "The sunlight here (Provence) is so intense that it seems to me that objects are silhouetted not only in black and white but also in blue, red, brown, and violet."[22] Artists, it seems, need a wider rainbow.

Led by Manet and Monet, French painters followed a theory of how we see light set out by Hermann von Helmholtz. It was a breakthrough idea based on the concept that light is a wave. Newton believed particles of colored light entered the eye. But when static electricity and batteries were being better understood, people like Helmholtz began seeing the body as an electrical machine, as well. Helmholtz said, "We see red, green, and blue" depending on what light-sensitive nerve cells get triggered. Three types of cones see these primary colors (although primary pigment colors remained red, yellow, and blue) and their secondary colors. Helmholtz also discovered rods — another type of cell in the retina. That's how we distinguish light and dark. We rapidly shift our eyes, allowing light to fall on fresh cones. Painters could now understand how complementary colors work together and after images are created. The Impressionists talked a lot about this three receptor theory and how "light works."

Our retinas do, in fact, have about 120 million photosensitive receptors or nerves called cones and rods. Rods can see about six hundred degrees of texture and contrast so they tell us "value." Values are colors that are combined with white or black. This is sometimes referred to as tone intensity. Cones, on the other hand, can recognize "hue" — that's the term we call a color we can see. Without these cones, we'd be surrounded by only grays, blacks, whites. Our cone cells fire when stimulated by light of certain wavelengths. Unless we're a tetrachromat, we have only three receptors in the retina, each sensitive to either red, blue, or green. The rods in our eyes perceive the quality of the color. Our retinas are just "go-betweens" bridging the phenomenon and the sensation.

Every quantum of light — that is each photon — acts on the retina by

---

[22] Ibid., 17.

decomposing one molecule of a visual color. Say purple. Then that molecule changes to visual yellow — its complement. But then the cones that perceive color rest and return to that visual purple again.

Our brains' right hemispheres perceive color more quickly than the left, but it's the left hemisphere that can name the colors and verbalize what we're seeing. Some researchers claim that violet rays stream into the brain left to right. Only primates, apparently, have brains capable of processing color information. When we visit the nocturnal animal buildings at our zoos, we'll notice a lot of red lights. And very active animals. Since they don't have rods in their retinas, they are fooled into thinking the red light is night. At night, when all the visitors are gone, the lights are white and the animals sleep.

As we get older, both men and women prefer shorter wavelength colors such as blue and green over red, yellow, orange. One theory for why people prefer blue when they grow older is that the fluids in our eyes grow yellowish with age; a child's lens will absorb about 10% of blue light; that of an octagenarian, about 85%, so the human eye may "thirst" for blue as the lens proceeds to filter more of it out. Interestingly enough, applied pressure on the eyeball can create the color blue.

We think baby girls like pink, and baby boys prefer blue, but some studies have proven that babies look at bright colors longer than at duller colors. They reach first for reds and yellows. Three-month-olds, for instance, will stare the longest at yellow. Then white, pink, and then red. I'm not sure what this all means, since I'll wager movement plays an equal role in attention span. But these studies seem to suggest that babies don't really care much for green, blue, violet, and certainly not black.

If you blink after viewing a color, you will have an after-vision. Usually in that color's opposite. Try this: stare at red, then look at a white surface. What do you see? Green? Or if you look at an object against a different colored background, it will change in color. Black letters in the evening appear red. When one's retina is stimulated, it can produce the opposite color. For instance, yellow demands purple; orange demands blue, and red demands green. Yellow will appear brighter on a black background than it will on white.

Light waves traveling at 186,000 miles a second bend around objects and even air and water. The range of light wavelengths varies but it's safe to say that at noon daylight levels out. People who spend their time measuring light waves tell us that light of 640 nanometers (a nanometer is one thousand-millionth of a meter) looks red whereas light of 540 nanometers looks green. Violet light is about 400. Red vibrates at a lower rate than violet. But that's not that's not very much of a difference. The ultraviolet end of the spectrum is around 359 nanometers and about 830 nanometers near the infrared portion of the spectrum. Most wavelengths below 500 are blocked from adult lenses by a protective yellow pigment layer on the retina. We usually can see colors in the 400 to 700 range. So, as you might guess, there's a lot in light that we can't see as colors.

The longest waves are called radio, followed by microwave, infrared, visible light, ultraviolet, x-rays and finally gamma rays. Truly sensitive people can see deeper into the infrared spectrum that most of us. Some can, for instance, see a glow from a hot iron in a completely darkened room.

Recent molecular biological studies on eyesight seem to indicate even a single amino acid can cause differences in color vision. At Johns Hopkins, researchers now think there is a genetic basis for ways, for instance, to see the color red. Caucasian men in particular "have a 'rosy' view of the world because of their greater sensitivity to red light."[23]

Color Deficiencies

A person who suffers from color blindness isn't really blind, just color-challenged, depending on which sensitive cones are missing. For instance, because of my age, I don't see short wavelength colors nearly as well as my granddaughter does.

More men than women have color recognition deficiencies. It may be as high as one in eight American men who are, to some degree, color-impaired. Some receptors in the retina may not be functioning and certain diseases may affect one's color senses. In the more technically advanced areas of our globe, the incidence of defective color vision is greater than in areas of high urban populations elsewhere. It's about one in twelve. The lowest incidence (1 in 50) occur in the Arctic and equatorial rain forests.[24]

---

[23] Charles A. Riley II, *Color Codes* (Hanover, NH: University Press of New England, 1995), 2.
[24] Varley, 37.

It was John Dalton, an eighteenth-century English chemist, who discovered he could see no difference between a laurel leaf and a stick of red sealing wax. Or a red dress and a tree. Color blindness became known as Daltonism.[25] A friend told me of how one of her friends asked her husband to bring in some tomatoes to eat from the garden. He said he couldn't find any ripe ones. She went out and brought in twenty-three very red ones. He really couldn't see that they were red.

We mothers can transmit this defect to our sons. Acquired color blindness may occur because of eye diseases or vitamin B deficiencies or exposure to certain poisonous chemicals. Lack of oxygen can temporarily cause problems in color recognition. Or snow blindness can cause people to see red, just as yellow vision can come from some forms of poison. Clouded cataracts can cause red vision, which is sometimes followed by blue vision.

Charles Riley in *Color Codes* relays some insights into color blindness by using the example of an artist who suffered a head injury and could no longer translate wavelengths he saw into color. The neurologist Oliver Sacks and Robert Wasserman explore what is called *achromatopia* in "The Case of the Colorblind Painter," a chapter in *An Anthropologist on Mars: Seven Paradoxical Tales.* The artist tries to remember the Pantone chart and work from logical memories of color, but reds have now turned black, and blues and yellows a pale gray, and he simply gives up. The authors sum it up this way: "The mystery of color constancy, or color judgment, seems to depend upon an immense inner act of comparison and computation, performed continually and faultlessly, every moment of our lives." [26]

Synesthesia: Seeing Color Through Other Senses

"All music is a rainbow!" Pablo Cassals said. And the Russian artist Wassily Kandinsky claimed happy sleigh bells have a raspberry jingle — a light, cool red like the ringing notes of a violin. Vermillion rings like a great trumpet. Church bells and contralto voices are orange. Shrill bugles, on the other hand, are lemon yellow and flutes create a light blue aura. In the 1920s Paul Klee used transparent interpenetrating planes of color to stimulate a harmonic blend of musical chords.

Synesthesia — the crossing of senses — has been a human trait since the time

---

[25] Faber Birren, *Color Psychology and Color Therapy* (University Books, 1961), 221.
[26] Riley, 319.

of Greece. Many musicians use color to describe what they hear. Liszt, for example, is supposed to have said, "More pink here!" And "This is too black!" Beethoven called B minor the "black key." Sunlight was the C for Rimsky-Korsakov.

I have a friend who saw colors as soon as she began playing the piano. "The first thirds in any octave — C, E, G — were like the primary colors. B was purple." I asked her when she knew that and she said, "I just always did." Like Messiaen, she has heard colors since she was a child.

Lyall Watson tells in *Gifts of Unknown Things* of a colorful Indonesian people living on one of the 13,000 islands between Asia and Australia. Parents there teach their children to hear color. Each vowel sound has a corresponding color. For instance, deep low pitches carry dark hues and high-pitched sounds are the brighter colors. The "I" sound is sharp white and the "O" sound is black. When they hear "U" they see blue. One little girl Watson writes about could locate mosquitoes in the dark by see-hearing a fine white light caused by their whine.

Most of us dream in color. In one particularly colorful dream a few years back, I was among a group of people standing around waiting for a predicted comet. Suddenly the sky became a holographic presentation of everyone's "whole records" projected there for all to see. Clouds and symbols appeared which everyone could "read" regardless of their various languages. Suddenly an impressive voice said, "Color the sky!" People began throwing crayons up into the sky and in a matter of a few dream-minutes the entire sky was colored. Then, since this seemed to be a powerful apocalyptic dream, Jesus appeared. He spoke to my younger son but I couldn't hear what he said. Like the Great Lion in the *Chronicles of Narnia*, he tells you only your story. When he approached me it was as if we were old friends meeting again. "I'll come again," he said, and left with parting words warning us of nuclear self-destruction. His parting words were "Love each other!" When I woke up, my fingertips were tingling. I looked down to see if they were glowing colors in the dark.

The Hebrew word for dream is *chalom*. It means "be healthy and strong." I still think about my "color the sky" dream, wondering if it might mean that we can color our future in hopeful hues, instead of painting it in Doomsday drab. We can imagine color as surely as our young son who at three said, "Mom, I can see that picture hanging on the wall of my brain." Children are blessed by clear "picture-seeing." And children report seeing color in their dreams more often than adults. Calvin Hall analyzed 3000 dreams a few decades back and determined that 29% of the dreams were in partial or full color and 7% more women than men dream in color.[27] And another study of deaf college students seemed to prove that 92% of them dreamed in color and their primary colors were very bright.[28]

Under various conditions such as migraine headaches, certain drug use, electrical stimulation of the brain and, obviously, by dreaming, color can be seen without one's eyes. Without light. How can this be? These conditions are exceptions to how we usually see colors. But it proves the brain can be stimulated to see color even without our vision. But if we hadn't had earlier color experiences, would we actually differentiate the colors?

The French Academy of Sciences in the early 1920s discovered that the skin is sensitive to light and that while blindfolded, sensitive people could "see" colors through their hands. And some people can "smell" colors. Helen Keller said she could understand how colors differed because she knew the smell of an orange is different from the smell of a grapefruit. To her, then, the color orange was "sticky sweet." She called white "exalted and pure"; green was "exuberant"; red suggested love or shame or strength. Without the color or its equivalent, life to her, she said, would be dark, barren, a vast blackness.

Sheila Ostrander and Lynn Schroeder documented some of this psychic-sensing work with color in Russia during the 1970s. Anyone who has seen the George Clooney movie *Men Who Stare at Goats* will recognize the U.S.-Russian race to harness super-sensitive energies during that time. Rosa Kuleshova was one of the Russian girls studied who could name colors through her fingertips, even over transparent paper or glass.

A woman from Michigan described how colors feel this way: "Light blue is smoothest. You feel yellow as very slippery, but not quite as smooth. Red, green, and dark blue are sticky… green is stickier than red, but not as coarse. Navy blue… has a braking feeling. Violet gives a greater braking effect that seems to slow the hand and feels rougher."[29]

---

[27] Robert L. Van de Castle, *Our Dreaming Mind* (New York: Ballantine, 1994), 298.

[28] Ibid., 253, 254.

[29] *Life* magazine, June 12, 1984.

Synethesia, apparently, can run in families. Vladimir Nabokov along with his mother and his son were able to see numbers and letters as colors.

Neil Harbisson, one of the TED presenters at www.ted.com/talks/neil_ harbisson_i_listen_to_color.html, talks about how he has been totally color-blind all his life due to a condition called achromatopsia. But then in 2003, computer technology allowed him to hear color through his skull as a bone conductor. He no longer lives in a gray world. An electronic eye sends out a signal and software "reads" color. He can hear Picasso and the colors in supermarkets sound like a rock concert. In the film he's wearing a pink jacket, blue shirt, and yellow pants. "Today is C major — a happy chord. If I had to go to a funeral I'd dress in D minor, which for me is turquoise, purple, and orange." He now perceives *beauty* differently. He can look at a beautiful face and it can sound terrible. He "hears" people's eyes. When the phone rings, it sounds green to him and Mozart sounds yellow. He now dreams in color as well. He had to memorize the names we give to color and then the notes he heard that coincided with those colors. But soon it became automatic. He can also "hear-see" colors we cannot with our eyes, in the infrared and ultraviolet ranges. Harbisson has started the Cyber Foundation, which offers people an opportunity to discover technology that extends our senses.

Body-Wrapped Rainbows

Auras

John Russell once said, "Color is energy made visible." Walt Whitman put it this way: "I sing the body electric."

Light is energy; color is light; therefore color is energy. Since we're electric-energy beings, it seems we are also walking rainbows giving off little electrical color displays. Carlos Castenada called it our "luminous egg." Some people believe our energy fields can actually extend in some cases, up to thirty feet around some bodies. The entire universe is filled with that force which the Hindus call *prana*. In the *Upanishads*, Hindu teachings claim our bodies contain hairlike veins full of white, blue, yellow, green, and red colors. We are made of light and color from the sun.

These globules of light and vitality continue to flash about in the entire atmosphere. They are almost colorless but they shine with a white or golden light. These forces are drawn into our bodies, some say into the center of our spleen, and are decomposed and broken up into streams of different colors. Our body colors don't follow the logical spectrum rainbow colors, the ROYGBIV colors, however. These threads of fire that bend around our bodies create our aura. Auric colors are likely connected to these magnetic atmospheric energies we have yet to really figure out. Human auras cocooned within our larger energy fields can extend two to three feet out from the body but they fluctuate, like the aurora borealis, so it's not easy to see something so fluid.

The outermost layer of color around our bodies is said to be the most closely connected to our spiritual selves. Some people call this the etheric sheath. It's apt to be a deep blue or violet. The head and lower portions have separate auric structures. Colors change depending on how we're feeling and moving.

Auras, according to some researchers, can be "read" differently, but they generally agree that auras can paint a picture of a person's overarching emotional condition. C. W. Leadbeater in *Man, Visible and Invincible* said dull and grayish browns along with green-browns are not happy colors. They show jealousy and fear, deceit and cunning. Black indicates hate and malice; deep red, anger; whereas a crimson red signifies sensuality or a loving nature. Orange reveals pride and ambition, but yellow depicts intelligence. Emerald green shows versatility and ingenuity. A pale, delicate green indicates sympathy and compassion. Dark blue usually indicates a deep religious feeling and a light blue or violet shows devotion to noble ideas. Some people may display all colors, as if they are wrapped in white light. Women and the elderly are apt to have larger auras, which average about six inches. Diseases can affect one's aura causing the aura to lose some of its sparkle and become rather murky. Auric healers use colors as a guide to determine inner imbalances.

Ruth Berger in *The Secret Is in the Rainbow* says that in order to see auras you must first think and believe in color. Feel the presence of your own energy first.

She suggests holding out your arms palms facing each other about fifteen inches apart and then slowly move the palms toward each other, noticing a resistance — that's the energy field. To see colors around people's heads and body, be in a slightly darkened room and squint a bit.

Love, as Berger sees it, creates a pink aura around us. Red in one's aura indicates a fiery excitement — a strong emotional force. Orange can signify motherhood, tolerance. Yellow in an aura, Berger says will usually be accompanied by a smile and an easy laughter. Light brown or tan in one's aura indicates outgoingness. Blue hangs around one when you are at rest — on a beach, meditating. It indicates a thirst for knowledge.

"We are composed of pieces of light. Our auras are celestial signatures."[30]

Dannion Brinkley, the writer of these words, was struck by lightning. As a consequence of his near-death experience, and his encounter with "Beings of Light," he has spent the rest of his life exploring life and death and ways to enhance our perception skills. He has created rooms with stained glass and colored light in his hospice work. The colors create a medium to travel between the worlds.

Walter Kilner in *The Human Atmosphere* encourages us to think of the human body as an envelope with three distinct parts. First, a narrow darker band a quarter of an inch wide next to the skin; then a second aura about two to four inches — very clear; then a third misty one about six inches across and the radiations shoot out at right angles from the body. They shift and change — longest coming from fingers, elbows, knees, hips, and breasts. He thought the color of health was bluish gray tinged with yellow and red. Duller and deeper grays indicate disease, but he diagnosed more from shape than from color.

Yogis usually sense the aura as fine bristles extending out from the body. When a person is sick, the bristles twist and snarl, are limp and chaotic. One female healer described seeing those colors as "wobbly Jell-O" when a person has a mental disorder. She also saw an "ugly deep red" color around the hips of prostitutes walking down the street.

---

[30] Dannion Brinkley with Paul Perry, *At Peace in the Light* (New York: Harper Torch, 1996), 16.

I first saw these filmy colorful magnetic vibrations in the early 1970s. We lived in a small Mississippi River town in Wisconsin that had a Jesuit high school and one of the teachers expanded his course to anyone in town who wished to take it. The class practiced telepathy and did experiments with viewing auras in a slightly darkened room against a neutral background. What I saw was a greenish-white light around a person's head, shooting up and fading quickly away. Exploring with my Jesuit friends who held Christ as close as I did made it all seem very safe and normal.

Like many others at the time, I was just discovering Kirlian photography. A Russian, Semyon Kirlian, back in the late 1930s had developed a way to photograph without a lens or camera or sunlight. In a secret method, a spark of some sort discharged onto a film emulsion and was captured directly onto film. He discovered rings of light around living objects: plants, animals, people. One day his wife, Valentina, tripped and injured her leg. He noticed that the stronger the pain, the brighter the colors. As the pain disappeared, the colors became more pastel. Today, an image of a relaxed person's finger taken in this special kirlian manner shows a blue-white glow. Strong emotions, such as anxiety, turn the aura a blue, then yellow, and finally a murky red.

I can understand why medieval and Renaissance painters painted bands of yellow around the heads of holy people and angels. It was called a halo or nimbus — a "glory light." They just painted what they saw, or what they thought they saw. When the background light is right, anyone can see auras. What colors mean, however, is certainly open to interpretation. It's possible that the aura acts as protection against outside psychic influences, as St. John of the Cross believed. These colors may protect you from those who would draw off your energy, for instance. Imagine your aura as a strong, clear, pure light — a white light all filled with Christed-colors. It's a bright spiritual armor.

Chakras

> *"Life is a luminous halo,*
> *a semi-transparent envelope surrounding us*
> *from the beginning of consciousness to the end."*

Virginia Woolf from "Modern Fiction"

Energy whirls around us and within us. To help us visualize how these spinning wheels vitalize our lives, and act as gateways, Hindu literature teaches us about the chakra system. *Chakra* is a Sanskrit word meaning "a wheel" or "a disk." A spinning vortex. They are sometimes called lotuses because they unfold, like a flower. How many "petals" each has varies in this seven-stepped system. From the bottom, the root chakra, associated with red, to the top, the crown chakra, associated with violet, there are 4, 6, 10, 12, 16, 2 and 1000 petals.[31]

Martin Brofman in his work on the Body/Mirror system says each of the chakras is energy that vibrates at a certain frequency and in a very logical and orderly sequence of seven vibrations. As we travel up the scale, the elements become more and more subtle, moving through the five physical elements of earth, water, fire, air, and ether, to the spiritual elements of inner sound and inner light. The heaviest element is on the bottom, the lightest on the top.

I have summarized these gateways between various dimensions this way:

Red/Root: "I have"; survival, groundedness and connected to the adrenal gland.

Orange: "I feel"; desire, sexuality, life force and connected to testes, ovaries, womb.

Yellow: "I can"; solar plexus, where ego is housed — willpower, but feelings, emotions.

Green: "I love"; heart balance, compassion, thymus and lungs, immune system.

---

[31] Anodea Judith, *Wheels of Life* (Woodbury, MN: Llewellyn Publications, 1989), 13.

Blue: "I speak"; communication, creativity, where we connect hypothalmus and thyroid.

Indigo: "I see"; third eye; intuition, imagination, dreaming, gateway to wisdom; pineal gland that produces melatonin.

Violet: " I know"; crown chakra; pituitary top of head — understanding, bliss, center of enlightenment.

Rudolph Steiner added a "peach" or "magenta" color above the violet for our spiritual center.

We can speak and pray into these various chakras to "unmuddy" their colors, to gather the colors together to make the various chakra points even stronger. *Hunab Ku: 77 Symbols for Balancing Body and Spirit* is organized by seven chakra colors and at the end of our book, my son, Joel, and I present a "Rainbow Reading" to further investigate each of the seven colors and how they can "soak in" to our bodies. "You will get a composite picture of what your body is processing right now. Ponder any blockages. Note any affirmations. Sense heat and pulsations, either moving from your red root chakra and up, or from your violet crown chakra and down your body. Keep in mind, the color green integrates the three chakra centers that are above and below. Your heart knows what is needed to keep you healthy and balanced. Breathe deeply into each new color."[32]

How amazing! We are rainbows, from the tops of heads to the soles of our feet.

---

[32] Karen Speerstra, Joel Speerstra, *Hunab Ku: 77 Sacred Symbols for Balancing Body and Spirit* (Berkeley, CA: The Crossing Press/Random House, 2005), 314.

Colorful Voices

. . . . .

ISAAC NEWTON (1642-1727)

England's Sir Isaac Newton was one of the greatest modern physical scientists who ever lived. The Great Plague closed down Cambridge so at twenty-three, he left Trinity College, moved back to his home in Lincolnshire, and intensely worked on his Principa — *his* Mathematical Principles of Natural Philosophy, *which wasn't published until 1687. He was elected to Parliament and was Master of the Mint until his death.*

He studied optics and during his post-Cambridge time he experimented with light and called this period his "prime age for invention." He later taught mathematics and laid the foundation for modern physics. He wrote on mechanics and gravitations, and one-tenth of his personal library was composed of alchemical treatises. He studied humanistic learning all this life, was fascinated by the Egyptians, and from their mysteries got the idea that the earth orbited the sun. Convinced that the Bible held secret wisdom of the universe, he learned Hebrew and read twenty different versions of the book of Revelation. He investigated and recreated the details of Solomon's Temple, and studied and wrote on Judeo-Christian prophesy. The economist John Maynard Keynes called Newton "the last of the magicians... the last great mind which looked out on the world with the same eyes as those who began to build our intellectual inheritance rather less than ten thousand years ago... he saw the whole universe... as a riddle, as a secret which could be read by applying pure thought to certain evidence, certain mystic clues which God had hid about the world to allow a sort of philosopher's treasure hunt..."[33]

Light is made up of minute particles. I believe everything is made of matter. It's inert. It's mechanical and precise. It's in motion and follows strict laws of cause and effect. There. Now you know how my mind works. But if the truth be told, I may be more alchemist than scientist. Alchemy helps me understand universal harmony.

---

[33] John Maynard Keyes, "Newton the Man" in *Newton Tercentenary Celebrations* (Royal Society of London, Cambridge University Press, 1947), 27-9.

I bought a prism at Stourbridge Fair and set up a darkened room where I could, like Descartes, study rainbows. When I passed sunshine through the glass — this was back in 1666 — I broke them up into separate ephemeral paths. My eyesight is rather poor, so I asked my friend to help me. Through a hole in my shutter, we saw a rainbow. At one time we had eleven colors; then five. We could really see six, but we settled on seven to match the notes in an octave. Or one for every day of the week. My friend thought we should add indigo since it's currently a favorite dye.

I chuckle at how John Keats thought there was much more to the rainbow than what I'd presented. In fact in the way he had with words, he poetically accused me of trying to "unweave a rainbow" and that philosophy "will clip an angel's wings." That wasn't my intention. Not at all. I was looking for cosmic patterns!

If I have made any discoveries, it's been more due to my patient attention than to any other talent. I coined the word "spectrum" from the Latin word for "apparition" — since "rainbow" seems so ephemeral. So ghostlike. Colors are a connection from this more "real" world to the next. When I bent light, I discovered that the weakest and darkest of the colors like purple were the most refracted. And the color least bent by a prism is red. I labeled three major aspects of how we see color: brightness, hue, and intensity. There are measurable mathematical patterns in color. How amazing!

Once I mixed yellow orpiment, bright purple, light green, and blue, and when I backed away from it a few feet, it looked brilliant white.

Colors circle back upon themselves from red through orange to yellow to green to blue to purple and to violet and back to red again. Around and around. Like life.

. . . . .

JOHANN WOLFGANG GOETHE   (1749–1832)

Goethe was a well-known German writer by the time he was twenty-five. He studied law in Leipzig but literature remained his first love. He traveled to Italy, served for a time in the military, and had a collaborative friendship with the poet-philosopher Friedrich Schiller. Goethe is best known for writing Faust, the tragedy of Doctor Faust, who makes a deal with Mephistopheles, the devil. He was a prolific poet and wrote many treatises, including one on the study of plants, and four novels. He began writing his Theory of Colors *in 1780 inspired, in part, by his skepticism of Newton's theory of color. Based not on any knowledge of physics, which he never claimed to have, it contained his own experiments and was published in 1810.*

If my eye were not of the nature of the sun, how could I behold the light? And if God's own power were not working within me, how could divine things be so delightful?

I remember walking across the park one day, past some yellow crocuses. Naturally, I stopped to admire them and when I turned away, the most amazing thing happened. I saw violet, yellow's opposite. But the crocuses were still yellow, so the violet had to have come from inside my mind. Maybe color isn't just about the external universe!

So this phenomenon of complementary colors isn't caused by light entering my eyes, but instead, how my brain sees them.

And it happened again. This time, I was staying at an inn and noticed, as the sun set, a beautiful fair-skinned girl in a red dress. I blinked and she became a dark-faced figure robed in a beautiful sea-green. Every color, it seems, forces its opposition.

I see the world as having three different classes of colors: physiological, physical, and chemical. Active colors such as yellow, orange, and red become even more energetic when they're combined with black or dark colors. But they weaken when they are combined with light colors. You can cheer violets, blues, and greens up if you combine them with light colors.

Air and light and clouds... how I love to study the sky. I still think about how Newton allowed light to pass through the hole in his window shade onto a screen and decided to experiment with a prism myself. But what I got were fringes of light around the edges of black and white patterns. It was distorted, troubled light. Thousands of overlapping spectra. What did this mean? Black and white leads to color! That's what it means.

I remember how I borrowed a prism from a friend and did my own experiments and concluded just the opposite of what Newton discovered. He focused a narrow beam of light in order to isolate the color phenomenon. I observed with a wider aperture, and there was no spectrum. I saw only reddish-yellow edges and blue-cyan edges with white between them, and the spectrum, when it arose, appeared only where these edges came close enough to overlapping. Color rises from the interaction of light and dark edges. So, I think Newton's theories about color are simply an old nest of rats and owls. If Newton were to describe a rose, he'd come up with a series of words about gray atomic particles and dry mathematical terms and would miss the beauty of what a sun-drenched rose really is. For heaven's sake, go outside! But to be fair to the old guy, I should say that he was mainly concerned with our special world and I am trying to take a longer, more inner view.

Light shouldn't be broken down, as Newton did. It's a "whole." I decided color is not the sole property of light. Instead, I like to think that the eye was made so that the *light* could see. I kept experimenting with color for twenty years. I came up with "plus" color and "minus" colors. "Plus" colors such as reds and oranges and yellows excite and enliven our feelings; "minus" colors such as blues, greens, and blue-ish reds make us more restless and anxious. I call some colors more lucid and others more serious. Others I call mighty, serene, and even melancholic.

I tell people: Study color out in nature, by all means! Close your eyes and open your ears and let nature speak to you. I wrote my doctrine of colors in 1810 with how I perceived the "color circle" to look. (Goethe's Color Wheel, page 149) I like to think it contains the doctrines of the ancients. Only two others have tried to do what I've done (to describe and classify the phenomena of colors) and they were Theophrastus and Boyle — generally ascribed to Aristotle.

Light, warm colors might be called positive and darker colder colors, those tempered with shadow, are negative. Both are needed for balance. Put red on one end, blue on the other, and in the middle you have green — the natural divide between light and shadow.

When I see color my eye is roused into activity. It seeks a colorless space next to it to produce the missing color — the color that creates totality in the circle of colors. This is the fundamental rule of harmony.

Colors are really half-lights and half-shadows. The retina is affected by brightness and by darkness. A dark object will appear smaller than a bright one even if they're the same size. Tycho de Brahe said the dark moon appears about one-fifth the size of a full moon. I'm sure he's right.

I like what Lodovico Dolce said in Venice in 1565 in his *Dialogue on Colors*: "If you wish to produce colors agreeable to the eye, put gray next to dusky orange; yellow-green next to a rose color; blue next to orange; dark purple black next to dark-green; white next to black... " See what we can learn from those who have gone before?

Color lives, as do we all, between heavenly illuminations and earth's dark matter. We hang, swinging between the two. Suspended by color.

Chapter Three

ARTFUL COLOR

Prelude

Mary Cassatt to Berthe Morisot
13, avenue Trudaine
Friday (Fall 1879)

Dear Madame,
Your letter found me at Divonne and I waited until my return here to respond. I
think I can buy something of Monet's. I wanted to do so before I left... my father
told me that he would buy a Monet when the others were sold... I will do what I
can but you know that it isn't easy to persuade the world.

I am so happy that you have done so much work, you will reclaim your place
at the exposition with éclat. I am very envious of your talent I assure you. This
summer I didn't get anything done, we traveled for nearly four weeks, in Pied-
mont and then to Milan and returned through Switzerland by Lake Maggiore
and Simplon. I saw many things to admire, beautiful frescoes, really I don't see
that the moderns have discovered anything about color. It seems to me that we
haven't learned anything more about color or drawing....

Affectionate friend

Mary Cassatt

A Young Artist

> *"Color possesses me. I don't have to pursue it.*
> *It will possess me always. I know it.*
> *That is the meaning of this happy hour.*
> *Color and I are one. I am a painter."*

Paul Klee, his notebook

I grew up in central Wisconsin. When my cousin David and I were ten, our aunt Bertha, the one who enticed us into all kinds of wonderful adventures, bought train tickets for the three of us to go to Superior — that mysterious city on the lake so far up north. We thought we might see polar bears. Instead, jack pines flew past our train windows. Later trips showed me that Superior was a railroad town, scatter-grown, and a place you pushed through to get to the zoo in Duluth. But the destination that hot summer day was an upstairs apartment on Superior's Main Street. We two young budding artists bounded up the wooden stairs to meet Uncle Fred, the family artist, and Ida, his saintly wife — our grand-mother's favorite sister. So favorite, in fact, that they had had a double wedding.

My grandmother Julia was soft and round; Ida was straight, angular, thin with a feisty head of red hair. Maybe it was all the turpentine she breathed daily. Fred was a railroad man, as transient as he was gifted. Every member of our family had at least one of his oil paintings — usually a lone wolf baying at a full moon. At our house, the wolf joined the only other piece of framed art that I remember: a print of "The Gleaners" by Jean Francois Millet. It was painted in 1857 and I never asked my parents why it hung in our 1940s and '50s home. So I grew up with one wolf surrounded by blue-white snow and three bent women working in that grain field, day after day. Millet's whole landscape is yellow fields and trees along the edge. A town peeks over the left-hand horizon. The foreground is a dark rich red-brown. The woman in the middle is painted in red tones, a bright carmine kerchief on her hair; the other two are in blues and browns. The woman in the left foreground is dressed in a silvery bright blue-gray, dove-gray, blue and turquoise grays. Low color thresholds make for easier access, perhaps, which accounts for people with very little art training loving it so. It was years before I saw the original at the Louvre. But that hot summer day in Superior, Wisconsin, we had no need for the Louvre, or even for prints. We had Uncle Fred right in front of us, the real deal, spreading pungent paint and communicating in grunts and coughs.

As David and I hovered near his suspendered shoulders, we watched him gesso a piece of wallboard with regular white wall paint. Fred rarely used stretched canvas. Then he blended blues into the white with his fingers. His fingers! Dave and I looked at each other in wide amazement, mouthing, "Can you do that?"

A tour of the apartment made it very clear that when Fred ran out of wallboard, he painted right onto the walls. When the scene was finished, he'd paint a frame around it. Aunt Ida had two-dimensional art wherever she looked. And whenever Uncle Fred's muse hit him, he'd paint over the wall and start all over again. I figured if Michelangelo could paint on ceilings, Uncle Fred could paint on walls.

That evening, before catching our southbound train, Bertha gave us the best present ever. We visited an art store — imagine a town with an art store! — and she bought us each a $10.00 boxed set of oil paints, some brushes (we already had our fingers poised for sky-painting) and a palette knife. We decided we could use an old plate for a palette. I'm sure that was the first time anyone had ever spent that much money on something for me that I couldn't eat or wear. All the way home, I rearranged my paints, slick with mysterious names. *Cerulean Blue. Burnt Umber.* Like Alice in Wonderland, I heard them crying out, "Try me, Try me!" One of Aunt Bertha's favorite sayings was, 'Take a chance. Columbus did." So both Dave and I chanced becoming artists, each in our own way.

I was blessed with another unmarried aunt. It was my Aunt Edna who introduced me to textile arts — embroidery — when I was four. This was the aunt who, when my parents traveled, cared for me on my father's home farm. At night I curled up with her in her big brass bed between icy sheets ironed so smoothly it was like sleeping between white paper. We spent summer afternoons sipping hot chocolate from fragile green-flowered teacups. She'd bring out dominoes and a button box and string. She taught me cat's cradle and how I could buzz a button in the center of a string the way Eskimo children played with bone and sinew. I've read that people of the North believe a spirit lives in the cat's cradle. You had to make the string dance faster and faster in order to beat the spirit at its own game. If they outmaneuvered the spirit, their hunt would be successful. The dark would not be overpowering. It was another way to peel back the night.

One afternoon Edna gave me a clump of bright pink floss, a needle, and a brand-new dish towel stamped with a large sugar bowl. "Do I get to do this all by myself?" I asked. "You sure do!" My half-inch stitches raced around the bowl and the design was beautiful. Together, we decided it would be a surprise gift for my mother, but of course the gift was really mine. The gift was called self-confidence and whenever I see pink, I am back there in that farmhouse confidently stitching. I was fortunate to have an art professor in college named John Rogers who taught me that there are no mistakes in art. "Only opportunities. Only character," as he put it.

Once I painted a fruit bowl still life for my husband's aunt Alice, a wonderful careful Dutch woman who never married but lived with her bachelor brother on a farm. Aunt Alice lived and died within the same square farmhouse, surrounded by the same furniture in the same arrangements, cooking the same menu for Thanksgiving dinners. When she got the framed painting, all ready to hang, Aunt decided the bananas were a bit too green. One day she asked me, "Could you please ripen them up?" Aunt Alice hadn't been privy to John Rogers' speech about "character" in art. So I took it home and added more yellow.

"Ripening up the bananas" has been a family joke ever since. All art is a work in progress and sometimes yellows do need to be a bit more "ripening," as even Van Gogh discovered. Aunt Alice always wanted to paint, but no one ever gave her permission to make mistakes, so she rarely tried. After she died, at her auction, I bought her childhood paint book along with a box of pristine watercolors. Sad little slabs of color still clung to the tin — unused. She had kept them "nice and new" for over seventy years.

On another occasion I had still another lesson to learn about painting with yellow. I discovered there are more ways than one to create green. I was invited to Sweden, to my son's university research workshop to paint dozens of ash wood panels — pipe shades — for the façade of a huge baroque organ that Goteborg University had built for Seoul, Korea. The organ builder, Munetaka Yokota, decided the ribbons that integrated all the acanthus leaves and rosettes, which I painted in *trompe l'oeil* to simulate three-dimensional wood carving, should be green. Alas, I had no greens. I had only cadmium yellow, burnt umber, and black at my disposal. But in a quick overlay of yellow and umber over black, the resulting green turned out to be exactly what he desired. He called it a "noble eighteenth-century green." It was an accidental color that could never have come from a tube.

Ancient Artists

"The oldest cave paintings yet discovered are in a cave named Chauvet in southern France. They are about 32,000 years old. The paintings show huge, vivid herds of animals spilling across the walls. In particular there are lions and horses all painted with individuality and a dynamism that makes them masterpieces. The lions are bent on the hunt and look fierce and wild-eyed. But cave bears were just as ferocious as lions, yet there is a wonderful, roly-poly bear with his head bent low as if he were sniffing flowers on the ground. The paintings there have all the refinement, subtlety and power that great art has had ever since."[1]

The first cave artists, men and women, used only black and red outlines; later these underground painters added a tannish red, orange, sepia by mixing red and black. For a rich red color, they ground up iron-oxide hematite ores. Red, the color of life. Fire. Blood. Fertility. Some archeologists have found entire cave floors covered with red perhaps to sanctify its sacred space.

Marija Gimbutas and others have indicated the color red is connected to how early people viewed caves and the Great Mother. "The caves, crevices and caverns of the earth are natural manifestations of the primordial womb of the

---

[1] Gregory Curtis, *The Cave Painters: Probing the Mysteries of the World's First Artists* (New York: Anchor Books, Random House, 2006), 16.

Mother. This idea is not Neolithic in origin; it goes back to the Paleolithic, when the narrow passages, oval-shaped areas, clefts, and small cavities of caves are marked or painted entirely in red. This red color must have symbolized the color of the Mother's regenerative organs."[2]

Altamira was the first painted cave discovered on Spain's northern coast. Its discovery made quite a stir right about the time Charles Darwin became known in England. People called the images frauds. After all, how could "unevolved primitive" humans create something so magnificent? Subsequent excavations in that area have unearthed masses of powdered red ochre, large patties of violet, vermillion, orange, and gray clay, all of which would have been excellent colors for early artists.

The skeletons that survive seem to indicate these people were generally healthy, as tall as we are, and may have lived fifty to sixty years. They lived in this southern France, northern Spain area of the Mediterranean in an unchanged environment for about 20,000 years. Their painting is unfailingly constant.

Discovered in 1994, Chauvet's paintings, like all other cave art, overlap and build on one another. It is supposed that the Neanderthal people who came later imitated earlier art and began using the colors that were already on the walls. These early artists stopped painting about 10,000 years ago. Experts now pretty much agree on how they did it, but continue to debate why. People study the composition of the animals, their placement, their relationship to the space and to each other and wonder: Are they clan symbols? Are the black and red stenciled hands with "missing fingers" just hand-figures with bent fingers forming a code? Do the hands reach into the rock and beyond? Do the animals emerge from another more shamanic dimension?

One October, my husband and I had the rare pleasure of visiting Lascaux II in the Dordogne Valley in France. It's a reproduction to the exact millimeter of the original cave that we ordinary people can no longer visit because we would further deteriorate the paintings. I left the Hall of Bulls and Axial Gallery reeling. Even though we weren't deep down in a vibrant cave like the original one just two

---

[2] Marija Gimbutas, *The Language of the Goddess* (San Francisco: Harper & Row Publishers, 1989), 151.

hundred yards up the road behind a chain-link fence, we felt we were on hallowed ground. Unlike a real cave, the walls weren't damp, we didn't slip on the rocks, or hear and feel water dripping. Still, the hushed atmosphere was absolutely shattering to my senses. The colors shimmered in the dim light that approximated early torchlight. I knew we were in only about one-third of the real Lascaux cave system, but the art we saw was completely true to what had originally been painted. The small-headed, thick-necked, spindly-legged horses that seemed to thunder around the walls all began with a thick black line for the mane and face. Then the artist sketched a light outline of the back and rounded belly either in red ochre or black, yellow, browns, or shades of red. Last, the artist sketched the hooves, legs, rump, and tail in black and then shaded them in. This was the sequence followed again and again, regardless of the horse's size.[3] And they kept painting them this way in this particular cave for at least a thousand years.

Our ancestors used little oil lamps to paint their magnificent art onto cave walls that bent and undulated underground. Indentations of natural rock indicated bison hips, mammoth legs, and leonine strength. With light and color, these artists created what they saw around them and even beyond what they could see with their physical eyes. Perhaps they thought a world existed beyond the solid dimension of the rock walls. However they viewed their sacred lives, they created soul-works and, ever after, that's what artists do.

Soul Works

"Mere color unspoiled by meaning
and unallied with definite form,
can speak to the soul in a thousand different ways."

Oscar Wilde

Whether we go to galleries and museums or not, art is a part of our everyday lives and so is artful color. But we first have to see it. "In the classroom, the teacher

---

[3] Curtis, 99.

explains that colors are not properties of things, but characteristics of reflected light: they are electromagnetic radiations which have a certain wavelength range; but when the class is over, teacher and students continue to speak of red apples and yellow grapefruit."[4]

When our older son was about fourteen, he received a wonderful gift from his art teacher, Loretta Grellner. She had handwritten, on her precious water-color paper, all the galleries and museums around the world, with their addresses, that he should one day visit. He thanked her, thinking, I'll never get to all these places. Now, decades later, he looks at that precious little book and realizes he's been to all of them. What a "pay it forward" gift!

When I visit a museum I all too often hurry around, peering at whatever is written to the piece to satisfy my intellectual curiosity. Who painted it? What is it named? What did the artist mean to "say" here? What did she mean by using these particular colors? I do this because I'm usually compelled to try to see more and more and more. Rather than sitting a ways off and contemplating a painting to see what it calls up in *me* I want to be fed. I would be better served to ask, "What do the colors mean to me? What is stirred inside me?" To truly enter the work, you have to step into it and out of it again. And then step back into it again.

I've heard that to allow your eyes to mix the colors, you should back up to view a painting at a distance eight times the painting's diagonal measurement. To view some of the gigantic contemporary canvases, you'd have to back up into the next block.

Once I broke my "hurry to see as much as possible" museum motto. It was five minutes to five when I climbed the steps of the British National Gallery. The guard said, "We're closing in five minutes, Madam," and I replied, "Then I guess I'll have to hurry." It was my first visit and since London's museums don't charge admission, I didn't pause for a moment to think, "what a waste of time and money for only five minutes." I entered, walked a few steps, intuitively turned to the right and there was a pot of Van Gogh's sunflowers. I spent my full five minutes absorbing one of our three holy trinity of colors as the Irish writer and poet John

---

[4]Jacques Maguet, *The Aesthetic Experience* (New Haven: Yale University Press, 1986), 8.

O'Donohue put it. He said yellow "casts glad brightness." When I descended the steps into the busy London street once more, every pore in my body radiated glad brightness.

Eight shades of beige and brown wool threads are embroidered onto Queen Matilda's famous Bayeux tapestry depicting the Battle of Hastings and her husband's conquering of England. Some of the blues remain nearly unfaded. We visited these well-preserved war-panels showing William's forty-two Viking ships launched against England on the very day we had walked along the coast of Normandy where just 878 years after William, seven thousand ships crossed the channel bound for France. The brown earth and rocks on Omaha and other landing sites no longer show blood-spots, but you can be sure they're still there as underpainting. Red and brown signify war — the muddy taking of lives just to prove one nation is stronger, more aligned with a greater good, richer, has better weapons and is more courageous.

If we were to take a trip back in time, we might wander into the Neolithic village of Çatalhöyük in southeastern Turkey, where we'd find peering from various rooms, as they have since 7000 B.C.E., white-headed bulls with stripes of black and red, together with red vultures. Gimbutus believed bulls, vultures, and a myriad of other early symbols, represented life, death, and regeneration. They were "Her" markings — The Great Mother's. The renewer of life. "She was the single source of all life who took her energy from the springs and wells, from the sun, moon, and moist earth. This symbolic system represents cyclical, not linear, mythical time. In art this is manifested by the signs of dynamic motion, whirling and twisting spirals, winding and coiling snakes, circles, crescents, horns, sprouting seeds and shoots... Even the colors had a different meaning than in the Indo-European symbolic system. Black did not mean death or the underworld; it was the color of fertility, the color of damp caves and rich soil, of the womb of the Goddess where life begins. White, on the other hand, was the color of death, of bones — the opposite of the Indo-European system in which both white and yellow are the colors of the shining sky and the sun."[5]

---

[5] Gimbutus, xix, xx.

Egyptians painted on papyrus, fabrics, walls, and statues. Some think even the sphinx was red at one time. When we see the remains of spare white statues from ancient times, it's easy to overlook the fact that the Greeks also painted everything in sight. Their main colors were black, white, red, and yellow but experts who have recovered these colors say they could mix 819 shades from those four basic colors.[6]

And Pompeii's lava-crusted walls were once decorated in brilliant reds, polished like glass.

Ishtar's Gate from Babylon's reign of Nebuchadnezzar during the 500s B.C.E. screams blue and gold in bold, glazed-brick relief expanses that stretch so far over your head, you feel faint just looking up. Stalking lions and alert dragons face off across vast expanses and fill the hall at Berlin's Pergamon Museum with a majesty rarely captured elsewhere. When we visited Museum Island the vast Processional Way drew us back to a time when color was king — or queen of heaven in Ishtar's case. Glazed, colorful animals, 575 of them in the original, created a religious complex — the Vatican of its day.

Romanesque pillars were ribboned with vivid color and statues carried all sorts of garish colors. Colors were arranged in a certain order, Andre Malraux reminds us, on statuary of the Middle Ages, not to just create a statue, but to *be* the Virgin. To *be* the Christ.

Sculpture has the advantage of offering a three-dimensional view. "A picture," however, "before being a war horse, a nude woman, or some anecdote, is essentially a flat surface covered by colors arranged in a certain order." That's the often-quoted definition of what lies within the borders of painting as described by Maurice Denis in 1890.

The philosopher Immanuel Kant, who founded German Idealism, was a man who felt that we have knowledge about absolute truths, about ourselves and our world, built into us in utero. He couldn't see the inner, spiritual beauty of color. He argued that color adds liveliness to what we are looking at, but color can't in itself make it beautiful.[7] Color is seductive. But, he said, it's design that's

[6] L. Moholy-Nagy, *Vision in Motion* (Chicago: Paul Theobald and Co., 1965), 162.

[7] Immanuel Kant, *The Critique of Judgment* (Oxford: Clarendon Press, 1952), 67.

essential. Kant held color in close check. "The Kantians feel that only in composition, rather than on their own, do color in painting or tone in music add to the beauty of the world."[8]

Most of us recognize famous art from art history books or brief visits to museums and galleries. But what did we actually see? And what colors captured us? Perhaps it was the red cruelty of war in Picasso's *Guernica*. Mona Lisa's sly smile? Andy Warhol's colorfully stacked Campbell's soup cans? Or the result of eleven centuries of Byzantine mosaics — cubes of colored glass that made saints and Godlike figures transcendent? Or O'Keeffe's sensuous flowers, "all chromatic microcosms that invite the viewer to enter and engage the forces of the palette on their own turf"[9]?

Matisse believed "the chief function of color should be to serve expression as well as possible... I put down my tones without a preconceived plan... The expressive aspect of colors imposes itself on me in a purely instinctive way. To paint an autumn landscape I will not try to remember what colors suit this season. I will be inspired only by the sensation that the season arouses in me: the icy purity of the sour blue sky will express the season just as well as the nuances of foliage."[10] He was quite taken with a new version of red called cadmium red. He liked its stability but he couldn't persuade Renoir to use it instead of his vermillion.

We've probably all heard of Picasso's blue period. Jung called the work he did then his mythical journey into hell. Color for him at that time took on the color of the underworld. Picasso's very dear friend, Casagemas, had just died and he painted him in his casket. Several times, using many shades of blue. Picasso called blue the color of all colors; it expresses "the sincerity... that cannot be found apart from grief." He called beggars and outcasts life's great sadness and often painted them in cold blues.

Van Gogh's little yellow house in Arles seemed to epitomize his necessity for yellow around him. "My house here is painted the yellow color of fresh butter on the outside with glaringly green shutters; it stands in the full sunlight in a square which has a green garden with plane trees, oleanders and acacias. And

[8] Charles A. Riley II, *Color Codes* (Hanover, NH: University Press of New England, 1995), 20.
[9] Ibid., 102.
[10] John Elderfield, *Henri Matisse: A Retrospective* (New York: Museum of Modern Art, 1992), 54.

it is completely whitewashed inside, and the floor is made of red bricks. And over it there is the intensely blue sky. In this I can live and breathe, meditate and paint." [11]

Reubens has been described as a "fleshy" man. He used a lot of reds in his painting. Blood. Noon. Summers. Plump women. Cheery cherubs. Botticelli used light pinks and greens — rainbow colors in his *Birth of Venus*. Spring. Youth. Renewal.

What artists associate with various colors on the canvas makes a world of difference. In fact, the Romantic Frenchman Eugène Delacroix once said, "Give me mud and I will make the skin of Venus out of it, if you will allow me to surround it as I please."[12] Titian's colors glowed because of what he placed next to each one. A friend of his once wrote, "Titian has displayed in his works no empty grace, but colors appropriate to their tasks." He created what his friend described as "broken color effects."

The English painter Turner, who when he died in 1851, left 350 oils and 20,000 sketches and drawings, was criticized for painting weak colors like "egg yolks." Another critic called it "soapsuds and whitewash." Nevertheless he kept on painting, attempting to capture sunshine and air. He matched his colors to the time of day: yellow for morning, red for evening. In a lecture he gave in 1818, he said yellow represented for him the medium, red the material objects, and blue the distance. Turner felt the three primary colors contained all of visible creation. His paintings of white frigates against glowing purples and violet skies on pale green seas are unforgettable. He would actually strap himself to the mast of a ship just to venture out into the heart of a storm. Later, he would "paint in tumultuous heavings and sobbings of color."[13]

Renaissance painters in northern Italy began to emphasize value over color. They limited their palettes and opted for more contrast of light and dark. They used grisaille — a monochrome grayish underpainting.

When the Impressionists came along they seemed to have said, "value, schmallue. Let's go for color!" They tried to capture air and color, often by

[11] Herkshel B. Chipp, *Theories of Modern Art* (Berkeley, CA: University of California Press, 1968), 34, quoted Ibid, 102.

[12] Paul C. Vitz and Arnold B. Glimcher, *Modern Art and Modern Science* (Praeger, 1984), 79.

[13] Diane Ackerman, *Deep Play* (New York: Random House, 1999), 65.

painting outdoors. Paul Cezanne felt *plein air* would teach artists more about their craft than anything else. That's because no color remains the same for very long outside. You have to capture the light quickly before it changes everything, he cautioned. He once wrote this about sunlight in Provence: "The sunlight here is so intense that it seems to me that objects are silhouetted not only in black and white but also in blue, red, brown, and violet."[14]

Van Gogh spread his blazing colors on the canvas like cake frosting. "Color is free!" he proclaimed — perhaps it was for him, since his brother Theo paid for most of it. We watch his red disks slip over the horizon and think Van Gogh must have worshipped the sun.

Claude Monet used his painting discipline to create his gardens in broad brushstrokes of breathing flowers. He preferred pure colors, solid colors to variegated, and richly patterned textures just as his kitchen was decorated. I looked out through his kitchen window to the porch and beyond to the gardens on a misty autumn day, thinking about how this impassioned colorist must have viewed early spring irises surrounded by light blue air, water lilies floating on pads of pink. (Monet's House and Garden, page 146-147) Standing on his green bridge, you could sense how he knew the mysterious ways light and air come together to form color. And when you look at all his haystacks, you realize he totally believed the real subject of every painting is light.

Édouard Manet preferred working in his studio. He like to place lighter color patches on top of darker ones, which was the opposite of what usually had been done: light colors first with overlays of darker colors. Suddenly, colors became objects in and of themselves. Manet didn't outline first but let the color become the boundary. Count Harry Kessler, who was rich enough to travel and meet "all the important people" and kept detailed diaries from 1880–1918, called Manet one of the great color theoreticians. He recorded in one of his many diaries his impressions of one of Manet's paintings of Berthe Morisot, his sister-in-law. "All done in forceful strokes, like the blows of a fighter... It is moreover curious that this genius for profiles and lines has created a revolution in the area

---

[14] Phillip Ball, *Bright Earth: Art and the Invention of Color* (New York: Farrar, Straus and Giroux, 2001), 174.

of color whereas his own coloring... is hard and unpleasant. Colors are strictly separated from colors by firm lines, and within the colors there is no shading. The total impression is closer to a mosaic than a painting."[15]

Kessler loved Renoir, with his models' cheeks often reddened by sleep, showing the flow of blood lurking beneath the skin. He saw in them wonders of color coming alive in the flickering and changing light. But he found the Impressionists' work to be "such orgies of hideousness and nerve-shaking combinations of colors I thought impossible outside a madhouse; violet trees in a red field and beneath a yellow sky, women with their faces all covered with red spots as if they had the measles, trees looking like demented serpents; I have never seen anything so terrible in my most painful nightmares... "

Well, it's true that Paul Gauguin did paint grass red and faces green on occasion. He even painted *The White Horse* in browns and greens. Werner Haftmann said, of Gauguin's work: "Color flows like a lava from a volcano."[16] Gauguin was trying to prove that objects can be relative colors rather than absolute ones. "Pure color," he once said. "You must sacrifice everything to it."

Edmond Duranty, a spokesman for the Impressionist movement, once said these artists proceeded by intuition and "little by little succeeded in splitting sunlight into its rays, and then reestablishing its unity in the general harmony of the iridescent color that they scatter over their canvases.... Even the most learned physicists could find nothing to criticize in these painters' analysis of light."[17]

Some Parisians in the 1880s hated Georges Seurat's pointillist work so much they actually poked his canvases with their umbrellas. They called him "the little chemist." But he didn't care. "I'm not going to do the mixing for anyone looking at this — let their eyes mix the colors from my dots." If you've ever seen that huge canvas, *A Sunday Afternoon on the Island of La Grande Jatte*, in Chicago, you know how dots can shimmer and vibrate.

Ogden Rood was an American who, in 1879, wrote about chromatics — all about dots of color and how the eye would blend them. It was translated into French in 1891 and influenced artists such as Pissaro, Seurat, and Signac. The

---

[15] Harry Kessler, *Journey to the Abyss* (Alfred A. Knopf, 2011, "Amiens-Canterbury, June 16, 1895," e-book edition)

[16] Werner Haftmann, *Painting in the 20th Century* (New York: George Braziller, 1982), 74.

[17] Andreas Blüm and Louise Lippincott, *Light: The Industrial Age 1750-1900* (London: Thames and Hudson, 2000), 20.

points of color, intended for the retina to mix, could become gray and cloudy — dreamlike. "The role of dotting (pointillage)... simply makes the surface of paintings more lively, but it does not guarantee luminosity, intensity of color, or harmony. The complementary colors, which are allies and enhance each other when juxtaposed, are enemies and destroy each other if mixed, even optically. A red and a green if juxtaposed enliven each other, but red dots and green dots make an aggregate which is gray and colorless."[18] Seurat died at thirty-one. But Pissaro lived longer and felt that the optical mixture of color decomposed various tones into their constituent elements and are, therefore, even more luminous than mixed pigments.[19] He later, however, abandoned the technique.

The French lawyer turned artist, Pierre Bonnard, usually worked with an eight-color palette. Like Van Gogh, he felt you never can have too much golden yellow. Red can be "power, royalty, opulence, but change it slightly and you're in for an exotic, erotic ride heading towards violence."

Degas so wanted to control color that he even changed frames, wall colors, and lighting before hanging a piece. "He was keenly aware of the variety of greens about him, from the 'apple green' to the 'vivid Veronese,' from turquoise from the 'powerful' yet sober gray green of the sea."[20] His friend Mary Cassatt, who often exhibited with him, used strong oils, vivid purples and greens around hands and brown-reds in faces. She was famous for her paintings of babies and children, so her earlier works are lighter and more pastel. But her colors become bolder as she aged.

Piet Mondrian, the Dutch abstraction painter with all his austere blocks of colors and lines, believed red to be more "outward" and blue and yellow more "inward and spiritual."

Then in the late nineteenth- and early-twentieth-century, Fauvism, named for the "wild beast," encouraged painters to use lots of pure color. Put feeling into it! It was so jarring to most critics that they cautioned pregnant women to avoid the shows lest they harm their unborn children. Cubists showed color's underlying planes; Rayonists painted spiked angles in all directions across their canvases.

---

[18] Floyd Ratliff, Paul Signac, *De Delacroix au Neo-Impressionisme, Paul Signac and Color in Neo-Impressionism* English Translation (New York: Rockefeller University Press, 1992), 108.
[19] Ball, 190.
[20] Chipp, 82.

Edvard Munch, the Norwegian who painted *The Scream* with tempera and pastels on cardboard, used oranges and yellows in his wavy sky as a way of describing to the world his inner pain and grief. His mother and sister had died and he was suffering from bronchitis and tuberculosis. Furthermore, he was surrounded by poverty. Henry Kessler, a European count who wrote of his travels from 1880 to 1918, noted in a January 1885 diary entry how he and a friend encountered Munch half-starved; the artist hadn't eaten for three days. He was living in Charlottenburg at the time. In Kessler's words: "A bitter mixture of turpentine thinner and cigarette smoke reaches your nostrils. Munch is still young, but looks already burnt out, tired, hungry in both the physical and psychological sense... He was overjoyed when I gave him sixty marks for a pair of engravings."

One evening as Munch walked along a fjord, he described being tired and sick. He felt wounded and saw wounds around him in nature. "I stood looking out across the fjord — the sun was setting — the clouds were colored red like blood. I felt as though a scream went through nature — I thought I heard a scream. I painted this picture — painted the clouds as real blood. The clouds were screaming."[21] Munch suffered from depression and mental illness. He grieved for the planet after the eruption of Krakatoa in 1883, "hearing" the planet screaming. Before he died, Munch described, in his inimitable Norwegian way that I recognize so well from having grown up surrounded by Scandinavians, many of whom could "do" morose very well, "I was born dying." In his paintings he tried to "dissect souls." He felt that sickness and dark angels had followed him all his life. No wonder he painted *The Scream*!

Joan Miro said, "I try to apply colors like words that shape poems, like notes that shape music." And James Abbott McNeil Whistler, an American who spent most of his life in other countries, used to label his paintings by color such as *Symphony in White; Variations in Flesh Color and Green; Harmony in Green and Rose; Nocturne in Blue and Green.* And his own mother's famous portrait, *Arrangement in Gray and Black No. 1.* He often painted young girls in front of muslin curtains — "a gorgeous mass of white," as he called it.

---

[21] Arne Eggum, et al, *Edvard Munch: Symbols and Images* (Washington, D.C.: National Gallery of Art, 1978), 39.

An American contemporary of Whistler's, Winslow Homer, was introduced to the Impressionists in France but came home to establish American watercolor as a respected medium, and as a result, painted light and color quite differently. He washed large areas of his watercolor paper with color that he blotted or scraped. The result was dramatic seascapes, mysterious rivers.

Expressionists such as Emile Nolde, Marc Chagall, Paul Klee, and Franz Marc used colors with great passion. Picasso and Braque and other Cubists often ignored color altogether but then color began vibrating and was revered as the actual soul of their paintings when Robert Delaunay, Hans Hoffman, Helen Frankenthaler, Mark Rothko, and Kenneth Noland came onto the scene. You can get lost in their solid colors. Nolde once said that he experienced color perceptively, tangibly, and emotionally.

"He had the gift of conveying with color, as if compulsively, where he had experience of seeing events past and present, mental images and visions, the entire 'theatrum mundi' of his unpainted picture. These pictures... erupted out of irregular shapes, flicks, paint runs, in a process of controlled change."[22]

"Something important happened to color in art in the 1960s.... Pop art and minimalism... an entirely new conception of color and was put into words, tentatively, by Stella, during a 1964 radio interview... 'I know a wise-guy who used to make fun of my painting, but he didn't like the Abstract Expressionists either. He said they would be good painters if they could only keep the paint as good as it is in the can. And that's what I tried to do.'"[23] A can rather than a tube! And if he and other artists couldn't "keep the paint as good" what did that mean?

Soon artists were using unbroken color. Mark Rothko, Barnett Newman, and Clyfford Still, for instance, spread luminous paint with no reference points. Color became a means to an end. "I'm not interested," Rothko said, "in the relationship of color or form or anything else. I'm interested only in expressing basic human emotions — tragedy, ecstasy, doom and so on... The people who weep before my pictures are having the same religious experience as I had when I painted them."[24] Lynn M. Herbert has written about Rothko in an essay called

---

[22] Jolanthe Nolde, Manfred Reuther, et al, *Emil Nolde: Unpainted Pictures* (Ostfildern-Ruit, Germany: Catje Cantz Publishers, 2001), 17.

[23] David Batchelor, *Chromophobia* (London: Reaktion Books Ltd., 2007) e-book edition, Chapter 5: "Chromophilia".

[24] Selden Rodman and Alexander Eliot, *Conversations with Artists*, (New York: Capricorn Books, 1961), 93.

"Regarding Spirituality." "Rothko sought the sublime in a form of purity through a fundamental use of color, line, and shape. He is best known for his painting in which mysterious rectangles of color appear to hover over a colored ground. Their rich and varied coloration engulfs viewers, drawing them into an other-worldly realm."[25] In 1964 when Rothko was sixty he was invited to create a series of paintings for a Houston, Texas, chapel designed by Philip Johnson. Rothko had longed for a chapel space and now he had his opportunity. He created large purplish rectangles unlike his earlier bright colors. The chapel was dedicated in 1971, a year after Rothko died, so he never saw the completed installation. People say his work conveys a deep sense of peace.

Trenton Doyle Hancock was born in 1974 and lived in Oklahoma and Texas. Influenced by Abstract Expressionism, he has created a group of paintings that work together to tell mythical stories about birth, death, life, afterlife. He calls one of his characters "Painter." "A mothering type of energy, synonymous with color, so it would only make sense that her energy would be all the colors, a rainbow of colors. With her array of colors, her spectrum, she represents hope and tolerance… Whenever bad things happen she can present us with a layer of color over the top of things to give something else to hope for… If there's no reason for color to be there, the piece will just end up being black and white."[26]

Colors seem to captivate Susan Rothenberg. She was born in Buffalo, New York, in 1945 and now lives and works in New Mexico. She has created life-sized images of horses and other iconic symbols, but it's color that calls to her. "I love red. I use a lot of red. I use innumerable tubes of white. I try to dirty down most of the colors that I use, rather than use them pure. Cobalt blue always gets a hit of something else to twist it out of its sharp, bright coldness… to use green out of context felt quite fresh… I love to work with twenty different colors of green."[27]

Beth Ames Swartz often combines ritual and art — red foods, red candles, red rocks. Passion sizzles and catalyzes her art. She said, "I see red. Fuming, flaring, inflamed, kindled, explosive." She paints the Red Eye of the Dragon, Jacob's Biblical stew and ritual wine, a sacrificial red heifer. "Her Alizarin crimson moves

[25] Art: 21 Art in the Twenty-First Century, Vol. 1 (New York: Harry N. Abrams, Inc., 2003), 69
[26] Art: 21 Art in the Twenty-First Century, Vol. 2 (New York: Harry N. Abrams, Inc.,, 2003), 27.
[27] Art: 21 Art in the Twenty-First Century, Vol. 3 (New York: Harry N. Abrams, Inc., 2005), 102.

from vermillion to claret, to mingle yet never truly merge, suggesting the edgy collision of fire and blood."[28] She says she continues to quest to rediscover the Shekinah, or the Divine Feminine, in her Red Sea series.

A Russian-born American, Jules Olitski, is also worth contemplating. He became one of our most famous color artists in the late 1960s and died in 2007. An Internet search on his name will bring up many of his paintings, which he said he wanted to look like "nothing but some colors sprayed into the air and staying there." You'll discover ways of seeing landscapes, for instance, in only pure color.

Another very playful color artist is an Austrian, Friedensreich Hundertwasser. He died in 2000 but not before creating a body of unparalleled creations. He had no studio and never used an easel. Instead, he traveled around, and placed his canvas or found materials out in front of him and captured in various combined mediums what he was looking at. The results are intense, radiant, active works of color.

Color becomes for an artist a way to make and make and make again. Why? Because, Adrienne Rich said, it is the artist's passion to "make and make and make again/ where such unmaking reigns." Our world often seems to be coming apart. So much "unmaking" does seem to reign. But color, as Titian said, is the true alchemy of painting and like all alchemical processes, color can change lead to gold! Each of us can use our creative imaginations to describe what we see, in our own way, with our own comfortable words. Diane Ackerman says artists continue to create "as a form of praise and celebration. To impose an order on the formless clamor of the world. As a magical intermediary between us and the hostile, unpredictable universe. For religious reasons. For spiritual reasons, to commune with the other. To temporarily stop a world that seems too fast, too random, too chaotic. To help locate ourselves in nature, and give us a sense of home."[29]

Where Artful Colors Come From

Ever since the cave painters crushed rock and mixed it with fat, artists' colors have come from the earth. They used calcite from the rock walls. They got black

---

[28] David S. Rubi and Arlene Raven, *Reminders of Invisible Light: The Art of Beth Ames Swartz* (Manchester, VT: Hudson Hills Press, 2002), 30.

[29] Ackerman, 136.

from magnetite and charcoal from wood or bone. Yellow came from limonite; browns from siderite; dark browns from pyrites. They got red from the madder root and yellows were found in the inner bark of some oak species. In fact, until the 1800s pigments for all artists came from the earth. Then synthetic paint colors were born. Pig bladders gave way to manufactured tubes.

Early polychrome pottery appeared all over Europe; the earliest note of color (around 5000 B.C.E.) in Egypt is from a vase with white lines on burnished red.

As early as 3500 B.C.E. the Minoans on Crete painted a red wash with deeper reds, black and white — and later blue. Red and black were their predominant colors, however, even after they added rose colors, gray-blues, red-browns, and creamy whites to their pottery and mosaics. Colorful pottery extended from England to China by about 3000 B.C.E.

Colored clay beads are probably the first created colored objects. Jewelry, it seems, has always been foremost in our minds! By blending one part lime and one part copper oxide with four parts quartz or silica, Egyptians created a blue called frit. It was a combination of chalk, copper, azurite or malachite, and sand all fired into a brittle blue that could be ground into paint. To make glass, as well as soap, you need alkalis. Soda and potash or nitron was used to make glass in Mesopotamia — Iraq and Syria — as early as 4500 B.C.E. Sumerian and Babylonian artists were powdering surfaces and heating them to glaze tiles and pottery and game boards.

On his trek around his known world, Alexander the Great eventually got to what is now Iran where, unfortunately, he burned the Persian city of Persepolis. According to Diodorus Siculus, a first-century Greek historian, "It was the wealthiest city under the sun... filled with precious objects." Lots of gold, no doubt.

Brilliant gold is rustproof and durable. No wonder people through the ages have chosen to wear it. And base their monetary system on it. In the Incan empire, the new rulers were sprayed with resin and gold dust, virtually turning them into living gold statues. After all, the sun god excreted all this gold for them. The Chinese, too, viewed gold as the essence of heaven. Jason went off in search of a golden sheepskin; Moses tried to keep his people from worshiping a golden calf. The Egyptians called their sun god Ra, the mountain of gold. Later alchemists tried to turn base metal into gold and called it their Great Work. Midas got entangled in it. The Black Hills Sioux called gold the *yellow metal that makes white man crazy*. For the Hindus, gold is the mineral form of light. And it is that yellow color of light that begs us to gild our souls with its promise of enlightenment.

Two manuscripts — ancient papyri in Greek — turned up in Leiden, The Netherlands, and in Uppsala, Sweden. Believed to be the work of an Egyptian artisan in the third century C.E., the one in Upsalla contained recipes for dyeing, mordanting (the process of "fixing" dyes to be stable), and for making artificial gemstones. The Leiden manuscript focuses on metallurgy — 101 recipes for gilding, silvering, and tinting metals including tricks to make copper objects appear like gold. Berthelot published a French translation of the Leiden papyrus, which, in many ways, sounds like a book the alchemists would have liked to get their hands on.

Color names often carried their origins: raw sienna, Spanish brown, burnt umber.

Red madder came from the madder root; cochineal red from a wingless insect living in the New World (another reason besides gold to invade) as well as in the scarlet oak in the Near East, Spain, southern France, and Italy. When the kermes insect is crushed and boiled in lye, the result is what the English called "crimson" and "carmine" which the French called *cramoisie*. They called ground cinnabar vermillion or "little insect" because it's like the dye extracted from the insects.

Blues, such as the colors the early Celts painted themselves with, came from woad leaves — a biennial plant native to southern Europe, but it was also found in Scotland. Getting the dye from woad was no small feat. It took the better part of a year from picking and crushing it to its final blue useable stage. First it had to be balled up and dried. Then fermented in a mass that had to be turned daily for up to nine weeks. Too much heat would destroy the dye. This color was known in Renaissance Europe as *bleu de Roi* most likely because only people as rich as kings could afford to buy it. Still, by the seventeenth century, thirty to forty tons a year were shipped to London, Antwerp, and Hamburg from Toulouse.

Indigo, however, came from India — a dye made from the Indigofera plants that grew there. It was a precious color, Pliny described in his *Natural History*, "which gleams with the hue of a dark rose... it's called in to appease the gods." In the late 1800s there were, in fact, about three thousand indigo factories in India. Britain bought most of the dye. In India dyers were once the unclean caste.

During medieval times, purple glass was made from manganese oxide. But purple dye has its own long and royal history. Purpua was a tiny whelk or shell-fish in the Mediterranean. It was called Tyrian purple, a sumptuous shade that Pliny the Elder described as "the color of congealed blood, blackish at first, but gleaming when held up to the light." Snails in the Dead Sea area also collected bromine, which turned purple. Market-driven Phoenicians around 1699 B.C.E. made family fortunes from selling it. The Greeks picked it up from them and began harvesting and squeezing the heads of mollusks. Each shell gave up only about a drop, so to get just one ounce of my perfect purple, you'd have to sacrifice about 250,000 shellfish. Piles of the discarded shells can still be seen around the Mediterranean. It was considered such a valuable substance that at one point in Roman history, if you were caught crushing even one of those little whelks, you could be put to death. By the fourth century C.E., only emperors were allowed to wear this purple color.

Vinegar was valued for more than just cooking. Verdigris or blue-green copper acetate, for example, came from corroding copper metals with vinegar fumes. And white lead is lead carbonate made with a salt called lead acetate. Lead strips were placed in clay pots that also had a separate compartment for vinegar and then the pots were stacked up and sealed over with animal dung. Vinegar fumes converted the lead to acetate; carbon dioxide gas from fermented dung combined with water to generate carbonic acid. White pigment would appear in a month or so.

The Pueblo potter Maria Martinez discovered her unique black-on-black pottery at San Ildefonso Pueblo, north of Santa Fe, quite by accident. She and her husband, Julian Martinez, perfected the glazed matte black ware by using a slip with rich iron content. Then, they encased the painted pots in sheep dung and fired them a special way in a makeshift kiln of scrap metal. For the Pueblo people, pottery is prayer in physical form — sacred earth, sacred food, sacred life.

Early Flemish paintings resembled stained glass. This may have been due in part to the fact that artists such as Pietar Bruegel put their apprentices to work grinding up actual glass to add to other minerals. For instance, they created "smalt" or a mid-color blue, from grinding up blue cobalt glass. Dark blue from azurite. Copper and malachite for greens. Sulfur and mercury for vermillion. White was actually lead-white. Painting could be a noxious, unsafe, and unhealthy profession. There is some speculation that Vermeer may have been affected by his toxic paint since his wife Catherine said he "died in a frenzy." Vermeer used a lot of white. Remember that wholesome stream of milk the milkmaid poured from her ceramic pitcher? She's standing in front of a creamy plastered wall, her head shrouded in a cloudy cap. Fresh white breadcrumbs lie scattered on the table. Or Vermeer's *Girl with the Pearl Earring*. The pearl is a crescent of white and her liquid brown eyes are set off by white, like her lacy collar. Two small white dots appear on either side of her mouth. White brings her alive, in spite of the fact toxic whites created so many problems for those who painted with them.

Van Gogh's mental problems may have been, if not caused, certainly exacerbated, by his poisonous paints. And there is solid documentation regarding Goya's bouts with paralysis, and delusions, even to the point of going into a coma. When he stopped painting, he got better.

Van Eyck, whom some believe invented oil paints, hated the varnish his colleagues used, calling it "brown sauce." So he devised a colorless varnish and added pigments for a brilliant result — a glow, like painted glass.

Like culinary experts, artists often cooked their paints. By heating yellow ochres in a process called calcining, "burnt sienna" was formed. Dutch painters bought the yellow ochre in France and then treated it and called it "English red."

Fresco means "fresh." Pigments were mixed with water right into fresh lime or gypsum plaster, which was typically made from sand and lime. A thick layer of plaster was applied on top of the pigment wash and repeated. At Pompei, they applied up to six coats of plaster. The final three were ground and polished to look like hard, glossy marble. Egg tempera lasts longer than oils, but it dries very quickly. It's made from yolks mixed with water to a creamy paste consistency.

Craft guilds enforced payment standards for artists and if a patron or customer wanted blue or gold in his painting, the price went up considerably. At one Florentine dye shop in the Renaissance, kermes red dye cost nearly twice as much as green and three times as much as yellow or light blue. It cost about ten times as much to dye cloth red as sky blue.[30]

Pigments always have to be mixed with a binder of some sort. In the mid 1400s people read Cennini's standard text, *Il libro dell' arte*, which told artists how to powder roots, grind rocks, crush insects, and bind them with linseed and walnut poppy oils. Later Giorgio Vasari wrote his handbook and Flemish painters became experts in drying and binding colors to canvas.

During Victorian times William Reeves figured out how to add honey mixed with gum arabic to pigment and Winsor and Newton added glycerine to lumps of color so they could be molded into neat little squares.[31]

"Better living through chemistry" brought more durable, cheaper, safer and more reliable paints. When new acrylics came in the twentieth century, artists could stain and dye canvas instead of painting on it.

Wheels of Color

We like to categorize things. And arrange them in various ways. Colors are no exception. Moses Harris, an engraver, created the first color wheel in 1766. Then in 1771 a man named Ignaz Schiffermüller came up with a circle of twelve colors that included not just a "fire red" but also a "fire blue." Color researchers continued to come up with graphic ways to describe hues, values, and intensities by creating their own circle and wheels.

Newton's wheel had seven colors. Goethe and Schopenhauer's, six. Ostwald came up with a spherical color system containing twenty-four hues based on red,

---

[30] Amy Butler Greenfield, *A Perfect Red* (New York: Harper Collins, 2005), 31.

[31] Victoria Finlay, *Color: A Natural History of the Palette* (New York: Ballantine Books, 2002), 18.

yellow, green, and ultramarine blue (which means "beyond the seas") and their secondaries: orange, leaf green, ice blue, and purple. Itten came up with a gray-scale spoked wheel made up of seven steps.

In 1810, the year in which Goethe's *Theory of Colors* with its color circle (Goethe's Color Wheel, page 149) was published, the young painter Philipp Otto Runge presented his work on a "color-sphere." (Runge's Color Spheres, page 150) His color system, published the last year of his young life, was described at the time as "a blend of scientific-mathematical knowledge, mystical-magical combinations and symbolic interpretations." In order to figure out the relationships of colors, he imagined a sphere or globe with colors arranged in a circle with the primaries — red, yellow, and blue — being separated by orange, violet, and green all equidistant from black and white. The middle of the globe was gray. The pure colors ran along the equator and could move in five directions. They could move up toward white and down toward black. And inward toward gray. To create it, he carefully mixed fifty drops of two colors. Then he painted half the area he wished to cover with each, spun the disk, added black, spun it again. He repeated this with nine different colors. His intent was to show the harmonies of color. He once wrote in a letter to Goethe: "If we try to think of a bluish orange, a reddish green, or a yellowish violet, it is like trying to imagine a southwesterly north wind." His sphere created the platform for all future color wheels and was not surpassed for a hundred years. Runge, no doubt, would have gone on to continue experimenting, but he died at thirty-three.

Albert Munsell, a professor of art at Massachusetts Normal School in the late 1800s, published his *A Color Notation* in 1905. Color names are misleading, he taught his students, so he devised a decimal numbering system. His color samples are printed in highly stable inks and have been used for decades as a reliable color system. "Chroma" is a term he borrowed to indicate the degree of saturation of a surface color. (Ellen's Saturation Tree, page 151)

Munsell's first wheel had ten colors. It became much more complex after that. In fact it grew to include fifteen hundred plastic chips. The Vatican currently uses a system for numbering colors based on Munsell's system. We continue to find unique ways of organizing colors, hoping to better understand and value them.

Colorful Voices

· · · · ·

LEONARDO DA VINCI (1452–1519)

Leonardo di ser Piero da Vinci was an Italian Renaissance man who not only painted and sculpted, but was an architect, a musician (he played the lyre well), scientist, mathematician, engineer, and inventor. He dissected bodies as carefully as he studied rocks and plants and animals. His journals, which he kept for thirty years, record his many interests. Twenty notebooks remain. He painted the Mona Lisa *in 1507 after* The Last Supper *in 1498. His famous* Virgin of the Rocks *was completed in 1508. He apprenticed in Florence in the studio of Verrocchio and later lived and worked in Milan. Four years before he died, he painted his famous self-portrait. For several years, he lived in Rome under the patronage of Pope Leo X and died in France at sixty-seven while in the service of King Francis I at Ambroise on the Loire.*

Who would have thought a bastard (really, my father married four times, but not even once to my mother) like me would have created such a stir? My earliest memory is when I was about two. I was lying in my crib. The window must have been open. A little bird flew in and opened my mouth with its tail. I love birds. I often pay vendors for their caged birds and then let them go.

The glories of nature sometimes overwhelm me. The earth is an awesome living organism. It breathes. The most magnificent thing is the sun. All souls have their source in it. I believe we are meant to live long. After all, my life is attached to a star; why would I turn back?

I predict the world will end in a deluge. And earthquakes. Red lava, blue water.

I study. Dissect. Sketch. I've collected brown beetles and black bats since I was a kid.

When I look at my machine-blueprints again, I remind myself that war is beastly madness. So why do I continue to devise destructive machines just to make kings and princes happy? My black and red charcoal sketches pile up.

Sepia washes of drapery. Horses. Maps. Architectural drawings. And all things with wheels. I play around with reverse images and mirror writing. And riddles. I love to solve riddles — the funnier the better. It's a pitiful master who can do only one thing well.

And, of course, sometimes I paint. Usually by commission, and I encourage my studio friends to do likewise. One must eat. My *servitors* remain faithful to the end and if they make any money from my work, good for them. I sell very little. And I finish even fewer. I'm easily bored. Too many other things seem to capture my interest. I frustrate my patrons and anger as many as I please. Still they came to me. Poor Sforza had to wait sixteen years for his blasted horse!

The mural of *The Last Supper* on the back wall of the Santa Maria Delle Grazie Monastery in Milan took me... let's see. I started it in 1495. I'd been preparing for years. But I guess, all in all, it took me three years. It's still not finished. Jesus and Judas still need more work. I worked hard at the contrast by placing Jesus in light and Judas in shadow. I wanted to use oil and tempera instead of fresco painting on fresh plaster because I believed the colors would be more vibrant. Unfortunately it flaked. Some days I'd just lie on the scaffold and imagine — or maybe make a couple of brush strokes and call it a day. I grouped the disciples in threes — each wondering who would betray Jesus. They still speak to me. John wears red over blue and Jesus is dressed in blue over red. I'm sure you will speculate about that "togetherness" of those two figures in the middle — some believe it's not John at all, but Jesus' beloved Magdalene. Or that John and Jesus were actually a couple. I don't really care what people think any more than I really care about sex. People will see what they care to see. It took me so long to find a model for Judas. I searched all the criminal haunts in Milan for just the right face. The prior kept asking me when I'd be finished. In exasperation, I finally said, "I can finish now. I'll use you as a model for Judas."

I'm smiling as I remember once giving a dinner for all the ugliest people in town. Then I sketched them. What fun! I'm suspicious of beauty — it's too light — too thin. I have no intention to improve on nature — nature is beautiful *and* ugly. Why disguise it? Besides, the beautiful is made more beautiful by contrast. Like light and shadow.

I live in great darkness. *And* great light. People say I invented chiaroscuro — a shadow is always affected by the color on which it's laid and deep shadows make for luminous bodies. Simple. Watch the light, I tell my students. Challenge every dogma. Forget what you've been told and just observe. Light, I've discovered, behaves like sound, ripples like water, bounces like a ball and hammers the heart. I like to study the eye. It embraces all colors and all beauty in this world. It is excellent above all other things created by God. It commands the hands to create. I tell my students, watch water move. Study the air. Paint the shadows. Paint liquid smiles. Take your time! Go for the details. Impatience is the mother of stupidity. And study clouds and flaking walls and all random shapes. Even a sponge thrown against the wall will create wonderful color.

Why is it so hard for me to explain color? Maybe it's because I don't trust color to reveal truth. It's just one of the ten attributes of painting: Color, Darkness, Light, Solidity, Form, Position, Distance and Nearness, Motion and Rest. I like the rest part.

I confess, I spend more time perfecting black and shadows in order to better capture its opposite, the light, than I do to color. Shadows are always darker when they have white around them. And a pale yellow, for example, will cause red to appear more beautiful than if it's opposed to a purple color. I have been intrigued by the colors of the earth my whole life. Nature possesses only eight colors. Blue air changes with mists and at different times of the day. So the blues must change as well. I don't flatter myself that I can retain all the colors and effects of nature. Therefore, I consult nature for everything. And if it doesn't come through my senses, I find it suspect.

I like muted greens and blues. I enjoy painting at dusk when the sun isn't so bright. Or in rainy weather. Earth tones. Warm glazes. Translucent browns. Maybe that says more about me than my paintings. Am I somber? Perhaps. I enjoy painting sfumato — smokiness by adding pigment over an underpainting of neutral grays and browns. Smoky blue. Veiled to white.

I pick up *DeColoribus* again and reread Aristotle's words. All color comes from sunlight, firelight, air, and water. I like the way he saw shaded versions of daylight. But what are words? Color can't be intellectualized. Like God's love — or life itself. It must be experienced.

. . . . .

VINCENT VAN GOGH (1852-1890)

Born in Auvers-sur-Oise in The Netherlands, Van Gogh is considered by many to be the most famous Dutch painter after Rembrandt, although his paintings brought him very little revenue and during his adult life he was financially, and emotionally, dependent on his brother Theodore. His letters to Theo form much of our knowledge of this bold painter, tormented by several unhappy romances, an aborted career in theology, and the art business. He went to Paris and met many influential artists of the time including Gauguin, Bernard, Toulouse-Lautrec. Still unable to sell much of his work, he opened an art colony in the south of France, at Arles. It was there he spent time in a mental hospital. The Potato Eaters was his first major painting, completed in 1885. He only painted about ten years, but in that short decade, he produced some 900 works. A recent biography suggests that he didn't commit suicide, as most history accounts tell us. And, in fact, he painted a half dozen more paintings after the crows in the wheatfield. He may have been, perhaps accidentally, shot by a couple of young Parisian boys on vacation who were playing cowboys and Indians, with a real gun they'd found, near the hotel where Van Gogh stayed in St. Rémy. They had recently seen a Buffalo Bill show in Paris. Vincent told his doctor not to investigate the shooting any further, thus protecting them. When asked if he had shot himself in the stomach, he responded to the doctor, "I believe I have."

Some days I forget to eat. All I want to do is paint. And make the colors ripe, mellow, generous. But there's never enough time. My brush flies faster and faster as I try to capture — what? I almost have it. Yellow-gray, blue-gray, green-gray. I can't get enough shades of gray. It's impossible to say how many green-grays there are. But if I have red, yellow, and blue, and my trusty black and white, I can make seventy tones. Pink-green and green-pink. Kindred spirits. And twenty-seven blacks. I can't stand to use black for shadows. No! Instead, I like black-green. I have to paint shadows in snow a blue or violet. Well, depending on the time of day. Indigo with terra sienna. A vigorous blue-black from Prussian blue with burnt sienna. When I hear people say, "There is no black in nature," I think, well, there is no black in colors either! But in their essence, black and white *are* colors. They can be as complementary to each other as red and green. Japanese painters know this.

It's paralyzing to stare at a blank canvas. "You're an idiot!" So I talk back. "Here, take this brush full of Prussian blue." Maybe I can trap whatever it was that those careful church-painters used to get when they painted gold halos around people's heads. I want my colors to give me depth and firmness. But if I don't keep my eyes open, all is lost.

I keep returning to that frankly green billiard table. I tried to express the terrible passions we humans have, by using acidic yellow light and bold reds and greens. My colors scream and whirl. They can, perhaps, even make you go mad. Four citron-lamps cast an orange and green glow. On the green counter there is a pink nosegay. A café is a place where you can ruin yourself, run mad or even commit a crime. I tried to paint the powers of darkness and make the colors create that atmosphere.

My palette is thawing. When I was painting the other day with my good marten brushes I noticed the change. I had some ugly reds and greens. They were vulgar colors until I added pink. I soften crude pinks with flatter reds. I break the color and now there is harmony.

The best way to know God, I have to remember, is to love many things. Coffee-colored clay. Cinder paths. Dug up earth after a pouring rain. Green beech trunks against yellow leaves. I need more yellow. How can I capture that young green corn without cadmium? I'll ask Theo to send me some more. I'll ask for some of that Ingres paper the color of unbleached linen too. What would I do without my brother?

I must use blazing colors and sometimes I spread them like frosting on a cake. Colors free me. My critics accuse me of just loading color into a pistol and shooting it onto my canvas. One even said my unmixed colors drip so much they land on the floor. They say I only paint with my thumb and then wipe it on my coat. Well, sometimes I do.

I am seeking for blue all the time. Cobalt is for the atmosphere. Carmine is like red wine, warm and lively. First I paint a violet haze, then a red sun, and a dark purple cloud with a fine red border. The sky reflects vermillion and a streak of yellow — green then blue. Not just any blue. Cerulean blue. But those colors that have no name are the real foundation of everything.

For three nights running, I've stayed up to paint at night and then I sleep during the day. Nights are more alive, more richly colored. I stick candles in my hat and paint the stars. Why should not the shining dots of the sky be as accessible as the black dots on the map of France?

Two people sit in a small room with their cat. I look at them, and remember Goethe. So I paint complements: long blue shadows on an orange rush floor. Shadows shimmer and shift. There are no absolute norms. I don't care if some people find my colors gaudy. I love them. I'm free to paint what I see. It's a happy form of painting. I can leave a painting "unfinished" to the average eye, but as one critic I was reading said, "Is a painting ever finished? Is it smooth? Polished? Fully formed?" Never! If that's what "finished" means, may I never finish. I leave brush marks; I layer a color in deep textures. I'm free to paint the air and make colors vibrate. I believe the painter of the future will be a colorist the likes of which no one has ever seen before.

I smile when I think of Paul. My friend thought European art was not only an error, but very corrupt. The more exotic, the better for old Gauguin. He didn't care what he said. Or what "primitive" colors he used. Horses could be green if they wished. When he visited me at Arles, where there is a yellow sky over everything, I welcomed him by spreading sunflowers over every corner of the room. Yellow is "Her" color. My Divine Sunshine.

I am trying to get at something utterly heartbroken. It may be that there is no God here... but there must be one not far off. But now I'm so tired. But if we are tired, isn't it then because we have already walked a long way?

Painting wears a person out. Maybe earth really is a study that didn't come off. I struggle to see a brighter light. A stronger sun. A different yellow. Yellow leaves against green trunks. I may decide to take leave of all these olive groves and wheat fields, and just fly away with the black crows.

. . . . .

GEORGIA O'KEEFE (1887-1986)

For seven decades, O'Keefe was an influential American art figure. Her work is known for precise clean lines and elegant simplicity. Born in Wisconsin, she studied at the Art Institute of Chicago and the Art Students League in New York and got her teaching degree at the University of Virginia. She met Alfred Stiegliz, the famous photographer, when she was twenty. He was forty-four. He promoted artists. He promoted her (from 1923 until 1946 when he died); they were married in 1924. Three years later, O'Keefe moved to New Mexico — Abiquiu and Ghost Ranch; her museum is in Santa Fe.

Feel that sun's power! I love it! I was, after all, born in Sun Prairie. It may be Irish hyperbole, but I have felt sunny and tall and powerful from as early as I can remember.

I've been drawing and painting since I was eleven. When the Wild West called, I said yes, I can teach. I wore black, black, like the charcoal drawings I sent Alfred. Like my thick black hair. Like my black crosses. Like Alfred's eyes.

I read the *Divine Comedy*. Ibsen. Nietzsche. Alfred sent me a copy of *Faust*. And I learned about Goethe's Divine Eternal Feminine — I was twenty-nine and Alfred photographed me with my one-woman show. "When I make a photograph, I make love," he said. Ah, indeed. Alfred needed people; I needed solitude. How else could I capture the blue skies and yellow corn?

Taos. Santa Fe. Abiquiu. Ghost Ranch. It's where the sun bids me paint. Blue skies. White bones. Everywhere I look, from the monsoon-drenched mountains and the red landscapes to the limitless sky that surround me, I see color. I often color-name my works: *Canna Red and Orange*, *Black Iris*, *Cow's Skull — Red, White and Blue*. I love Asian art. I love rocks that slit into nothingness. I love their bold forms. I see green gold, red gold, yellow gold with blue and pink and lavender in strips and spots. Colors stack up. I wedge them. Curve them. I go to gray and black places where wrinkled surfaces and bands of color wrap me until I think the whole world has turned into just what I am seeing.

Gray crosses. Indigo spirals. Canyons. Striated rocks. Yellow arches against a deep blue sky. Flowers wrapped in light. Blue and green music.

My gray ashes now mix with the windy landscape near Ghost Ranch. Ghosts all around. Gray, gray, swirling seashells. Waves on Lake George. Shadows on adobe. Charcoal on paper. Dust to dust. Ashes to ashes.

Chapter Four

COLOR CODES

Prelude

"He appeared like a flash of azure and turquoise shining out from the edge of the dark woods. Not illuminated but luminous, as if he himself were source of tinsel and flare come down from the exquisite sky incandescent, radiant, incarnate. He flickered in the shadows of the pine and hemlocks like a sapphire jewel and then vanished as quickly as he had appeared.

"Later, after a quick check of the field guide confirmed my vision I read that indigo buntings are not really blue at all, but black, which left me wondering about light, about how the diffraction of the day's brilliance as it shines through the structure of feathers can create color. How optic nerve and retina had transformed the spectral rays of light into the jewel-toned color I thought I saw...

"It seems color is as fugitive as time or memory... Everything we see is an interpretation of light filtered through our eyes, our memories, and our experiences. In other words, the sky blows blue because we blue it. We find comfort in blue skies and associate them with good times. We imagine an azure elsewhere beyond all we can see and populate it with a host of angels and saints and our dearly departed...

"Blue feathers, blue waters, blue sky...we assign colors to birds and elements and what we most yearn for, hoping to turn the ineffable into something indelible."[1]

---

[1] Thom Rock, *Blueberry Fool: Memory, Moments, and Meaning* (Eugene, OR: Resource Publications, 2011), 70, 72, 73.

Indelible Colors

Thom Rock's beautiful words from his *Blueberry Fool* remind me of what my friend Jonna told me about having accidentally killed a yellow bird with her car, and feeling terrible. The next morning a very rare indigo blue bunting came to her bird feeder, as if offering her azurine forgiveness. Upon hearing her story, I went back to what Goethe had said in his *Theory of Colors*: "If our doctrine of colors find favor, applications and allusions, allegorical, symbolical, and mystical will not fail to be made, in accordance with the spirit of the age."[2] Jonna's color sense found favor and, for her, indigo blue became indelible.

We pause at the produce counter of our favorite grocery store, or at a farmer's market, and judge the ripeness of fruit or vegetables by the colors we associate with "ripeness" and "ready to eat." We think we know what colors "mean," but it's tricky to code colors and then to decipher all those codes.

Warm colors (reds, oranges, pinks, browns) advance; they move in on you and make the space seem tighter; cool colors (blues, greens) recede, expand. All colors, even what we might call the neutrals (black, white, beiges), are influenced by the company they keep. And we often know them by their intensity. Color can change dimensions and create optical illusions. Colors morph.

When our older son was about five, he said, "Hey Mom! Look at this. It's a butterfly and it's white until it flies. Then it's blue. Isn't that neat?" A butterfly daring to be both white and blue? Quite amazing. White butterflies masquerading as blue have been discovered before, but the trick it to discover them again.

If someone asks you what is your favorite color, what is your response? Was it always? Ask people in your family. Do the men and boys choose different colors than the women and girls? In one study of 21,000 people, blue ranked first, then red, green, violet, orange, and yellow.

Color invites us, like those designer bower birds, to decorate and redecorate using color. For a time, our family lived in a Lutheran parsonage that had a very, very high kitchen ceiling. Knowing how warm colors advance and cool colors recede, I decided to paint the ceiling orange. Mind you, this was in that

---

[2] Johann Wolfgang von Goethe, *Theory of Colors* (Translated by Charles Eastlake, 1840), 332. (Kindle edition, BLTC Press, 2008).

bygone decade when orange was a pretty acceptable decorating color. But you know, before I tell you, what happened as soon as I tapped the lid back on the paint can. The ceiling came crashing down! And you can bet it was the first thing people looked at when they entered the kitchen.

Color remains an effective and inexpensive way to change the mood or shape of a room, to help decide how formal or informal it is, and even give it its "gender level," as some interior designers say. People with poor eyesight can benefit from light, clear room colors. And thank goodness, hospitals and other institutions no longer use that "certain" shade of green.

Healing with Color

> *"Who has not observed the purifying effect of light...*
> *especially of direct sunlight upon the air of a room?*
> *Go into a sick room where the shutters are always shut*
> *and though the room has never been polluted*
> *by breathing of human beings, you observe a close, musty smell*
> *of corrupt air, unpurified by the effects of the sun's rays...*
> *Where there is sun, there is thought... Put the pale,*
> *withering plant and human being into the sun,*
> *and if not too far gone, each will recover health and spirit."*

Florence Nightingale, *Notes on Nursing*

What is healing? Making one's self whole? Coming to terms with one's fears and failures? Feeling safe? Soothing one's discomfort? Lessening pain and discomfort? Learning how to live with limitations and difficulties? Finally grasping what it means to love ourselves? If this comes close to describing the healing process, the big question is: "Can colors really help to heal a person?"

Florence Nightingale's take on healing should have come as no great surprise. After all, as Pliny pointed out, for six hundred years Rome had no physicians.

Instead they used sunlight, exercise, vapor baths. And in Asia Minor early Persians practiced a form of color therapy based on the emanations of light. Without full-spectrum sunlight, it's a pretty well known fact that one can get rickets and other bone diseases. And then there's *bilirubinemia*. That's a fancy word for a pathologic jaundice — a yellowing of the skin in newborn infants. It can occur in as many as 17% of all premature babies. If not treated, it can cause deafness and even brain damage and death. A doctor named Richard J. Cremer and his staff in England began to notice in the late 1950s that when bassinets were placed near a window, the babies who occupied them had less jaundice than those placed farther from the light. Controlled experiments were carried out and it became apparent that if a jaundiced baby was placed under a blue light, with eyes protected, he or she was healed. It's called phototherapy — light therapy.

It's likely that the Egyptians knew all about the healing properties of light and color. They had, according to some sources, temples where people could go to be treated by bathing in certain light-colors prescribed by their healers. The floors of some temples in Karnak and Thebes were green and by using certain crystals, color healers regulated sunlight to fall on patients. Lists of "color cures" were recorded as early as 1550 B.C.E. They mainly used six colors: red (*desher*), green (*wadj*, which means "to be healthy"), blue (*khesbedj* and *irtiu*), yellow (*kenit* and *khenet*), black (*khem* or *kem*), and white (*shesap* and *hedj*). We know this because mineral compounds last a very long time. Green gemstones such as malachite, turquoise, and jade were particularly valued. If these gems weren't available they sometimes used a green glazed quartz. Chapter 77 of the *Book of the Dead* makes reference to the deceased becoming a falcon whose wings are of green stone, referring to new life and rebirth. The green heart scarab was placed in the dead person's heart cavity.[3] A tiny red stone was often placed in the heart cavity along with the scarab. Red was associated with the blood and power of Isis and green more aligned with Osiris. Black symbolized death, the underworld, and the night, as well as fertility and resurrection. White alabaster carried implications of purity. Other color cures in early Egypt

---

[3] Anita Stratos, "Ancient Egypt: Breaking the Color Code" (From the website: Humanity Healing International, http://community.humanityhealing.net/forum/topics/ancient-egypt-breaking-the-color-code).

consisted of using white oil, red lead, the testicles of a black ass, black lizards, indigo, and verdigris — a green copper salt used to treat cataracts.[4]

At the time of early Christianity, Celsus healed with colored plasters to relieve wounds: black, green, red, white; Hippocrates, Galen, and the Arabian Avicenna also diagnosed with an eye to hue. Early healers used red sulfide of mercury — cinnabar — or as it was once called, "the blood of dragons," for some diseases and burns. Today we call it Mercurochrome.

Dr. Paracelsus (1493–1541) was an alchemist doctor. He said we're not here to make gold from lead, but to make medicines. Disease at the time was believed to be caused by contaminated blood. Hence the leeches. But people back then believed color and light were valuable agents for health as well. Paracelsus used prayer, music vibrations, color, elixirs, talismen, charms, herbs, and diet, in addition to bleeding and purging.

Many people remain skeptical about light and color's therapeutic value. "It's not scientific. It can't be quantified. It's voodoo. It's not certified by the AMA." Many positive and innovative things can be suppressed for various reasons — more having to do with who profits than what might benefit the patient. But light and color therapy may be less "woo-woo" than some might initially think.

A Dane named Niels R. Finsen was one of the first pioneers in light research. He founded a light institute for treating TB. Now, people who suffer from SAD (seasonal affective disorder) can buy light boxes, which they are encouraged to sit under for about thirty minutes every morning. Light therapy like this is measured in "lux" (the measurement of light intensity — distance away from a specific light source) as opposed to "lumen" (the amount of light generated by a bulb at its surface.) To be effective, white fluorescent light therapy must deliver about 10,000 lux. To put this in perspective, most homes have lux levels of 100–300. Offices, about 700 or below. White light is safe, according to experts. It has been used for over twenty years. Some people are pushing "blue light" therapies, but clinical research is still dubious about that method.

---

[4] Helen Varley, ed., *Colour* (London: Marshall Editions, 1983), 46.

The Mayo Clinic in Rochester, Minnesota, has researched the benefits and side effects of using a light box for the treatment of SAD as well as depression, obsessive compulsive disorder, and some sleep disorders. To treat SAD they use phototherapy along with psychotherapy and medications. The reduced levels of sunlight in fall and winter may disrupt our circadian rhythms and lead to feelings of depression — "the blues." A drop in serotonin and melatonin levels might also throw our bodies off and affect our moods. They discovered that more women than men are affected and family history may also play a role. Light therapy is one of their first lines of treatment. They find that it generally starts working within two to four days and causes few side effects. The Mayo website states: "Research on light therapy is limited, but it appears to be effective for most people in relieving seasonal affective disorder symptoms." They suggest getting only high-quality therapy boxes.

Some bathtub manufacturers have built colored lights into their units so bathing can be therapeutic and relieve stress. Colored lights can increase one's melatonin (also an antioxidant) and stimulate the pineal gland, which can strengthen one's autoimmune system.

Some counselors use therapeutic color. For example, a type of Hawaiian counseling session often begins by imagining the body suffused by blue, green, purple, and white light, to bring peace and healing to the body, mind, and spirit. Being surrounded by certain colors and colored lights feeds different parts of the body. Our body seems to know, instinctively, what colors it needs. When you are bored or depressed, try thinking about what colors you're "missing." Which colors might make you feel differently? Our minds speak in color codes when words are not necessary or unavailable. We just need to listen to what our body is telling us. It seems to know that bright colors can speed up brain activity and make the heart beat faster and increase blood pressure. Calm cool colors and dim lights can reduce blood pressure — slowing body and brain functions. For more insights into how color can speak to us, turn to "The Meditative Palette" at the end of this book.

Thanks to another pioneer in light and health research, John Ott, we've learned a great deal about full-spectrum lighting — artificial lighting that tries to create nature's full color range. We now know that full-spectrum lighting makes plants grow and people healthier. You don't get this from incandescent or fluorescent bulbs or sodium vapor lights. Without full-spectrum light, we can develop brittle bones, eye strain, headaches, irritability, sluggishness, and sleepiness, hyperactivity in children, some kinds of cancer, more cavities in teeth. Chickens will lay fewer eggs and cows will produce less milk. When zoo officials installed sunlight-simulating lights in the Burnett Park Zoo in Syracuse, New York, the animals started having many more babies. Light is a nutrient and affects not only fertility but the whole endocrine system. It triggers certain hormones. Russians practice light therapy on their mine workers, insisting that they spend at least a half an hour in natural light or under full-spectrum artificial lighting. Women who are kept out of the sunlight for long periods of time cease menstruating. It may be folklore, or it may be true, that Inuit children are generally born nine months after the advent of spring when the arctic sun returns and restorative light returns.

Edwin Babbitt, born in 1828, was the son of a Congregational minister in New York. He taught for a while and then began receiving spiritual insights. He accepted the truths of all scriptures and prophets of all nations and studied harmonic convergences. Although he had no training as a doctor of medicine, he started practicing as a "psychophysician," and, like others during that Victorian era, began working with magnetisim, clairvoyance, psychic forces, and with color in a technique he called "chromo-therapeutics." Red, he said, was the center of heat; yellow the center of luminosity; blue the center of electricity; colors were to be used with their complements.

He developed a special cabinet called the "Thermolume" using natural sunlight; a "Chromo Disk" — a funnel-shaped object that localized light and could be fitted with special filters to hold over various parts of one's body that needed color healing; and "Chromolumes" or framed stained glass windows to be placed in a southern exposure window. Blue light, for instance, was focused on inflamed areas such as wounds; yellow on the brain, the liver, the abdomen. He arranged the colors according to "harmonic contrast and chemical affinity." (Babbitt's Chromatic Harmony, page 152) The colored glass was sequenced from light yellow down to blue in about sixteen different hues. He would focus color on parts of the patient's body by moving his or her chair in relationship to the light coming through the colored glass. People who needed skin treatment would wear a white garment and get a full color bath. Green, he said, was good for toning up the back; yellow for the bowels; orange for nerves. He also drew up a list of colors as they related to various chemical compounds and prepared drinks using colored bottles of water.

Babbitt said he drew from the work of Baron Riechenbach — an Austrian scientist who experimented in his castle near Vienna. The Baron had the resources to conduct thousands of experiments and came up with a vital "force of nature" he called "Odic Force." Odic light has flowed through our universe for millions of years. Nature (and color) is eternal, he said. Babbitt decided odic light appears in five forms: incandescence, flame, threads, streaks or nebulai, smoke, and sparks. Reichenbach said human beings are luminous all over our bodies — but especially on the palms of the hands, points of one's fingers and toes, from one's eyes, and portions of one's head. Emotions send out various colors, he determined. Unlike the aurora borealis, which can be seen by everyone, only the more sensitive people can see the auric colors and psychic lights. Babbitt wrote that the left hemisphere of the brain receives blue and radiates out the warmth of red; the right brain radiates the blue forces and receives the red more strongly than the left, which is stronger in intellect. The right is stronger in "organic life."[5]

Faber Birren said red light was used in Europe more than in America for treating various maladies including reducing pain in postoperative incisions. Red produces heat in the tissue and dilates the blood vessels; blue has bactericidal properties and is said to increase the output of carbon dioxide in certain cold-blooded creatures.

Blue has also been prescribed to cure headache, high blood pressure, and intractable insomnia. Yellow applied abdominally seem to increase the flow of gastric juices — and may stimulate the bowels.

---

[5] Edwin D. Babbitt, *The Principles of Light and Color* (edited, annotated by Faber Birren, University Books, 1967), 267.

Color rays absorbed through the skin can affect all the glands, blood cells, and chemicals within your body. Hair dyes and clothing colors can, in fact, affect the entire body. People who heal with color aim to reestablish body balance and release tension and illness caused by a particular color starvation. Color, they say, can be introduced through colored foods, exposure to the sun, room décor and clothing, stones and gems as well as meditating on color. They also say natural color is a more powerful healer than any color in glass, filters, or dyes. The purer the colors, the more penetrating the rays and therefore, the faster the body's reaction.[6]

One can find numerous books on techniques for healing with color including dream work, reading auras, color meditations, concentrating on colorful mandalas, burning colored candles, using colored water therapies, and ... One of them on my shelf begins with this caveat, which is good to ...: "Color therapy is not meant to be a panacea for every health dif... ...er is it meant to be a prescription. We cannot prescribe colors like ... When we use color therapies, we are simply employing preventa... ...are participating more responsibly and actively in our own health ... The techniques are holistic guidelines..."[7]

Reds and oranges tend to excite us — hence the preferred décor in most restaurants. Surrounded by hot colors (the colors that advance on you like reds and oranges) people eat faster and allow restaurants to serve more patrons; blues and some greens slow eaters down. They're relaxing colors and make people want to sit around and talk.

We use color words to describe our states of mind: "I'm in the pink," "I'm green with envy," "I just told a white lie," "I feel blue," or "I'm so angry, I'm seeing red!" But we don't normally think of colors themselves as making us feel that way. Nor do we think of colors as being capable of changing how we feel. Yet color does impact our daily lives and obviously has for centuries.

---

[6] Morton Avery, *The Power of Color* (New York: Avery Publishing Group, 1989), 100, 101.

[7] Ted Andrews, *How to Heal with Color* (St. Paul, MN: Llewellyn Publications, 1992 and 2001), Kindle edition, front matter.

How We Code Colors

Look around at all the codes we've built into colors. For instance, the American Cancer Society uses various colors for cancer awareness. We've all seen the pink ribbons and bracelets for breast cancer awareness. After my own diagnosis, I'm "up close and personal" with teal for ovarian cancer. Prostate cancer is blue; childhood cancers, gold; leukemia, orange. Liver, emerald green; esophageal, periwinkle blue. Bone cancer is yellow. Kidney, kelly green; bladder, yellow. General cancer awareness is lavender. I'm not sure how the colors are assigned, but I find it interesting that uterine cancer is peach — the most "spiritual" color, according to Rudolf Steiner. Our ability to procreate and the source of so much ideological contention regarding women's bodies and reproduction is marked by a color that, for some at least, points to how we might relate to dimensions beyond our physical bodies. And how we learn to honor the mother as well as her newly forming child.

When I receive chemotherapy, my nursing team reminds me to eat a variety of foods with bright colors. The more colors the better. Colorful foods contain things like antioxidants and bioflavonoids. So I reach for purple grapes and strawberries and sweet potatoes, blueberries and carrots. Beets, black cherries, blueberries, asparagus, red cabbage. Brown rice, beige oatmeal, and tan nuts. And pomegranates. The American Dietetic Association suggests eating red foods such as those sweet strawberries, watermelon, pomegranates, and tomatoes to protect our cells and guard against heart disease and some cancers; blue and purple foods such as blueberries protect memory function; purple cabbage, purple potatoes, purple tomatoes, and grapes contain antioxidants that protect our arteries from heart disease; yellow foods such as corn can protect against macular degeneration; orange in carrots and sweet potatoes can lower cholesterol and prevent strokes; green in leafy greens can protect against cancer.

The autumn when I was pregnant with our younger son, my favorite "lie down" time was when the sun slanted through our bedroom window past a huge tree with yellow-orange leaves. In some dark recess of my brain I must have known about how temperature causes a loss of chlorophyll in certain yellow pigments in the cell membranes of the leaves, but I didn't care where the color came from. Reds and oranges bathed both of us in their sweet syrupy warm richness. It was a happy pregnancy.

When our bodies are in balance, color therapists tell us, they filter out of white light all the colors they need. We've learned that full spectrum or natural sunlight can actually increase fertility, decrease cavities, produce red blood cells, and even cut down on hyperactivity among children. All without drugs.

We might call some of the uses of color purely superstitious. But, then, knowing the positive effects a placebo can often have, perhaps if you *believe* evil can be avoided by wearing a red wool bracelet, maybe it can. Since evil was once thought to enter through the left side, you should wear the bracelet on the left wrist. Or, if you believe red underwear will protect you from scarlet fever, it might. Or, if you're Scottish, who knows, a sprain might be helped by wrapping it in red wool. In Scotland, Hungary, Portugal, Norway, Denmark, and Germany, red strings along with bits of red cloth were tied to animals for protection. Red charms from red coral protect South American newborns.

Avicenna in the eleventh century dressed and covered his bleeding patients with red cloth. Edward II's physician made sure everything in his bedrooms was red to thwart smallpox. English physicians once wore scarlet cloaks. Since red coats hid the blood, that's the color the British army began wearing. Frenchmen wore red neck scarves as bloody reminders of what the guillotine did — and then, ironically enough, red became the color of revolution. In Japan red was believed to overcome nightmares. A red ribbon is still thought to promote long life in China. More currently, some University of Texas researchers determined that if athletes wore red clothing, or concentrated on the color red, their muscle strength would be increased. (And/or, perhaps, their libido.)

Red Dye No. 2 was banned as a carcinogen in 1976. Since then, there has been a cochineal (the cactus insect) revival. It was once called *grana* for the "grain-like" insects that made it. During Elizabeth I's reign pirates confiscated shiploads of these crimson cakes as "cochineal fleets" made their way to China and Turkey from the New World. In 1575 eighty metric tons found its way to

Spain and spies worked very hard to break up the Spanish monopoly on this red "gold." By 1990 a cochineal renaissance was in full swing and the world production reached one million pounds, 80% of it coming from Peru and the rest from Chile, the Canary Islands, Bolivia, and South Africa. This red additive is called E 120 and currently about two million pounds are shipped around the world a year. Now vegans have another "animal product" to worry about as cochineal or E 120 makes its way into red foods.

Our younger son's eyes are very blue and when we visited Turkey, people stopped on the streets to stare and smile. Ataturk, their hero who revolutionized Turkey, also had blue eyes, we learned, and people began calling our son "Ataturk!" We saw blue disks sewn onto baby strollers and babies' hats for protection against the "evil eye." Apparently these magical blue "eyes" go back to the time in Persia when a bit of turquoise was placed in the eye of a roasted sacrificial lamb and then put into an amulet case and sewn into a child's headdress for health and protection.

Feng Shui's Color Codes

Even landscapes can be healed through color, along with sound and movement. "As each phenomena of the multidimensional world has its own sound vibration, it has also a characteristic color quality, as well as its own movement code. Working through sound, color, and movement (dance) it is possible to enter into an interaction with all of the different aspects of a place or landscape. These are wonderful creative tools for being creative within invisible worlds, especially if healing, tuning or balancing a landscape or environment is needed." [8]

While we might not ordinarily think of *feng shui* (fung shway), which translates as "wind and water," as insightful use of colors, it has the potential to heal and energize landscapes, interior spaces, and our inner selves as well. Feng shui is an ancient practice used by Chinese astrologers and acupuncturists to tap into Tao wisdom and chi's living power. Each of the five elements (wood, fire, earth, metal, and water) has a corresponding color and shape. Carol Wheelock of Feng Shui Vermont says, "By honoring all the elements, you will create

---

[8] Marko Pogacnik, *Sacred Geography* (Great Barrington, MA: Lindisfarne Books, 2007), 216.

an environment that supports not only you, but also those with whom you share or invite into your space. In the process, you are also honoring the natural rhythms and cycles of nature."[9]

Feng shui's coded colors are also tied to geometric figures. Reds and oranges, represented by triangles and pyramids, symbolize the upward energy of south. This is associated with all the crimson birds of luck and success, especially the red phoenix.

Whites and pastels, associated with circles and ovals and metals and minerals, symbolize "white tiger energy" of the west, and autumn and protection.

Blues and other darker colors including black represent water — anything that flows. This is winter energy and it flows downward. This is the dragon of the east.

Greens are column shapes like trees. Wood means growth and strength. It's the budding, nurturing, outward growing energy of spring. Frogs and terrapins or tortoises bring in the energy of the north.

Yellows and earth tones, like brick and adobe, are earth energies — rectangular, flat shapes, the energy of the harvest and the center where all others meet. Like everything on earth, yellow, too, is transformed and moves around.

Alchemically Speaking

As I write this, huge electrical storms have been passing through our region. What happens when lightning strikes? It can bring great changes including, at times, even death. My aunt and uncle lost their home twice to fire caused by lightning. Now and then, you hear of people's brains even having been changed from lightning.

According to the prophet Mohammed, God hides behind 70,000 curtains of light and darkness. If the curtains were to be removed, the Divine Light is so powerful that everything would be consumed by lightning.

Jacob Boehme was an alchemist, like many thinkers of the sixteenth century. He used code words such as "lightning" to explain how life breaks off

---

[9] Carol C. Wheelock, "feng shui questions," *Everchanging Magazine for Body Mind & Spirit* (Burlington, VT, May/June 2004), 5.

from a Divine Source of Eternal Light and enters the matter that makes up our elemental world. It enters us. Like all alchemists he peppered his manuscripts with symbols. The sign for lightning made an equal-armed cross. It meant that our "lightning-Christ" descended to earth. Alchemists devised various symbols for different minerals and elements. For instance a cross with a little circle on top was the sign for copper and for Venus. A circle in the center and four crosses going out in four different directions was the symbol for salt. Carl Jung and others picked these symbols up. Jung would later liken our intuitive flashes to lightning.

When lightning strikes sand, sand can become glass. There's a word for this "petrified lightning": *fulgurites*. It's from Latin for "thunder." After realizing that lightning could create glass, people began mixing sand and soda ash and limestone with metallic oxides for wonderful colored glass.

Our essence as humans, Jacob Boehme and others believed, was composed of salt, or salniter, the chemical from which all salts come. We're chemical beings. He equated our spirits to sulfur and our love to mercury or quicksilver, which mirrors life itself. There was gold in the "stone" or our souls, he preached. But also lead — all that is gray and most melancholy. Silver is like the moon, and feminine; gold is like the sun, and masculine.

"The holy art" of alchemy or *al keme*, which means "black earth" and refers to the dark Nile mud, may have first been practiced in Egypt but it was the Arab culture that kept it alive and introduced it to Europe. They called it "oneness of existence." It became a time-honored system of dissolving matter and then hardening it again. The process of transforming leaden "stuff" into golden "stuff" was called an *opus contra naturam* —the work of opening nature, breaking it into "better" stuff. With its sexual overtones of conception from the male seed, sulphur, and the female seed, mercury or quicksilver, a mystical change takes place.

Chyma means "to smelt" or "to cast." So you see, it's a short step from *alchemy* to chemistry. The god Hermes or Thoth is thought to have presented this art of purification and transformation in four stages to humans for their use. It's all described in a sixty-eight-foot-long roll called the Emerald Tablet found at Thebes, which contains eight hundred prescriptions, remedies, and alchemical formulas. It was likely written by Hermes Trismegistus, who was said to be "The Thrice Greatest Master of All Arts and Sciences." And it involved color, as alchemists believed the divine entity was closely associated with light. Hermes unquestionably also tried to heal with color. One papyrus exclaims, "*Coe verdigris ointment*! Come then verdant one!" Come, Green One![10] In alchemical parlance, "argot" means the "art of light," and it's connected to a hidden language. In French, *oevert* means "open"; *vert* means "closed" as well as "green." So a "green language," sometimes called "language of the birds," is a secret, closed language intended only for initiates, or people trained in the hidden meanings of alchemy. But the power of color and symbols can no longer be controlled or hidden. Color alchemy is now for everyone!

When alchemist craftsmen fired up their glass beakers to transmute base metals such as lead or mercury into gold and silver, they expected the process to follow a color sequence and, if they got their formulas and temperatures just right, the result would be a "peacock" or "rainbow" at the end. This spectrum of colors was believed to come from the peacock's eye. Peacocks were visible symbols of transformation since when they molt, they seem stripped of all color, but then they are transformed once more into creatures with radiant rainbow plumage.

The peacock, they believed, is "the bird which flies by night without wings, which the early dew of heaven, continually acting by upward and downward ascent and descent, turns into the head of a crow, then into the tail of a peacock and afterwards it acquires the bright wings of a swan, and lastly an extreme redness, an index of its fiery nature. The peacock's eggs... contain the fullness of all colors. Amazingly, there were supposed to be 365 of them. The golden color could be produced from the peacock's eggs... The light of Mohammed has the form of a peacock, and the angels were made out of the peacock's sweat."[11]

Alchemists believed the colors that resulted from this process — The Great Work — came from The Spirit, which ultimately bathes the entire universe. In

[10] Faber Birren, *Color Psychology and Color Therapy* (New Hyde Park, NY: University Books, 1961), 15.
[11] Carl Jung, *Mandala Symbolism* (Bollingen Series) (Princeton, NJ: Princeton University Press, 1972), note 124, p. 47. Originally from Aptowitzer, "Arabisch-Jüdische Schöpfungstheorien" 209, 233.

other words, holy colors. "What alchemy really means is something which has attained to such excellence, such nearness to perfection, that it offers a glory, an expansion of life and understanding, to those who have been brought into contact with it."[12]

The "philosopher's stone" was the term that encompassed all the mystic conditions that allowed the alchemist to cook the ingredients in their "pelicans," their glass beakers with long necks, and go through seven predictable stages. First black (*nigredo*), then through gray to white (*albedo*), yellow (*xanthosis*), red and then purple (*losis-kingship*). Finally, a holy or primal state: silver or gold. As more heat was added, more vivid colors appeared in the molten metals. Now, it's unclear exactly what was cooked. Mercury was the "king" of metals... at times silver and at times red. It was the "guide" to the rest of the process. Silver was a stand-in for the moon, water, or the feminine. Sulphur was symbolic for "sul" or sun, light and "phur" or fire. Masculine.

Alchemy is filled with symbols. The "green lion," for example, represented green vitriol, a corrosive liquid used in many alchemical formulas. Often the lion is shown swallowing the sun and is a symbol for gold. The phoenix, like the peacock, represents the final stage of perfection.

Because the first alchemical stage was black and the next was white, much emphasis was placed on the "white lily, "white dove," "white swan" and the "black raven." Goethe thought colors came from mixing dark and light or black and white. Where black and white meet — the magic in the middle — is the threshold where creativity and transformation take place. White is often seen as "the father" and black "the mother." The Black Virgin. Isis. In Egyptian symbology, the high priestess sits on a throne between two pyramids: one black and one white. Shakespeare painted the polarities in scenes with the dark Moor and the white Desdemona.

The next alchemical stage after that is yellow or red. This is called the red lion, the philosopher's stone, the grand elixir. In later Christian ceremonial processions for the Black Virgin, or Our Lady Underground, only green candles were burned.

---

[12] Robertson Davies, *Happy Alchemy* (Toronto: McClelland & Stewart Inc, 1997), 3, 4.

By the fifteenth century alchemists formed a guild, which was rather religious and certainly political in nature. They wore red "Phrygian" caps and were the forerunners of chemists as they studied nature's secrets, cured disease, and shared formulas. Around 1600 Rudolph II of Prague invited artists and alchemists to his royal Bohemian world. There they investigated ideas, geometric gardens, and of course, color and its relationship to nature's hidden powers and to music.

Carl Jung began studying alchemy in 1928 when he got a copy of the Chinese classic, *The Golden Flower*. He even connected a family member back to some seventeenth-century alchemists in Mainz. "Jung differentiated between two forms of spiritual light: *lumen dei*, the light proceeding from the spiritual realm of a transcendent God, and *lumen naturae*, the light hidden in matter and the forces of nature. The Divine Light may be experienced through revelation and spiritual practices that give us access to our transcendent self. The Light of Nature needs to be released through inner alchemy so that it can work creatively in the world."[13]

Jung saw in the alchemical process a color-like "squaring of the circle, from trinity to quaternity — three to four — linked with the mandalas he so loved. When a dream or mandala lacks red, blue, green, and yellow, Jung inferred the absence of some essential characteristic.[14]

An authentic alchemist wasn't just a "puffer," someone who worked the bellows to stoke the fire, as Chaucer described them with brains "troubled with the smoak of their own furnaces" but rather, he was a serious adept, a holy person who knew how one's soul could become incorruptible, like gold. But first the "base metal" such as "guilt" or "sickness" has to be "burnt away" and purified before you congeal into something more "pure" — union with God. We're stuck in matter; alchemy is the freeing process.

Science, religion, and "natural magic" were, at one time, three very close friends. We still practice alchemy when we cook. Our kitchens become our labs and we combine and transform ingredients by peeling, slicing, spicing, and

---

[13] Llewellyn Vaughan-Lee, *The Return of the Feminine and the World Soul* (Inverness, CA: The Golden Sufi Center, 2009), 101-102.

[14] Charles A. Riley II, *Color Codes* (Hanover, NH: University Press of New England, 1995), 309, 310.

heating. Doctors and nurses are present-day alchemists when they heal with chemicals and procedures.

Alchemy is all about pursuing our spiritual quest in the physical world as it was given to us. It is the art of transmuting our reality into "something else." It's a way of mixing the sacred and the profane. Each of us is an alchemist when we begin to view differently our bodies and our spirit. When we replace distraction with mindfulness, turn bewilderment into clarity and transform enemies into friends. After all, "Each thing has to transform itself into something better, and acquire a new destiny."[15]

"Everything on earth is being continuously transformed because the earth is alive... and it has a soul. We are part of that soul, so we rarely recognize that is working for us."[16] This process was once called "celestial agriculture." It was built into buildings and paintings and even into our understandings of the universe. Brian Swimme's groundbreaking work, *The Universe Is a Green Dragon: A Cosmic Creation Story*, is an alchemical vision of our universe being green because it's alive and filled, as are dragons, with fire. We are faced with the task of shaping and discharging this fire in a manner worthy of its numinous origins. Are we creating something beautiful for our planetary home? Swimme encourages us not to waste it on trivialities or revenge, resentment or despair. We have the alchemical power to forge cosmic fire.

Culture Codes

We think we know what *culture* means. It's what we're surrounded by. It's what we "buy into." We might say our U.S. culture is one of fast food, faster cars, and very little control of privately owned weapons. Our culture is filled with independent creatures, free to exploit and become rich and richer; but many us think banding together for the common good is also a very good idea.

Here's how Stephen King defines culture: "Culture is the shape a place takes when it's inside the head of its people — all the habits, attitudes, and values they take for granted."[17] What do we take for granted? How readily might that change? Simone Weil said culture means to be rooted in perhaps the most

---

[15] Paulo Coelho, *The Alchemist* (San Francisco: Harper San Francisco, 1993), 78.

[16] Ibid., 171.

[17] Stephen King, *On Writing: A Memoir of the Craft* (New York: Scribner, 2000), 43.

important and least recognized need of the human soul. What are these needs? And might a more enlightened view of color help us meet them? Do "elders" view color — and I mean *spiritually*, not with more weakened eyes — differently than younger people?

We know different cultures gravitate toward particular colors. Car manufacturers, for instance, don't intend to sell many white cars to Asians because white is recognized by many Asians as a symbolic color of death. Red is the traditional bridal color for many eastern cultures instead of white. Even though fire hydrants and fire trucks have for decades been red, people now realize that red is a hard color to see at night. So now emergency vehicles are usually yellow-green.

When I grew up in Wisconsin, yellow oleomargarine was banned. What was available was pasty white and you had to add a packet of yellow dye to make it look like butter. We were, after all, The Dairy State, and people trusted cows more than chemists so laws were passed to protect butter sales. But my aunt Mildred, the margarine mule for the family, would drive to Iowa where yellow "ole" was legal, and then clandestinely pack her trunk with a whole lot of "buttery" margarine for the rest of her sisters. After all, like boxed cake mixes and packaged "everything" in the early '50s, margarine was the "modern way to cook."

Take notice of all the colors you see next time you're in the grocery store. Which ones grab you? Among other things, you'll notice that bread is often packaged in a yellowish, brownish wrapper to make the bread look more appetizing. It's our culture!

How We Code Colors

When thousands of Ghengis Khan's Mongols thundered across the plains to a new city, he first raised a white tent as a warning that the people under siege should surrender quickly. If they didn't, he raised a red tent signifying that they would kill every male of fighting age. If they still hadn't surrendered, then the black tent was raised meaning nothing would survive and when they left there would be bare scorched earth.

I live in what's called The Green Mountain State, named *Vert-Mont*, for our Green Mountains. We weren't part of the original thirteen colonies. The Republic of Vermont was born on July 8, 1777, and Vermonters still value their independence and remember our first motto: "Freedom *and* Unity." Both. We still celebrate Ethan Allan and our Green Mountain Boys, those hard-driving, hard-drinking, hard-fighting boys who captured the largest British fort in North America: Ticonderoga. Never mind that not one shot was fired in that takeover, mainly because the British soldiers all had the flu.

Charleston green, a dark almost black-green, was devised after the Civil War, during the Reconstruction period when only black paint could be found in large quantities. It was mixed with a little yellow and now all the historical buildings in Charleston, South Carolina, are to this day this sanctioned deep shade of green.

Forest green is always a favorite in Germany and Austria. But the Masai people in Kenya traditionally wear reddish-brown. Kente cloth woven by the Asanti people is coded with meanings, just as the tartans in Scotland originally held clan origins. Those Scottish plaids were so threatening that the English, during the Scottish Clearances, banned the wearing of tartans, as well as the playing of bagpipes since they rouse warlike emotions. Zulu beads formed coded shapes to indicate their own villages and histories by the ways in which they were attached and each color had both positive and negative meanings. Blue could mean sky, sea, or faithfulness, but also could have unfriendly connotations. Yellow meant wealth, but also could mean dry and hateful. Green stood for grass and cows and contentment but could also indicate jealousy or illness. Pink was a sign of status and kept promises but it also stood for laziness and being poor. Red meant love and strong feelings, but could mean anger and being heartsick. White always means purity and spiritual love and had no negative connotations. Black was for marriage and renewal, but could also be sadness and disappointment.[18] Bands of colors woven with specific threads could protect the person wearing them. White, in many African cultures, is usually a

---

[18] Willow Bascom, *Many Colors Many Cultures* (self-published), 51.

priestly, shamanic color. Red, often worn by blacksmiths (who some stories say invented the color to portray fire), is also the color for older people who carry fiery knowledge and wisdom. Hunters and young boys wore yellow in some African cultures and black clothing was compulsory for anyone who was sad or in mourning. Or was just ending something.[19]

Purple, pink, or green kimonos don't sell well in Japan. They prefer the more gentle colors found in serene water and wood. In Barcelona, we noticed that Gaudi, for instance, chose to work with his beloved Catalan colors based on mountain colors, red-orange clay, flashing Mediterranean waters, and brilliant sunshine yellows.

We've been adding paint to our bodies ever since our Neanderthal ancestors spread colored flower petals on their dead and marked them with red ochre, a symbol of life. White body-paint clay is a sign of mourning to the Papua New Guinea people. Shamans and medicine people around the world have always tattooed and painted their bodies with local color-substances, as have tribal warriors. Initiation rites often involve particular color symbols that can be readily interpreted by one's family and clan. Ancients used green malachite, kohl, red ochres. Black kohl may have been a deterrent to flies getting into one's eyes, so it may have been a useful paint as well as a beautiful, decorative one. Egyptians even painted their mummies before wrapping them in linen. Cretan woman gilded their nipples. Rouges and lip gloss go way, way back. We've all seen pictures of Queen Elizabeth I with her white-powdered-mask face. White lead! English women quickly imitated her style, even using an egg-white varnish to keep their faces from dissolving in the rain. Saffron and henna are still marks of ceremonial splendor among many women in Hindu and Muslim cultures. At Indian markets, likely the most colorful markets anywhere, even today you can find a green vegetable powder that stains skin red. Mounded piles of saffron, vermillion, ochre, and turmeric are for sale around temples for ceremonial body painting and colorful rituals.

---

[19] Dominique Zahan, "Colour Symbolism in Black Africa," *Color Symbolism* (Eranos Yearbook, 1972), 61, 62.

Red is a symbolic color favored by writers and musicians the world over. In 1274, Dante met Beatrice when they were only nine. She wore a crimson dress. From that moment on, he said, "Love ruled my soul." We certainly remember the red stigma imposed on Hawthorne's Hester Prynne, whose red "A" was attached to her breast in "rich scarlet cloth fantastically embroidered with gold thread." And who can forget Scarlett O'Hara? Furthermore, it's no accident that Bizet's operatic heroine, Carmen (carmine), wears a short red skirt. And surely you remember, as vividly as I do, the little girl in the red coat in the otherwise black and grayness of the movie *Schindler's List*? What did that coat say to you? Her death was THE tragedy. One person's story is more compelling than a million, which is, as Joseph Stalin said, merely a statistic.

Any red, the contemporary Abstract Expressionist Robert Motherwell said, is "rooted in blood, glass, wine, hunters' caps, and a thousand other concrete phenomena."

For the Chinese, yellow is the center of the universe. It's the color of royalty. Red and orange means happiness and joy; blues and greens stand for vitality and harmony. White for people in China brings connotations of purity (hence the wedding color), and black is for beginnings. Red, green, and gold are particularly associated with luck. For many Western people, white is noble and good; black is evil. Traditionally, many Black African cultures viewed white as evil and death, whereas black is good, fertile, living, dynamic. I wish I could read all the colorful tiles in the Alhambra, which are religious codes. It's obvious that what colors "stand for" lies in the eye of the beholder. And names of new colors carry codes as well.

Master dyers during the reign of Louis XIV at Versailles created a new color to make crawling lice less noticeable! How practical. They called it *puce*, which is French for "flea." Puce, which for any color-name-deprived readers (aka men who are still trying to figure out what mauve and taupe are) is a dark purplish red, like the underbelly of a louse. Soon it became all the rage in France. But in all fairness, it's a color few can agree on. Some even think puce is green. I personally place it between Pantone's sangria and deep claret, if that helps any.

One of my favorite little books is called *Colorstrology* by Michele Bernhardt. It "combines astrology, numerology, and the metaphysical power of color," according to the jacket. You look up your birthday and find "your color." Now, I need to tell you that I've always loved that blue that falls more on the gray than the yellow side of the scale. I loved wearing my favorite wedgewood blue business suit. And as I recall I wore that same colored blue two-piece wool dress on the snowy December night my husband asked me to marry him. This color is named for the English china guru, Josiah Wedgewood, who in the mid-eighteenth-century had a factory in Stoke-on-Trent. He noticed how raw materials baked in his ovens at varying temperatures turned from red to yellow to white. (Incidentally, Wedgewood's research around color and temperatures led Max Planck in 1900 to birth the quantum theory based on the temperature of the sun.) Wedgewood became the royal potter to Queen Charlotte, and Catherine of Russia once ordered a little set of dishes from him: 952 pieces. Most of what he turned out was more creamy than blue and he created Basalt black and Jasper red pieces as well. Nevertheless, wedgewood is the name for my favorite color, this luscious blue that borders on deep violet. So, when I bought *Colorostrology*, naturally I turned to my birthday to see what my color was supposed to be and... wait for it... wait for it... it's wedgewood. For someone "creative, youthful, and efficient," it says. This color resonates with peace and love, it says, and wearing it or surrounding myself with it calms my nerves and lightens my spirit. Well, there you have it!

We've come to associate certain colors with certain emotions, but that certainly is not the case for everyone seeing or painting with a particular color. Red doesn't have to mean anger or aggression. Nor does black have to be associated with grief or depression. For many black is attractive, restful, mysterious, and positive. Nor do yellow and orange always mean joy and cheeriness. Colors themselves hold no psychological meaning.

But we all recognize red crosses and red crescents as signs for emergency vehicles. And Eleanor of Aquitaine and her women would canter up on their white horses to Knights Templar staging areas armed with red fabric crosses and needles and thread. Stitching red crosses to the knights' white tunics marked them as soldiers in "God's army" headed south to retake Jerusalem.

Magic formulas were usually written in red ink. The Ebers Papyrus, a sixty-eight-foot-long manuscript that dates to 1500 B.C.E., gives all headings, names of diseases, and drugs, in vivid red — most likely from vermillion ink mixed with goat's fat. In Christian manuscripts, the directions that are not part of the actual prayer or service in a prayer book or liturgical guide are printed in red and called *rubrics*, a word that means "red."

Dolores Cannon explains that the Essenes, those pre-Christian Dead Sea Scroll writers, used color as codes. They wore colored headbands tied across their foreheads: gray for young students, green for a seeker who is above the student level but still seeking; blue for masters, indicating inner peace; white for elders — those with ultimate attainment — those at total rest; red bands for visitors — those who have come, not to join, but to study for awhile.[20]

Without getting into why people once wore amber-orange beads around their necks for sore throats (there are loads of gem-healing sources available) or why people spend, on average, a minimum of $2,000 a year on jewelry in the U.S., it's interesting to try to figure out why we value gems so highly. We know their value varies according to their brilliance, the cut, the color, the purity and durability, and how rare they are, but there may be more underlying cosmic reasons. David Marcum, an expert in gem investments, says, "A gemstone's origin is locked in the secrets of the formation of the cosmos." He explains that our sun is not capable of creating anything heavier than carbon. Yet the earth holds a lot of other galactic debris including exploding stars. That's why we so value chemicals such as chromium, manganese, vanadium, and iron — the stuff that makes emeralds green, rubies red, and sapphires blue. Pearls and amber of course are from oysters and resins, but crystals are something quite unique. Complete purity in gem minerals, however, is not that interesting because they're not colorful. Diamonds with their clear reflective natures are in a whole other category. But for most gemstones, the harder and more durable,

[20] Dolores Cannon, *Jesus and the Essenes* (Huntsville, AR: Ozark Mountain Publishing, 1992), Kindle edition, Chapter 5 "Description of Qumran."

the richer the hue, the more attractive. Rubies are thought to increase one's libido. Violet and "cool" colored stones tend to be quieter. We wear our "birthstones" for various individual reasons.

Crystals vibrate and form energy fields around gemstones. They actually form three-dimensional patterns in the gemstone's atoms causing each color to vibrate and transmit energy differently. Think back to crystal radio sets for a moment. Crystals can be charged in a couple of ways: by sunlight, running water, and rushing wind. Gem therapy was practiced in medieval times and is studied and used by many healers today. Rubies, diamonds, sapphires, and emeralds have clear, pure color and hardness — and are rare, so they're valued.

Red, blue, yellow, green, and white colors were most often formerly associated with unseen benefits. For instance, red stones were thought to protect you from fire and lightning. Blues were associated with virtue and faith. Yellow would likely bring happiness and prosperity. Green was for fertility and white carried heaven's protection.

And then there is orange for amber. "Amber" actually means *elektron*, or the substance of the sun. It is a miraculous forty-to-fifty-million-year-old pine resin creation that produces an electric charge when stroked. Chopin supposedly rubbed amber before playing the piano, perhaps because it eliminates perspiration. There are, amazingly enough, two hundred and fifty different colors of amber — the rarest being blue and green. My few pieces of amber jewelry are all orange and rust-flecked and mostly a brownish pumpkin hue. We've all watched the *Jurassic Park* movies so we know that various things can get trapped in this old resin. Some Italian researchers recently found some mites frozen in amber droplets that are 230 million years old! Pliny poetically said amber is formed by trees' tears or the dew of sunbeams. When our family traveled to the Baltic shores of Poland, we got to visit an amber water "mine." I learned that if amber floats it's real. If it sinks, it's a fake resin creation. Caveat Emptor! Our tour guide said there's enough amber along the Baltic coastlines to last for another thousand years... but at what rate of "buying"? And "enough" for what, I wondered. You have to be licensed to "mine" the water pumps and amber mining is strictly regulated by Poland's environmental standards. Still many people get it illegally and you can find amber bits while walking along a beach, especially after a storm. When amber is sawed or cut, it gives off a pleasant fragrance many believe to be healing. They point to the fact that none of the amber cutters ever died from the plague that ravaged other nearby areas.

Long before that visit to the amber-works, I had a dream about holding a rectangular piece of amber next to my solar plexus and in my dream I flew. "Fly" and "amber" — my dream self was humorously pointing to that wordplay. When I woke up, I asked my "dream self" what it all meant. Here's what I wrote in my journal: "*Trust yourself. You have the tools within you. You don't need 'help' from the outside. Use your own 'wealth.' Amber's better than gold in this respect — to teach you how to unlock the enclosed 'fly' or 'mosquito' from long, long ago. Why the solar plexus? It's the center of creation. Use your emotions for forward propulsion. Fear. Anger. Joy. Don't encase and encrust them inside you. Let them out and use them.*"

The Estonians colorfully decorate their folk costumes, as we learned in Tallinn. There is a traditional form of embroidery that comes from a particular lake region west of Gdansk. Three shades of blue for the sky, the Baltic, and the inland lakes; red for blood; yellow for the sun; green for the trees, and black for the mystery of it all. They use tulip designs and it's very recognizable. Men and women, both, create these costume designs and they're worn on the back and the front. These colors played a huge role in the Estonian "Singing Revolution." Under Communist rule, one-third of all the people living in Estonia gathered at a large outdoor concert hall in Tallinn — 300,000 of them — wearing their traditional folk costumes and singing their "forbidden" songs. The Russians had banned all folk songs and made laws that Estonians could only sing Communist worker songs. Braving arrest, they proved power in numbers and so outnumbered the few Russian soldiers stationed there that they sang their native songs, wearing their native colors, and they got their independence in 1991.

Surgery staff dress in green for a reason. Green is the complement of red. If the surgical team stared at red wounds (and blood) for a long time and then looked at white, for instance, they could have disturbing after-images. Color researchers tell us that this is the same reason people working on anything red for long periods of time (lipstick, red fabric, any red surface) will need green around them to keep them from getting nauseous and dizzy. It's much the same principle as experienced in nurseries using blue bilirubin lights. They need to introduce yellow for the nursing staff who otherwise would get dizzy and some even nauseous from too much blue.

Colors convey messages, if you know how to read them.

Sacred Colors

According to the Torah, God told Moses to instruct the Israelite people to make fringes on the borders of their men's garments and at each corner to put a thread of blue — a very particular blue made from the shell of a sea creature. This would remind Jewish men of their sacred responsibilities. But blues were hard to come by. Then someone observed that if dyeing were done on a sunny day, the result was blue; if done on a cloudy overcast day, the result was more purple. So to get the "holy blue," sunlight was combined with the rotting bodies of the murex shellfish. And the high priest Aaron's garments were to be made very colorfully, as well. The undergarment was blue with the lower edges trimmed in embroidered pomegranates of blue, purple, and crimson. Gold, blue, purple, red yarn, and twisted linen threads were worked throughout. And the colors had to be made from traditionally tested recipes. The Talmud even gives chemical tests for detecting fraudulent use of ritual dyes.[21]

Moses' brother Aaron's breastplate (and all other high priests that came after him) must have been a sight to behold! The breastplate was of "gold, of blue and purple and crimson yarns and fine twisted linen… square and doubled."[22] It was worn close to the priest's heart, and a nine-inch pouch was fastened with a gold chain and blue ribbons on the outside. Inside the pouch were fortune-telling stones called the Urim (meaning "lights") and the Thummin (meaning "perfection" or "truth"). The stones were the same shape and a priest could draw one for "yes" and one for "no." No one knows for sure how the Thummin and

---

[21] Spike Bucklow, *The Alchemy of Paint* (London: Marion Boyars Publishers Ltd., 2009), 31.
[22] Exodus 28: 15-17.

Urim worked, but some think the stones functioned in conjunction with the breastplate. Mormons describe the scrying glasses Joseph Smith used to translate their sacred text as the Urim and Thummin. Masonic legends state the Urim and Thummin were recovered from Solomon's Temple and may have become part of the Templar's treasury. Yale still uses it as their shield/coat of arms: Lux et Veritas — Light and Truth.

On the breastplate were twelve precious stones corresponding to the twelve tribes of Israel — one for each of Jacob's twelve sons born to four women: two wives and two maids. The stones were placed in four horizontal rows of three stones each. The name of each son was engraved on each stone:

1) Red jasper, sardinus — Reuben, the first; Leah's son.

2) Topaz or serpentine — Simeon; Leah's son.

3) Carbuncle, emerald, or green feldspar — Levi; Leah's son.

4) Emerald, ruby, garnet — Judah; Leah's son.

5) Sapphire lapis lazuli — Dan; Bilhah's son, Rachel's maid.

6) Diamond, jade — Naphtali; Bilhah's son, Rachel's maid.

7) Hyacinth, jacinth, amber — Gad; Zilpah's son, Leah's maid.

8) Ruby, agate — Asher; Zilpah's son, Leah's maid.

9) Amethyst, purple quartz — Issachar; Leah's son.

10) Beryl, yellow jasper — Zebulun; Leah's son; then Leah bore a daughter, Dinah.

11) Onyx, malachite-turquoise — Joseph; Rachel's son.

12) Jasper-jade — Benjamin, the last; Rachel's son; Rachel died in childbirth.

The priest wore a blue ephod under it all — a garment of "gold, blue, purples and crimson yarns, and of fine twisted linen, skillfully worked." On each shoulder he wore two onyx stones set in gold filigree. On one were engraved the first six names of Jacob's sons and on the other, the last six.[23] Our present-day monthly birthstones are said to be patterned after this ancient priestly system. No one really knows exactly what the high priest did with these stones. Or why they were called the stones of judgment. But it sounds like divination to me.

St. Jerome came along and wrote about the hidden meanings of color in the Exodus tabernacle and how it described the whole universe. The twelve jewels, he said, linked to twelve colors, arranged in four tiers of three as being the twelve stones on which the heavenly Jerusalem is built. And at the same time, they are the twelve colors or stones of the zodiac and each of the four groups of three represent the seasons. He argued that even though the pagans used them, that doesn't mean Christians can't. Jerome said white linen or flax is earthlike; purple from the little sea snails represents water; the hyacinth color is likened to air; and scarlet represents fire. Later on in the thirteenth century, Pope Innocent III chose these four colors for church vestments, even though they differed a bit from Exodus' high priestly colors.

The early Chaldeans watched the night skies and arranged the zodiac onto a wheel. The ancients assigned colors to each planet: Aries was pure red; Taurus, red-orange; Gemini, pure orange; Cancer, orange-yellow; Leo, pure yellow; Virgo, yellow-green; Libra, pure green; Scorpio, green-blue; Sagittarius, pure blue; Capricorn, blue-violet; Aquarius, pure violet; and Pisces, violet-red.

Navajo ceremonial sand paintings, like Buddhist mandalas, form intricate, colorful but very temporary pieces of art. These ephemeral creations are meant to last only a few hours. But in that short time these "otherworldly spaces" have the ability to heal the one who is invited to sit in the middle of this traditional ceremony. The Navajo word for "religion" means "moving about ceremonially." Since the universe is alive and interdependent, they firmly believe a ritual ceremony can restore balance and healing. Balance and symmetry are essential and the painting brings order out of chaos.

The sandpainting or *iikááh* is a place of entry — a holy altar. Each design

---

[23] Exodus 28: 21-30.

is created by several people working together from the center outward. Traditions dictate the precise placement of colored sand or grain. The background is filled with black or white wavy lines. Feathered prayer sticks mound up the earth east of the hogan's doorway where the ceremony is taking place. This invites the supernaturals' presence and then the figures are placed on the painting — usually black and yellow for a male and blue or white for a female. Male figures have round heads; female, square. The patient may sit on the painting for several hours as the "singer" works. A sand painting can assist in healings in the following ways:

1)   It attracts the supernaturals and their healing power.

2)   It depicts the supernaturals and identifies the patients with their healing powers.

3)   It absorbs the sickness from and immunizes the patient.

4)   It creates a ritual reality in which patient and the supernatural dramatically interact.[24]

In some esoteric traditions, colors are also associated with particular days of the week. Sunday is the day of yellow and illumination. Monday is the day of divine love, represented by the color pink. Tuesday is the day for the color blue, symbolic of faith and the will of God. Wednesday is green for healing and truth. Thursday has two colors: purple and gold. Both of these colors are symbolic of service to others. Friday is white, denoting purity. Saturday is violet, symbolic of freedom and transmutation.

Colors can also denote harmony of the seasons. Winter solstice is associated with white. The white light that surrounds Christmas. The golden white midnight birth of a new sun. Autumn equinox carries tremendous power with an exquisite blue. Spring equinox calls up red, for new life. And the summer solstice is associated with a luminous gold.

The colors for our four directions differ according to various ancient cultures. The Tibetans, for instance, say north is yellow; south, blue; east, white

---

[24] Trudy Griffin-Pierce, *Earth Is My Mother, Sky Is My Father: Space, Time and Astronomy in Navajo Sandpainting* (Albuquerque, NM: University of New Mexico Press, 1998), 43.

and west, red. Going back to old Ireland, we find they believed north was black, white the south; purple the east; and a dun color for the west. For the Chinese, black is also north, but red for the south, green for east and the west is white.

The Maya people of the Yucatan decided the east, where the sun was born, was the color red. The north, white; west was where the sun "died" so it was black, and south, connected to the sun, was yellow. They had a fifth color as well — the underworld, which was turquoise. Many of their fresco murals are still intact. Some friezes on their temples still show fragments of color. What we now see as drab gray stone was once elaborately and brilliantly colored — just as the Greek statues and friezes were when they were first carved. It is said that once even the sphinx's face was painted red.

In America, some Navaho people still ascribe colors to their sacred mountains and directions. Dawn comes each day from the southern blue mountains. The eastern mountains are white and cause daylight. Western mountains are yellow and bring twilight. The mountains to the north are black and they cover the earth in darkness.

Literature, too, can carry color messages. Leslie L. Lewis once prepared a structure chart of *Ulysses* by James Joyce for her "Joyce Lecture" at Chicago's Institute of Design showing, among other things, the colors attributed to every one of his eighteen chapters.[25] John Hollander, a contemporary poet, writes a great deal about color arrangements and actually has a character named Roy G. Biv.[26]

The author Edward de Bono wrote a book on problem-solving called *Six Thinking Hats* in 1985 using the metaphor of six colored hats. Like the Seuss character, Bartholomew Cubbins, we can "put any number of these hats on" but many of us just keep wearing the same colors more easily than others. Our brains are "sensitized" to them, so they're comfortable to wear. These hats, he explains, aren't "really us" but rather the way we develop strategies for thinking about particular issues. De Bono identifies six distinct states in which the brain can be "sensitized." In each of these states the brain will identify and bring into

[25] L. Moholy-Nagy, *Vision in Motion* (Paul Theobald and Co., 1965), 347.
[26] Charles A. Riley II, *Color Codes* (Hanover, NH: University Press of New England, 1995), 250.

conscious thought certain aspects of issues being considered (e.g., gut instinct, pessimistic judgment, neutral facts). The trick is to wear *all* the colored hats.

Many of us associate the color purple with bruising and sexual violation as Sofia's swollen, eggplant-colored face reminded us in *The Color Purple* by Alice Walker. Her book was published in 1982; the film version premiered in 1985 and the musical play debuted in 2005. Celie, in the story, is the Southern Black woman who writes letters to God about her life as daughter, wife, sister, mother, and friend. Shug Avery, the blues singer, becomes her salvation. Throughout the story, it is Celie who is the center of her community of women and the one who knows how to survive. One day Shug says, "I think it pisses God off when you walk by the color purple in a field and don't notice it." Walker, who calls herself a Southern Woman of Color, recently wrote about the bruising of Mother Earth and a new way of being: "A system of governance we can dream and imagine and build together. One that recognizes at least six thousand years of brutally enforced complicity in the assassination of Mother Earth, but foresees six thousand years ahead of us when we will not submit."[27]

Purple certainly can have negative connotations. For instance, a friend of mine has a daughter who works in a mental health facility near Boston. One of the residents seeking treatment there had, as most mentally ill people do, a "trigger" that can set her off and destroy any equilibrium she may have built up to that point. With some sleuthing, the staff finally isolated the trigger point: the color purple. So anyone working with her or caring for her in any way was cautioned against wearing anything purple.

David Batchelor has written a book called *Chromophobia*. In it, he describes how some people attempt to purge color from culture, to devalue it, diminish its significance and deny its complexity. They do this in two ways, he says. First, by claiming a particular color is foreign, vulgar, even pathological. "Not us." The second way is to regard a particular color as dangerous, or at the very least, trivial and not worthy of serious consideration. They argue that color has "fixed laws" so it's therefore easier for artists to learn to use than for them to

---

[27] Alice Walker, from "Democratic Womanism," as read on "Democracy Now!" Amy Goodman's radio show honoring Alice Walker and the thirtieth anniversary since the publication of *The Color Purple*.

master the more difficult art of drawing. On the hierarchy of tools artists usually employ, color, therefore, has been relegated to a lower rung.

Not everyone believes, as Roland Barthes did, that "color... is a kind of bliss... like a closing eyelid, a tiny fainting spell."[28] Batchelor reminded me of a movie I'd seen a few years back: *Wings of Desire*. We are taken back and forth between a spirit world of black and white and a sensuous world in full color. An angel falls from grace — into color — and asks what every color is called. If this metaphor is apt, we "fall" into color. But, must color be controlled and classified? Scaled and "scriptured?" Is color "less than true" like the patches sewn on Kurtz' clothing in *Heart of Darkness*? Is it just cosmetic? Or can it also be mystical? Something that touches us very deeply?

"We have come at color from many different directions; we have seen it seep into the world and flood over it; we have seen it rubbed out and covered over; we have seen it kill and be killed and give life and deny death. But whichever way we have come at it, it is difficult to avoid the conclusion that color is a very peculiar other."[29]

I can't think of any color I'd consider "other." I claim them all. But I have special fondness for purple and violet.

As a child, I hiked up a hill behind the family barn to pick violets for my mother. Johnny jump-ups, we sometimes called them. I had my own field of purple and I noticed it every spring. My mother had a peculiar vase. It was a creamy iridescent swan with an open back. When I got back from my climb, the swan had a purple back filled with the delicate, short-stemmed blossoms. Thirty years later, she wore a lilac pantsuit to her wake, and rested in a casket whose interior was painted in sprays of violets. Looking down at her, all I could think of was a swan vase filled with purple flowers.

We like to ascribe color names. For instance, we call a chess-playing machine that can analyze 200 million positions per second Deep Blue. Since the late 1990s, we've called children with blue or violet auras *indigo children*. Nancy Ann Tappe was one of the first to recognize them as special. They have large, clear

---

[28] Roland Barthes, *The Responsibility of Forms: Critical Essays on Music, Art, and Representation* (Oxford: Oxford University Press, 1986), 166.

[29] David Batchelor, *Chromophobia* (London: Reaktion Books Ltd., 2007), Kindle Book, Chapter Three.

eyes, and are, by and large, precious, often hyperactive, and easily bored. They were "foretold" by Edgar Cayce as representing a new form of humanity. These children "see" angels and other beings in the etheric realms. They "know" who they are and are not afraid to let parents and teachers know. They need little sleep and have an affinity for languages. Naturally, given their talents, they find our educational system hampering and even detrimental. They're very intuitive nonconformists and will let you know what they need — even what foods they think they should eat. They'll usually prefer vegetables and grains. Studies have been conducted especially around "attention deficits" and indigo children. Hay House offers several books on the topic.

As far back as 1985, Michael Scallion "saw" these children coming. He called them "Children of the Blue Ray." They come, he noted, as "peacemakers" and teachers. "They are drawn to color in a grand way. They will work with color in such a fashion as many today might use the pencil and ruler for sketching… You will find them drawn most to pastels, and in particular, to the color mauve, or hues of mauve."[30]

Kandinsky correlated musical instruments to colors: violin, a cool red or yellow; trumpet or drum, vermillion; church bell or a strong contralto, orange; flute, light blue; cello is darker blue; double bass, midnight blue. English horn is violet, he said; pauses in music are white. All of *Tannhäuser* is considered by some to be blue: *Parsifal*, green. Mozart has been associated with the color blue; Chopin, green; Beethoven, black. Music can take on various colors. Categorizing specific compositions is so personal, yet some works just "feel" like these colors.

We all do this to some degree. For instance, if you think of "red" music, you may think of John Philip Sousa marches. "Red" music is forceful and stark. It radiates raw power like rock music and dramatic operas. "Orange" music is more celebratory — festive and triumphant, like wedding marches. "Yellow" music is joyous and happy, light and fun. Think of most of Mozart. "Green" music is filled with peace and compassion and the luscious beauty of nature. Think

---

[30] Gordon-Michael Scallion, *Notes from the Cosmos* (West Chesterfield, NH: Matrix Institute, Inc., 1997), 280.

of practically everything Claude Debussy wrote. "Blue" music inspires truth and beauty, purity, structure and form. It's radiant. Chopin. Bach, Beethoven, Handel. "Indigo" music brings an awareness of spirit — wonder, awe, and mystery. Handel's *Messiah*, for instance.

And finally "violet" music is about love and oneness. Here we "come home" to our source. This music is transcendent. Remember John Tavener's *Song for Athene*, which was performed at Princess Diana's funeral?

The Finnish composer Jean Sibelius also saw colors as musical tones. He once told a stove builder who asked what color he wanted his stove, "F major," which would have been for him a dark red. They didn't know his code, so they painted it green.[31]

It is said that Richard Wagner wore silk next to his body in colors that harmonized with his compositions. He felt that one's nervous system responds to color's subtle radiation so he often dressed in orchid, blues, pale mauves, and golden tones.[32]

Because Jean Auel so carefully researched *Earth's Children*, her series set in prehistoric Europe, I took special note of her description of colors in her final book, *The Land of Painted Caves*.

A Zelandoni wise one explains the five sacred colors to our heroine, Ayla. "The first color is red. It is the color of blood, the color of life, but just as life does not last, the color red seldom stays true for very long. As blood dries it darkens and becomes brown, sometimes very dark. Brown is an aspect of red, sometimes called old red. It is the color of the trunks and branches of many trees. The red ochers of the earth are the dried blood of the Mother, and though some can be very bright, almost new looking, they are considered old red... When red fruits such as strawberries are dried, they turn to old red."[33] Green, the color of leaves and grass, is also the color of life. Yellow, the color of sun and fire, although, "there is also much red in both, which shows that they have a life of their own. You can see the red in the sun mostly in the morning and in the evening. The sun gives us light and warmth, but it can be dangerous. Too much

[31] Varley, 197.
[32] Ibid., 76.
[33] Jean M. Auel, *The Land of Painted Caves* (New York: Crown Publishers, 2011), 94.

sun can make the skin burn and dry out plants and watering holes. We have no control over the sun... Fire can be even more dangerous than the sun... Not all things that are yellow are hot. Some soil is yellow, there is yellow ocher as well as red ocher... and of course many flowers show its true color. They always age to brown, which is an aspect of red. It is for that reason some argue that yellow should be considered an aspect of red and not a sacred color in its own right, but most agree that it is a primary color that attracts red, the color of life."[34]

The ancient speaker then goes on to explain that the fourth color is "clear." It's the color of the wind and of water. It can show all colors as in a reflection on a pond. "Both blue and white are aspects of clear. When you look at the wind, it is clear, but when you look into the sky, you see blue. Water in a lake, or in the Great Waters of the West, is often blue, and the water seen on glaciers is a deep, vivid blue."

The fifth sacred color is "dark," sometimes called black. "It is the color of night, the color of charcoal after fire has burned its life out of the wood. It is the color that overcomes the color of life, red, especially as it ages. Some have said that black is the darkest shade of old red, but it is not. Dark is the absence of light, and the absence of life. It is the color of death. It does not even have an ephemeral life; there are no black flowers. Deep caves show the primary color of dark in its truest form."[35]

Stained glass, Malraux said, is "impassioned crystallization, the blaze of color, kindled by the Prophets."[36] Glass was invented about four thousand years before sparkling walls lined European cathedrals. Sacred glaziers during the twelfth and thirteenth centuries burned beechwood and used the ash to get manganese and iron. They used three wood-burning furnaces — one for heating, one for cooling, and one to melt the blown glass into sheets. Copper oxide created white glass as well as red and green by using various cooking temperatures. It was all quite unstable and sometimes unpredictable. Reds and blues were the most difficult glass colors to create. Stained glass artists worked at their benches often flashing up to forty coats of glazings just to get the right

---

[34] Auel, 96.

[35] Ibid., 97.

[36] André Malraux, *The Voices of Silence* (New York: Doubleday & Company, Inc. 1956), 41.

hue and luminosity. For these ruby reds they overlaid green, purple, brown, and yellow. What made matters ever more challenging was that they couldn't view their work until it was actually hung.

During both world wars, the people of Chartres in France saved their famous stained glass windows by burying them in mines or in the cathedral's crypt itself. This was no small feat since the 116 glass windows in that one church cover the equivalent of an acre of space. When the cathedral burned in 1194, the western wall was miraculously saved. One window in particular hung there in the smoke like a giant jewel-encrusted brooch. It's called "The Blue Virgin Window" (page 228) because of its rich blues against a ruby-red background. Calm and commanding, always the queen. Chartres' glaziers, al-chemists in their own right, created a blue so intense and so beautifully lapis-lazuli that no one has been able to duplicate it since.

Henry Adams in *Mont-Saint-Michel and Chartres* points out that the cost of these windows was extravagant — "almost like grinding up sapphires..." — but whatever it was, the glassmakers seem to agree that this glass of 1140–50 is the best ever made. "The men who made it were not professionals but ama-teurs, who may have had some knowledge of enameling, but who worked like jewelers, unused to glass, and with the refinement that a reliquary or a crozier required."[37] "The longer one looks into it, the more overpowering it becomes until one begins almost to feel an echo of what our... ancestors, drunk with the passion of youth and the splendor of the Virgin, have been calling to us... no words... could revive their emotions so vividly as they glow in the purity of the colors; the limpidity of the blues; the depth of the red, the intensity of the green; the complicated harmonies; the sparkle and splendor of the light, and the quiet and certain strength of the mass."[38] He calls the windows a cluster of jewels and a delirium of colored light.

Stained glass windows, even the kind less grand than at Chartres, invite us to read the iconographic meanings from them after we revel in their sheer beauty. The splendid play of colors in light can bring us to ecstasy, as the blue tiles and

---

[37] Henry Adams, *Mont-Saint-Michel and Chartres* (Princeton, NJ: Princeton University Press, 1905, 1933), 135.
[38] Ibid., 137.

windows in Istanbul's Blue Mosque. Color in these gothic church settings have, as the painter Maurice Denis said, "a magnificent power over the spirit... a smiling gravity... a revealed truth... a serious conviction of Christianity."[39]

Remember those large Buddha statues of Bamiyan in Afghanistan? The ones the Taliban blew up? They marked the home to lapis mines. One statue was originally painted red; the other blue. Now they're lying in the dust.

Most lapis lazuli comes from Afghanistan, but it was also available in ancient Sumeria and Egypt. It's a form of limestone very rich in the dark blue mineral lazurite and early people believed it imitated heaven. No wonder, then, early king-gods were surrounded with blue — and gold, of course. From the sun.

Colors were coded, along with various intricate knots, into the five-thousand-year-old Quipu or knotted cord "writing system" used by people of the Incan Empire and their ancestors along the coast of western South America. Using fibers, color, and knots, they recorded transactions and events including population census and tax information, the output of mines, and food and crop updates as well as poems and legends. Their runners efficiently carried them, sometimes in large wrapped balls of string, over ten thousand kilometers of roads running twenty kilometers at a time. Gary Urton and Carrie Brezine, Harvard anthropologists using computer database analysis, claim that by combining fabrics and colors, their intricate knot system contains a seven-bit binary code that can carry more than fifteen hundred separate units of information. Because of their age, the faded colors are harder to interpret — most are brown. But yellow cords have been discovered and by the knots, it's believed they indicate the maize crop information. Wool cords of oranges, reds, yellows, and beiges were also used. Every color of string meant something: yellow was gold; black was time, blue was sky and gods; red, their deep purplish red, stood for the Incas themselves. Red cords meant battles; knots, how many people had died. They made red from the cochineal, orange from the dried seeds of the annatto plant, a deep pink from the brazil tree wood. They fixed the red dye with a mordant of tin or alum, which bit onto the color and made it stick to the textile.[40]

---

[39] Robert Branner, Ed., *Chartres Cathedral* (New York: W. W. Norton & Company, 1969), 234.

[40] Victoria Finlay, *Color: A Natural History of the Palette* (New York: Ballantine Books, 2002), 144.

In order to make their dyes stick to the fabric, dyers in Europe sought valuable tin or alum from Champagne, France, as well as from Smyrna on the Turkish coast. Rumor has it that Henry VIII married Anne of Cleaves just to get his hands on her alum.[41]

In the Christian Trinity, colors carry various meanings:

Red: masculine/Father; color of will, action, command; fiery, explosive.

Blue: feminine/Mother; color of reflection, nurturance, secrecy, formation, waters; passivity, acceptance, Holy Spirit or Sophia.

Yellow: androgynous, the heavenly Child, color of the intellect and learning, meditation; it can give and take, wait or act.

Christian priests and ministers still wear liturgical vestments created, perhaps not as rigidly as the High Priest Aaron's, but nevertheless, colorfully. And each color represents a worship season and connotes a theological thought.

White: light/innocence, purity, joy, glory; used for Christmas and Easter.

Red: fire, blood, charity and generous sacrifice; used for the season of Pentecost.

Green: nature, hope of eternal life; green symbolizes new life and is used in the liturgical season when no other colors are appropriate.

Purple: affliction and melancholy; used during Advent and Lent. Some churches use blue for Advent.

Black: sorrow, death; the liturgical color of mourning.

Terry Tempest Williams[42] tells her story of going to Ravenna to learn about mosaics and how to make a tessera — a cube that plays with light. Williams' teacher told her that because the glass surfaces are irregular, they increase the dance of light and many colors create one color from a ways off. She could learn the technique in about fifteen minutes, he said, but it would take a lifetime

---

[41] Finlay, 144.

[42] Terry Tempest Williams, *Finding Beauty in a Broken World* (New York: Pantheon Books, 2008), 6.

to master it. "A mosaic is a conversation between what is broken."

Mosaics were first created in Mesopotamia around 2500 B.C.E. Colorful Greek pebbles gave way to cut glass cubes and colored terracotta. They were set into intricate geometrical designs. When Joel and I visited Delos, we saw the famous mosaic pavement of Dionysus riding on a panther in the House of Masks. I was struck by the beautiful intense green colors. The Romans used more regular repetitions of equal units of color to create more uniform textures. Metallic tesserae, gold and silver cubes, were added to the glass cubes to make up Christian mosaics. Anyone standing in St. Peter's Cathedral has been first fooled, as I was, into thinking the mosaics were paintings. Red tesserae were scattered on cheeks to make the mosaics come alive. Under Constantine colored glass replaced stone and the colored cubes in Byzantine mosaics, like the ones in Hagia Sophia, were sometimes placed at angles to reflect the light of candles.

Show Your Colors!

According to the Norse *Edda*, early Scandinavians imagined a rainbow-bridge, Bifröst, which connected Midgaard, where we all live, to Asgard, home of the gods. The bridge had three colors: red, gold, and blue. Mythologists suggest those colors represented the three social classes of early Norway: gold for the nobles, red for freemen, and blue for slaves. Viking shields hanging on the sides of their dragon-prowed boats displayed red for battle, gold for royalty, green for health, blue for the sea, white for purity, and black for death.

England's King Richard in 1197 made a rule called the "Assize of Cloth," which essentially confined the lower class to wearing gray. Charlemagne also ordered peasants to wear black and gray. Only aristocrats in medieval Europe could wear scarlet.

In the Qing dynasty (1644–1911) it was the law that a shade of yellow could only be worn by the emperors. As recently as 1949 during the Maoist revolution, it was dictated that people, regardless of their rank, all had to wear blue. Thai monks wear saffron-colored robes, Tibetan monks and nuns wear orange or red robes, while Zen Buddhist monks wear brown or black. The Christian Franciscans wear gray; some Benedictines wear gray and others black robes; the Cistercians, white; the Dominicans, brown. Carthusians wear a black cloak over a white habit. Carmelite nuns wear brown; cardinals wear red, of course.

Varna means *color* in Sanskrit. Ancient Indians texts described the four original races or castes and their ascribed colors as follows: the Brahmans or priests, white; the Kshatriyas or soldiers, red; the Vaisyas or merchants and business people, yellow; and the Sudras or servant class, black.

Heraldry codes go back in Europe to when knights jousted and rode to war. They needed to identify families and ranks so they devised a system of rules called "blazon." Sort of like public school ties. Colors or tinctures and metals were intricately combined in various ways to be quickly read, even from the backs of speeding horses. There were two standard flowers in heraldry: the rose and the lily. But the colors for the shields as well as the knights and horse attire varied, as did the various designs.

White: purity

Red: courage, zeal, and sacrifice

Blue: piety and sincerity

Yellow gold: honor and loyalty

Green: growth and hope

White or silver: faith and purity

Black: grief and penitence

Orange: strength and endurance

Purple: royalty or rank

The British novelist Anthony Trollope wrote two and a half hours every day before setting off for the post office where he worked for thirty-three years.

He introduced the red pillar mailboxes still used for outgoing letters all over Britain today.

Our own university system uses colors to tell at a glance who is in which department or "school."

Scarlet: theology

Blue: philosophy

White: the arts and letters

Green: medicine

Purple: law

Golden yellow: science

Orange: engineering

Pink: music

Dan Beck and Christopher Cowen explain in their states of human development system called *Spiral Dynamics* that we all carry various types — or colors — or memes within us. At the bottom of this at times messy spiral of nine color categories is our "Survival Sense." They call this one *beige*. Think Freud. It covers about 0.1% of our adult population.

Next is "Kin Spirits" or *purple*. About 10% of all people are at this stage; they're seeking harmony and safety in a mysterious world.

The third stage is what they call "Power Gods" and the color is — no surprise — *red*. This is a feudal mindset and still captivates about 20% of the people. Think Nietzsche.

The fourth stage is "Truth Force" and it's *blue*. This is a mythic order and it tries to bring order and ensure the future. About 40% live here. It's here you'll find a lot of fundamentalist thinking.

The fifth tier is called "Strive Drive." It's *orange*. Think Wall Street and Descartes. About 50% fall into this one. It's mostly about strategy to prosper and gain power.

The sixth tier is called "Human Bond" and it's *green*. These folks are against hierarchies. About 10% of the population is here, striving for more pluralism. They value communication; they explore the inner self and value others.

After this green stage, moving to what the authors envision as the seventh category, we have what they call the "Flax Flow." Only about 1% of the people are here. It's an integrative stage and its color is *yellow*. People in this category strive to align systems.

Then at the eighth stage, we find "Whole View," and its color is *turquoise*. Only about 0.1% are here. They experience holons and waves.

Finally, at the ninth stage, called "Integral Holonic," people find themselves very close to what Chardin called the Noosphere. Its color is *coral-peach*. Few people are here, but we are all striving to reach this level of understanding.

This quick overview does not do justice to this brilliant and thoughtful look at our colorful transforming potential, but those wishing to know more can find many books on Spiral Dynamics.

Colorful flags proudly wave over all cultures. How do we feel about our own red, white, and blue? Pride? The Stars and Stripes tug at our hearts, especially when we see coffins draped in them. Most flags are red, white, and blue with green and yellow coming in as next choices. France used a red, white, and blue tricolor flag and other nations followed suit after their revolutions. Greece and Israel's are blue and white; the pan-African colors are red, green, and yellow. During a party in Weimar in the winter of 1785, Goethe had a late-night conversation on his theory of primary colors with the South American revolutionary Francisco de Miranda. This conversation inspired Miranda, as he later recounted, in his designing the yellow, blue, and red flag of Gran Colombia, from which the present national flags of Colombia, Venezuela, and Ecuador are derived.

The rainbow flag has been used by the LGBT pride movement since the 1970s. The original one was hand-dyed by Gilbert Baker of San Francisco and had eight stripes:

Hot pink: sex

Red: life

Orange: healing

Yellow: sun

Green: serenity with nature

Turquoise: art

Indigo: harmony

Violet: spirit

Eventually, the hot pink was dropped. The current LGBT flag contains six stripes, no longer including turquoise or hot pink. Rainbow-striped flags have often been used by various groups to represent hope for difficult causes.

Thangka (meaning "to unroll") or traditional Tibetan prayer flags are also called *Dar Cho* (*Dar* means "to increase life, fortune, health, and wealth" and *Cho* means "all sentient beings.") They stand for luck, happiness, longevity, and prosperity and date back thousands of years. Each of the five colors corresponds to an element and the colors are always in this order: yellow, earth; green, water; red, fire; white, air, wind or cloud; and blue, space. The most familiar symbol is the Lung-ta or Wind Horse, which is "Wish Fulfilling Jewel of Enlightenment" and usually occupies the middle space. Texts of short sutras or various mantras appear in pictorial or written forms.

We name and code what is important to us. By naming it, we actually *see* it. And by naming colors and what they mean to us, by *seeing* them, they will begin interacting with us. If we love colors, we will value them and we'll begin to see them in new ways *everywhere.*

Colorful Voices

· · · · ·

EDGAR CAYCE (1877–1945)

Edgar Cayce, born on a farm near Hopkinsville, Kentucky, grew up in a religious home and later became a Sunday school teacher. As a child, he had obvious psychic abilities — for instance, when he was six or seven, he told his parents he could talk to relatives who had recently died. He slept with his head on his schoolbooks and developed a kind of photographic memory of the information inside them. At twenty-one he developed paralysis of his throat muscles and had great problems talking. He decided to try self-hypnosis and asked a friend to help him achieve a self-induced trance and then record what he had to say. This launched his role as the "sleeping prophet" when he recommended his own medication and therapy, which restored his speech. Soon it became apparent that other people could get information from the tranced Cayce. After doing these readings for forty-three years, by the time he died he left over fourteen thousand documented records of telepathic-clairvoyant statements he had given to over eight thousand people. In 1931, Cayce established the Association for Research and Enlightenment, the A.R.E. center in Virginia Beach, Virginia, a nonprofit educational organization to preserve and study the information he was receiving. His son, Hugh Lynn Cayce, was president until his death in 1982. All of Edgar Cayce's indexed "readings" are at the A.R.E. and much of the original information stored in three-ring black binders has been published, often by "category." For instance, 2,500 readings were called "life readings" — people who received them got a picture of their own soul's progress through former experiences on earth. Others are on Biblical topics such as the Essenes. Others are on such topics as Atlantis, dreams, psychic abilities, etc. One is called Color, *published in 1973 by the Edgar Cayce Foundation and introduced by Roger Lewis; it forms the basis of the following.*

I didn't set out to investigate color, but like other areas of research, I kept getting information about how our pituitary, for instance, transforms the colors of light rays into vital energy. Color is nothing but vibration and vibration is movement. It's like electricity. But color is a more creative vibration than electricity. It's all God-force. We learn more about color by meditating on it. That's how our consciousness grows. When various glandular colors are depleted or out of balance, we are not well or whole.

We all come into this life with a "soul" mission. Mine, obviously, was to dispense information to people who were seeking it. We all search for harmony and beauty. Color helps us.

Color is part of all of our planets, just as the planets are part of the universe. If we begin our search for deeper meaning with a spiritual attitude, we'll discover that mind is the builder and the physical body is the result. Around the body is an aura. It's good to mentally "wrap it" in a blue light. It seems people won't be able to accept the possibility of color therapy until we all accept the truth about our auras, and learn how to "read" them.

Red in the aura stands for force, vigor, energy. Orange for thoughtfulness and consideration. Yellow for health and well-being. Green is the color of healing.

Blue the color of the spirit. Indigo and violet indicate a search for a cause or a religious experience. The perfect color, of course, is white, and this is what we are striving for. If our souls were in perfect balance, then all our color vibrations would blend and we would have an aura of pure white.

Our color choices can be wonderful and abundant or skimpy and dull. Orange is the color of the sun. Vital and life-giving. And blue has always been the color of spirit — the symbol of contemplation, prayer, and heaven. I find the deeper blue shades are best to wear or surround ourselves with. Pure emerald green, especially if it has a dash of blue, is the color of healing — strong, friendly, helpful. A lemony green, on the other hand, can be deceitful. But I keep reminding myself, all forces in nature are one.

I remind myself that we are all guided by color, tone, and vibration. The Great Physician met the needs of the individual — whether by the spoken word, vibration, or other means, by recognizing the divinity in each soul. Let light, harmony, peace be our personal application.

. . . . .

CHRISTOPHER ALEXANDER (b. 1936)

Born in Vienna and raised in England, Alexander is a Fellow of the American Academy of Arts and Sciences, professor emeritus, author, mathematician, and architect. He has written many books including his ground-breaking The Timeless Way of Building and Pattern Language. *Much of his information on color comes from the fourth book,* The Luminous Ground, *of his multivolume series:* The Nature of Order.

When I work with color I know immediately either I've "done it" or I haven't "done it." If you make a window slightly wrong, you can't tell immediately. Not so with color. A red that's trying to be a brilliant red and falls short shows up immediately. I not only see it, I feel it. I keep asking, why does a color look the way it does? If it feels dead, it's obviously not *living*. When color is whole, I experience it in a single field — pure unbroken unity. This is "inner light." To "make inner light" we have to use unequal amounts of different colors.

As a kid, I was impressed by St. Teresa. Maybe it was her doubt and confusion that appealed to me. And her honesty.

All my working career I have tried to explain what is living in buildings and in the natural world. I keep searching for the "I" (or sometimes I call it the "ground") that exists everywhere — in every leaf, in every stone, in every picture, every room. I even look for this inner light in grains of sand. Something compels me to search and search and search. I keep wanting to *experience* reality. And reality is full of color — saturated with it. I see color in every line, every point, every shadow.

To be an artist, you need a teacher. It is for this reason, above all, I began collecting carpets. I think of those dyers who worked in early carpet weaving. Their apprenticeship lasted fifteen years. At the end of it, they were expected to make a color that no one had ever seen before. Then they could be a master dyer.

Every color I see invites me to see the actual *quality* of that color. Color is palpable and I can hear it talking to me. My mind wants to analyze every color's beauty and harmony. Why does this color look this way? Persian miniatures. Turkish carpets. Mosaics and tiles. Vermeer's work. Or Van Gogh, Gauguin, Matisse, Bonnard. Buildings on Greek islands. Meadows. Water. I keep searching for the inner light — brilliant, intense colors lying next to subdued and muted ones. Nature does that all the time. You spot an intense color but then it interacts with other colors and suddenly everything gives off even more light!

After I've seen it, I try to duplicate it. If I want to make a red glow, I'll surround it with a luminescent green. A mid-sea green with white green and patches of yellow. I layer colors and sometimes chop into red with my palette knife to release a bit of yellow underneath. Colors like to appear in families. But just as in families, each color has to be individually strong and vibrant.

I think back to a cactus growing in the Berkeley Botanical Garden — it was maybe forty feet long. It was in a rock garden surrounded by thousands of small shimmering purple flowers. At least that's how it seemed until you got close and then you could see that each flower was varied from deep purplish red to a pale reddish blue, dark blue-purple, violet, pale blue-purple. It all had life!

In any composition, each color links up and talks to the one below it and the one above it. Or across from it. When I see or imagine colors truly working together, one color always dominates and other smaller areas of color also play a major role to create a wholeness. A hairline of another color between two colors works magic. It's why carpet weavers weave a white thread between major colors. It brings unity to the abutting colors. Good colors are mixtures. I love created subdued brilliance.

I suppose it's because I've had mathematical training, but I have come to believe that color depends on geometry. Spikey shapes penetrate other color shapes. Squares and circles of color create magical interplay. Local symmetries. Wholeness in geometry contributes to the inner light sometimes found in color. I find this difficult to explain, but I experience it. Color isn't something just "stuck on." It establishes wholeness. When color is living, it reaches our inner Self.

Ah, *wholeness. Unity.* Those words continue to intrigue me. What makes things cohesive? Hang together? Deeply interlock? And what makes color whole? They work together to create peace and calm. The pattern of tones is beautiful, then they shine with an inner light. There is a deep interlock that creates this light and it's a light anyone can recognize without being an artist or a colorist. I recognize that light because I know it also exists in me. There is at the heart of all things — everything — a single voice. It speaks in all tongues and holds blackness and thickness and light.

When I look at colors now, I squint to see if an inner color is there — a color with inner light. There are thousands of possible colors, but there are only a few that really bring the light to life. I find this light to be mental and emotional as well as physical. When I see this inner light in myself, I am able to see it in others and in other things as well. Then I am able to reproduce it and share it with others.

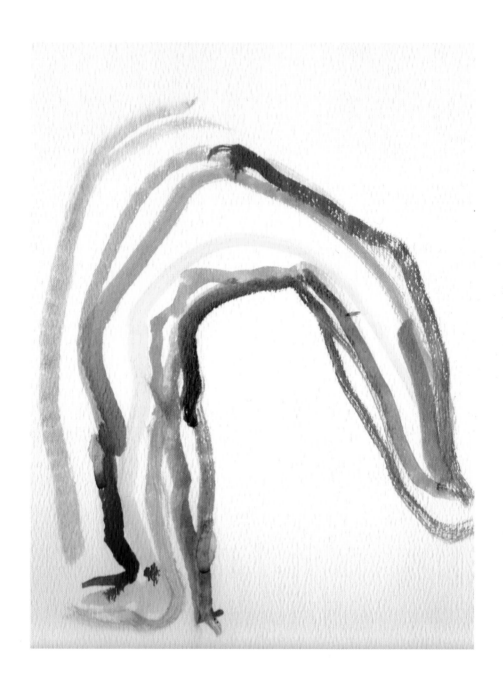

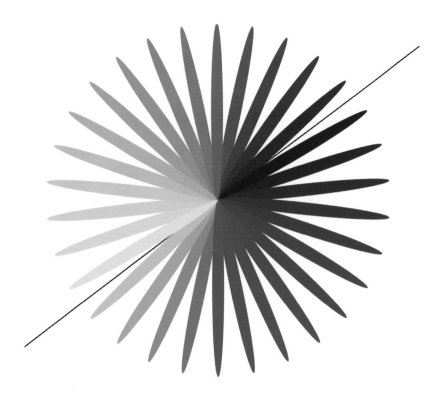

A color wheel in 30 steps. Starting with red at the top, move 5 steps to orange, 5 steps to yellow, 5 steps to green, 5 steps to purple and 5 steps back again to red. Each color's complement is directly across from it on the color wheel. The line at 45 degrees shows the division between warm and cool colors. Colors above the line are warm, colors below are cool.

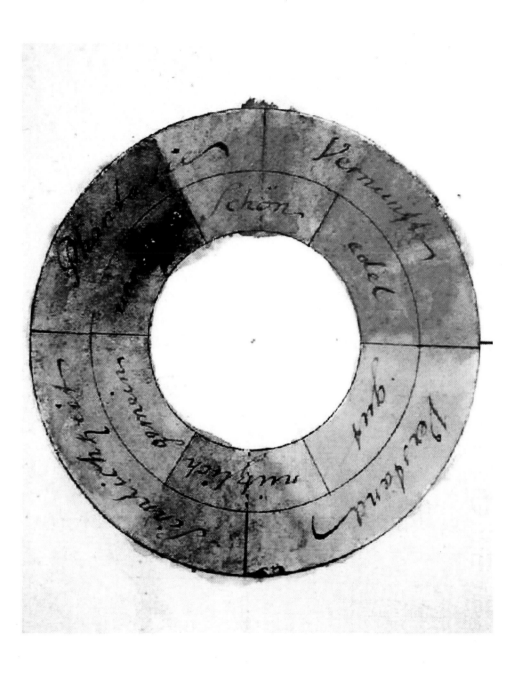

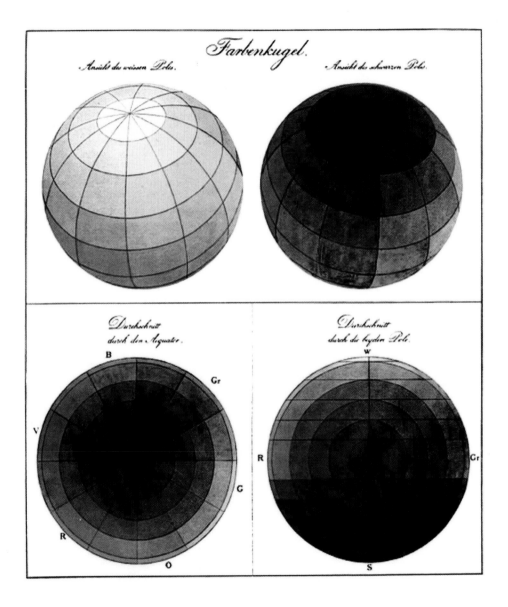

Color Tint and Saturation. The end of each branch is the true color. The leaves on the top of the branch are tints (adding white) and the leaves on the bottom of the branch are saturations (adding black). The left side of the tree is warm colors, the right side is cool colors.

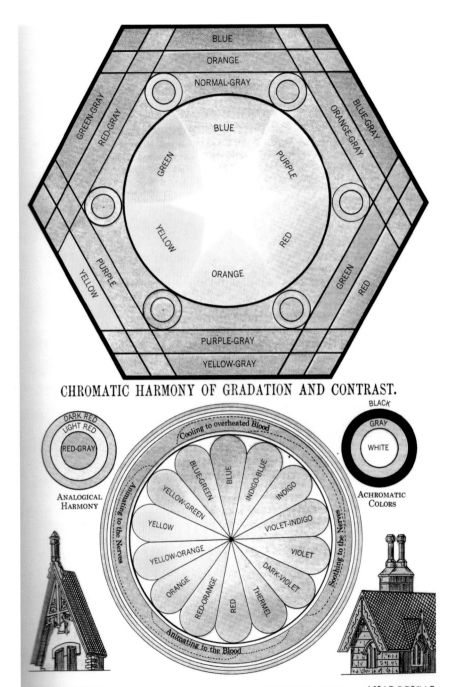

CHROMATIC HARMONY OF GRADATION AND CONTRAST.

ANALOGICAL HARMONY

ACHROMATIC COLORS

CONTRASTING HARMONY

CHROMATIC COLORS PLACED OPPOSITE THOSE WHICH FORM A CHEMICAL AFFINITY WITH THEM

ANALOGICAL HARMONY

Chapter Five

HOW COLOR FEEDS THE SOUL

Prelude

There is, I've been told, a magical city called Shambhala, the sacred city of light. Some say it's in Tibet hidden beneath eons of sand. Others claim it's protected in a hidden valley that can only be discovered by traveling through a holy mountain. Or it may be poised as a gateway to Siberia. Still others believe it quietly lies somewhere in Asia, but is connected to all the continents by a series of subterranean passages.

Buddhists call it the Pure Land, the Mother of Cities, and, over centuries, they have carefully constructed its secret north-country geography. James Hilton wrote about it in *Lost Horizon* and many movies have used it as a theme, including *Shangri-la* in the 1960s. Nicholas Roerich, who served in the FDR administration, held the belief that through art and beauty, all major religions could one day come together in peace. He traveled to India, Mongolia, and Tibet in 1924 in search of this special city.

Shambhala may be a place hinged to another plane — a spiritual one intended only for enlightened earthlings. This mystical place, thought to be protected by a group of dedicated adepts who are guiding our evolution, is filled with peace and tranquility. And, I am convinced, it's a place filled with fabulous colors. Shambhala, it has been said, can be experienced only through rigorous and disciplined practice based on holy writ and one's laser-like will and perseverance. It has been predicted that this far-away hidden place will appear again — around 2424 C.E. when our regular world declines into the darkness of war and greed. It will be a "golden age." But can we wait that long?

One wise lama once told a seeker, "You won't have to travel far. Shambhala is in your own heart."

"Color sounds the command of the future.
Everything black, gray, and misty has already sublimated
the consciousness of humanity. One must again ponder
about the gorgeous flower colors which always heralded
the epochs of renaissance."

Nicholas Roerich

"Mere color unspoiled by meaning and unallied with
definite form can speak to the soul in a thousand different ways."

Oscar Wilde

Our Souls

Are we bodies with souls or souls with bodies? It's an age-old question. We know our physical bodies will die one day, and like many others, I believe my soul is that part of me that will go on living — just as it has in the past, but with different earthly experiences, perhaps, than the "last times." Hildegard of Bingen believed the soul passes through the body like sap in a tree. "We are watered by Divine Breath, we blossom, grow strong. The soul sustains the body and the body sustains the soul." The twelfth-century theologian Meister Eckhart in his *Sermons and Resources* said, "God is in all things as a state of being, as activity and power. But only in the soul does he give birth, for although all creatures are as it were a footprint of God only the soul is naturally formed in the image of God."

Ah, so it's our *souls* that are formed in God's image. No wonder it's so hard to understand what our souls are made of. We can no more truly understand our souls than we can begin to understand God. Or how our minds really work.

Plato thought the soul was like the eye. In *The Republic*, he said, "When resting upon that on which truth and being shine, the soul perceives and understands and is radiant with intelligence; but when turned towards the twilight of becoming and perishing, then she has opinion only, and goes blinking about."

St. Augustine also called the soul "she." She is most effective, he said, when she loves rather than simply animates the body. Meditation and concentration or contemplation are inner processes that belong purely to the soul. The soul is somehow intricately bound up within our nervous system according to what Rudolf Steiner said. It's our souls that enable us to think, will, and feel. When we consciously "work" on our own souls ("feeding" it color, I believe, is one way), we make our bodies more outwardly like our souls.

"She" has five capacities that can be trained:

1)   Control the direction of thought.

2)   Control the impulses of will.

3)   Practice calmness in both joy and sorrow.

4)   Display positiveness in our attitude toward all of life.

5)   Show an impartiality in our attitude toward life.[1]

But what is the soul — really? And how does it differ from "spirit"? Rudolf Steiner has given an illustration[2] that helps us understand how everything is one, but there are different aspects to each. He says our souls are a kind spiritual messengers carrying knowledge beyond this lifetime. Nothing is lost on the soul that has made an impression on it during its sojourn with the physical body. We have three soul-states: waking, sleeping, and the in-between.

What I've learned in studying Steiner is that we are composed of several "bodies" like those colorfully painted stacked Russian matryoshka dolls. Starting inside first with the "smallest" is our physical "doll self." Next comes our etheric "doll self," usually arriving when we're about seven years old, Steiner says. Without it, our physical body would soon decay. This is the "doll" that

[1] Rudolf Steiner, *An Outline of Occult Science* (AnthropoSophic Press, 1922, a public domain book, Kindle version) adapted from 314.

[2] Rudolf Steiner, *The Apocalypse of St. John* (out of print, 153, but revised by M. Cotterell in 1958 and can be read on the Rudolf Steiner Archive website: http://wn.rsarchive.org/Lectures/GA104/English/APC1958/ApoJon_index.html)

gives us our aura colors. On the outside of that is our astral "doll self." We acquire that body along about the time we're fourteen. The ego "doll self" is there all along, but most present, along with the astral body, when we dream. When we're awake, the astral body interpenetrates the etheric and physical bodies, bringing order and organization to our lives, according to cosmic laws. Both our spirit and our soul are a part of us and when the physical body dies, they both separate from us. But they hover around a bit — some say for three days before slipping off over another living threshold into a "place," for lack of a better word, that is neither up nor down nor near nor far, but rather another vibrational dimension. Some people can access this "other vibration" to various degrees even while in their physical bodies. Then the ether body dies and the astral and ego soul bodies continue on.[3]

I decided to form my own interpretation of Steiner's illustrations by creating a replica of one of my husband's wonderful lemon meringue pies. Think of yourself as being this whole yummy pie. Not just a sliver — the whole thing.

Other states...I'll enjoy later

my Ego

my Astral-body   my Spirit-
                        Self
          my
          Sentient Soul

my Etheric-body   my Life-
          my   Spirit
          Intellectual/mind Soul

my Physical-   my Spirit-
body   my   Soul   human
          Consciousness

This is all me.

---

[3] For more on Steiner and "soul bodies" see Karen Speerstra, *Sophia — The Feminine Face of God* (Studio City, CA: Divine Arts/Michael Wiese Productions, 2011), 301-306.

As you can see, my "meringue-soul-pie" has three horizontal sections. Three soul-regions. And each has a comparable body and spirit component. During my evolution, my Sentient Soul, as Steiner describes it, transforms my Astral Body; my Intellectual/Mind Soul transforms my Ether Body; and the formation of my Consciousness Soul transforms my Physical Body. Eventually my Ego Self absorbs it all. And then after that — well, I guess we just keep on going toward our Divine Purpose. To Steiner, Ego meant something quite different than Freud and Jung's definition of that word. It's more like my "Big 'I'" or my "Oversoul." "The Real Me." I sometimes call it my Larger Self. Perhaps it's that 90% of our DNA that scientists have a hard time identifying so they simply label it "Junk DNA." I value it all—an abundant luscious crust, sweet yellow tangy goodness and a mound of meringue.

You may find the Sentient Soul as intriguing — and as baffling — a concept as I do. The soul's substance and being are tender and impressionable, according to what Karl König said in his book *The Human Soul*. It's through our senses and our feelings and emotions that we give our souls information. He draws on Rudolf Steiner's descriptions of our sensory systems. And we have more senses than we may have initially thought. Apparently, we have at least twelve! Our bodies and our souls work together through all our senses. König defines our senses this way: *touch* (our boundaries), *the sense of life* or body well-being, the *sense of movement* which conveys to our souls how various parts of our body relate to other parts, and our *sense of balance*. He calls these four senses our lower or "bodily" senses. Next come senses that are turned more to the outward world. They are the *sense of smell, taste, sight*, and *warmth* or temperature. The last four allow us to penetrate into the "soul-sphere" of our surroundings. Since the soul itself is sound and tone, according to Steiner, the final four senses are *hearing*, the *sense of word* (which tells us if the sound we hear is noise or speech), the *sense of thought* (which conveys the meaning of a word or phrase), and our *sense of ego*. This is the soul's capacity to experience the immediate presence of another body or voice. Since the soul dwells in a realm of rhythm and repetition (heartbeats, and breathing) "as soon as the rhythm stops, the soul must leave the body for another realm."[4]

If we can feed and "work" on our souls, I was curious how to do that. Once again Steiner provided clues for what I can practice every single day. So I copied them into my journal and added my own comments in parentheses.

A firmness in ethical judgment (Know why I think and act the way I do and be resolute about my choices.)

Certainty of character (In other words, know who I *really* am.)

Keenness of conscience (Keep it sharp.)

Courage (Be brave!)

Wakefulness (Wake up!)

A resolute iron will (Never give up.)

An indifference to pain (It doesn't mean I won't have it — I just don't need to give in to it.)

Love (Honor and love everyone and everything.)

Absolute calmness (Meditating helps. So does keeping a calm center.)

Patience (Something I need to work on every day!)

Willingness to receive grace and inspiration (Be open.)

Willingness to endure the time of inner ripening — spiritual gestation (In other words, don't force the lotus to open. I've come a long way since Sunday school — and I still have much to learn.)

Sven Birkerts says in *The Guttenberg Elegies* that the soul waxes in private and wanes in public. That seems reason enough to spend a lot of time in quiet meditation. And to avoid crowds if we wish to address our soul-needs.

Rudolph Steiner, when he created the Waldorf Schools and worked out the curriculum in 1919, instructed the teachers to "receive the children in

---

[4] Karl König, *The Human Soul* (Floris Books, Anthroposophic Press, 1959), 95-99.

reverence, educate them in love and let them go forth in freedom." They learn to value light and color. Students recite this daily morning prayer:

> "The sun with loving light makes bright for me the day;
> The soul with spirit power give strength unto my limbs;
> In sunlight shining clear I reverence, oh God,
> The strength of humankind
> Which you have graciously planted in my soul,
> That I with all might may love to work and learn.
> From you comes light and strength.
> To you rise love and thanks."

Like the Waldorf children, we may come to understand that God dyes our souls — at least that's how the Gnostic Gospel of Philip puts it. "God is a dyer. As the good dyes, which are called "true," dissolve with the things dyed in them, so it is with those whom God has dyed. Since his dyes are immortal, they are immortal by means of his colors."[5] And from the same source: "Truth did not come into this world naked but in symbols and images. The world cannot receive truth in any other way."

Richard of St. Victor, a contemporary of Hildegard of Bingen's and a native of Scotland, believed the soul has three components: imagination, reason, and intelligence.[6] Imagine, for a moment, being a blacksmith. You're holding a black iron bar in the fire. Soon it begins to glow white and then it turns red. Our souls are like that, he said. When the soul is plunged into the fire of divine love, it loses its blackness. "And lastly, it grows liquid, and losing its nature, is transmuted into an utterly different quality of being. And as the difference between iron that is cold and iron that is hot, so is the difference between soul and soul, between the tepid soul and the soul made incandescent by divine love."[7]

Incandescent is a word frequently used to describe our souls. Boris Pasternak said, "It's not the earthquake that controls the advent of a different life, but visions of incandescent souls."[8]

[5] Willis Barnstone, ed. "Gospel of Philip," *The Other Bible* (San Francisco: Harper & Row, 1984), 91.
[6] Robert C. Broderick, ed., *The Catholic Encyclopedia* (Nashville, TN: Thomas Nelson, Rev. Ed. 1990).
[7] Andrew Harvey and Anne Baring, *The Mystic Vision* (San Francisco, CA: HarperSanFrancisco, 1995), 62.
[8] Ibid., 173.

When I think of "incandescent" I think of those the egg-shaped, less efficient light bulbs with filaments that we're supposed to be phasing out. Still, regardless of their present worth, an incandescent bulb is a radiant image, a hot, electric, in-your-face kind of clear light.

The ancient Egyptians believed there are, depending on sources you read, either five or nine parts to the human soul: the *Ba*, the *Ka*, the *Akh*, the *Sheut*, and the *Ren*. The *Ba* is most readily recognized as the soul-part of the person living on earth, and the *Ka* is the soul-part after the person's death. The *Ka* stays close to the body. When they finally get together, after death, the soul is called the *Akh* or *Akhu*. The *Sheut* or *Khalbit* presents the shadow part of the soul that sticks pretty close to the *Ba*; and the *Ren* is the name of the person — a vital part of that person's soul. Added to those five are: the *Sahu* or the incorruptible spiritual body; the *Sejkhem*, the personification of the person's life-force, which lives in the afterlife with *Akhu* or *Akh*. The *Ab* or *Ib* is the heart — the part that would be weighed by Ma'at after death. (Is it a coincidence that in Hebrew, *ah ba* means "Heart Soul"?)

Plato imagined that people have different colors in their souls, different metals. Some people foster basic values that cause them to seek God above all. Their souls are gold. People with silver souls seek power; people whose souls are bronze seek security. And people whose souls are "iron like" only seek pleasure.

Colors, Christian mystics claim, are hidden within the "Mysterium of God" but shine through the "Mysterium of Nature" as a living light. Sophia, wisdom, the Feminine Divine, stands in the white color or the "housing of God" as Jacob Boehme put it. It is through her that the corporeal manifestation of God takes place. Through her *All-Color* comes all colors. Steiner says that Lucifer dulls her brilliant colors sometimes.

According to Boehme, colors initially appear in the sphere of the angels — those free spirits that are created after the nature of God. In his book *The Aurora*, Boehme writes of how color flashes through the holy angels and from the light of the Son of God. Some flashes are purple, bright, and clear. Flashes, like flowers in a meadow. Some light-flashes are strong, like a green precious stone. Some appear as a greenish-red; some are the quality of heat, yellowish and reddish. "Some are the strongest in the quality of love and those are a glance of the heavenly joyfulness, very light and bright, and when the light shineth on them, they look like light blue, or a pleasant gloss, glance, or luster."[9] Our earthly colors pale in comparison.

But we can take heart. Even though we're still only able to see earth colors now, there are more to come! Our souls learn from the world, but are constantly circling "home." Souls are, as the fourteenth-century English anchoress Julian of Norwich explained: "One to God, unchangeable goodness..." The soul keeps our past and collects treasures from our everyday living and records it all so we can later view it, remember, and evaluate this life. If there is judgment after death, it's our own soul-assessment.

In spite of the fact Hildegard of Bingen described the soul as "round, symmetrical and beautiful," in one of her painted illuminations, she portrayed the soul as a golden jeweled "kite" — a square suspended in a star-studded dark blue sky. The "kite" is filled with eyes. A gold ribbon flows down from the bottom tip into a woman's pregnant belly. Love, she said, is at work in the circles of eternity and we're all brilliantly colored in the dawn.

Warrior cultures such as the Aztecs believed souls of their dead went to a very colorful place filled with flowers, butterflies, and brightly feathered birds. "The Lord of Flowers, Xochipilli, must be the personification of the soul."[10]

Surely few things are more colorful than flowers. I picked a gladiola this morning whose deep colors moved flawlessly from black-purple to indigo to violet and white in the centers. Whenever I approach a particularly beautiful flower in our gardens, I thank it for being alive. I revel in its color. And I delight in the fact that we have such beautiful gifts to share with others. For instance, we're able to supply our little church with cut flowers from spring to fall. The perennials: yellow daffodils, white Shasta daisies, violet and purple irises, pink and rose peonies, creamy Solomon's Seal, blue lupines, lilies in yellow, orange, and rust are followed by dahlias and gladiolas of all colors. Perhaps one of the

---

[9] Jacob Boehme, John Watkins, *The Aurora* (1914 edition). (John Watkins/John Clarke, 1960), 269-272.

[10] Laurette Séjourné, "Lord of Flowers," (*Parabola*, Summer, 1996), 17.

reasons our marriage has been so colorful for nearly five decades is because we paid special attention to our wedding flowers. Thanks to a loving sister and Kodani Florist's from Hilo, Hawaii, we had huge bouquets (and I mean huge!) of showy red-orange birds of paradise, waxy red heart-shaped antherium, and pink, yellow, and white plumeria, along with dozens and dozens of large white orchids and butterfly orchids in glorious violet shades. What amazes me about flowers is how they speak to abundance. No matter how many I pick, it seems there are just as many more.

Becoming one with this colorful and abundant "God-force" within us, our Divine Center, was the goal of artists like Kandinksy and Malevich, Philipp Runge, and later, in America, for Rothko and Newman. And, as we have already discovered, Goethe believed in the spirituality of color. These people wanted to plumb the depths of the World Soul as well as their own souls, using not just their senses but also their inner consciousness.

Thomas Cole, one of the leaders of the Hudson River School of landscape painting in America, echoed Ralph Waldo Emerson who wrote: "I am part and parcel of God." These color-capturing artists stood by Niagara Falls and other mighty rivers and with their brushes poised to proclaim: "We are what we behold. We are united with this natural splendor because we are all in harmony with nature and the Divine."

Nourishing the Soul Through the Darkness

When colors reach right in to our interiors, our hearts "leap up" as Wordsworth put it. We see color and we feel less impoverished — we feel more full. Our souls can tell our bodies which color it needs for various purposes. All we need do is meditate and listen. I think of colors as emails to the soul — messages that are readily available to everyone, but only I am on the recipient line of a particular color transmission.

I woke up one morning awash in dream colors of stress. I had been surrounded by a brownish, yellowish, green environment. I don't remember the details but I know what I was seeing were *not* happy colors. When my muscles tense, they seem to turn from a healthy reddish-pink to this brownish yellow-green. I needed to consciously "think" the pink back.

An Italian artist and designer, Bruno Unari, said, "Ugly things are ugly in much the same way the world over." It's true. While we may debate what's beautiful or not, it's easier to agree on "ugly." And I'd argue it has to do with a lack of color. Our coral reefs, for instance, are rapidly turning from healthy pink-peach to dirty leech gray. We have created not just one ugly ten-mile-long floating garbage reef in our oceans, but some claim now there are five more floating out there. We know how landfills and dumps look. Very little color. We've seen videos of Camden, New Jersey — the city with the highest crime rate in America. Someone is shot every thirty hours in this poverty-stricken stretch of our own country that looks like a broken-windowed, pot-holed war zone. We know what war looks like. Some of us up close. America has engaged in six wars just during my lifetime! It's dusty, dirty, smelly, and filled with shades of grays and blacks and damaged browns. And, of course, bleeding-red. All places of no-color suck the life from us.

We've grown up believing there is light and dark fighting against each other — but we are living a new story now — one in which we no longer need dualities. This is hard to imagine, particularly when we even divide up our states into red and blue. But as President Obama has pointed out many times...we are the purple states. We are one. And we need both the light and the dark. Opposites can come together in new ways, now. Empoverished Camden and rich Philadelphia can reach across the water to come together. People can resolve their ideological differences if they but realize we are one people, one planet. All blessed equally with light and color. Vaughan-Lee says the light of the soul is not a foreign substance. We all have it. If we have breath, we have access to the light. Light is everywhere but sometimes it hides under a bushel, as the Bible puts it. We are the lamps. We have plenty of lamp oil. And we have the spark to light them. "The world has to awaken from its sleep of forgetfulness — it can no longer afford to forget its divinity."[11]

---

[11] Llewelyyn Vaughan-Lee, *The Return of the Feminine and the World Soul*. (The Golden Sufi Center, 2009), 158.

I take heart from people like Donna Hicks, who is dedicated to resolving conflicts and has written so eloquently about our role in making this happen. In *Dignity*,[12] she says dignity is a birthright. Respect is earned but dignity is a gift we all have. However, if indignities aren't named and addressed they take on an invisible destructive energy of their own. To protect our lives, we either fight or withdraw. But there is another way — "Tend and befriend." Conflict stays alive, Hicks says, when people do not feel acknowledged and when their voices are not heard. People need recognition for what they have suffered. She reminds us that war is the inevitable consequence of choosing to resolve differences by force. Each of us, she reminds her readers, has the capacity to violate the dignity of others as well as to honor it.

Together we can confront the collective darkness. We no longer need to live in a black and white and gray world, but first we have to name and confront the darkness around us, without blame, but by taking responsibility. This is both exhilarating and demanding, Vaughan-Lee reminds us. And frustrating because there is no map. But we can feel the colors vibrating all around us. Part of what we are now becoming aware of is how different levels of reality interact... how light flows and unfolds. We watched Egypt for eighteen days going from a dictatorship to an open revolution, an evolution fed by the ethereal connections of Twitter and Facebook and the Internet. We watched a collective consciousness take hold. Light spreads rapidly.

We're like the children in Frances Hodgson Burnett's wonderful book *The Secret Garden*. We all long to find this garden. Our hearts know the way; we all hold the key. But it seems as if we're living tangled up in choking brambles and surrounded by vine-encrusted gates and walls of overgrown ivy. There are many paths into this colorful garden if we just remember how to get in. It's overflowing with colorful idea-flowers that need tending, nurturing, watering. The garden contains the heart's wisdom. No wonder we all seek it. A little girl, a crippled boy, a father's hardened heart. We play different parts of this drama.

There is a line from her book I hold close and reread often: "At first people

[12] Donna Hicks, *Dignity: The Essential Role It Plays in Resolving Conflict* (New Haven, CT: Yale University Press, 2011).

refuse to believe that a strange new thing can be done, then they begin to hope it can't be done. They hope it can't be done because it means seeing the garden in a whole new way... Then they see it can be done. Then it is done, and all the world wonders why it was not done centuries before." It is a little girl who holds the key in the story and it is the feminine who can now heal. The mysteries of color and the soul are feminine attributes we all share. The pink-white lotus opens. The fiery poppy beckons. There are ninety-six Sanskrit words to portray love. Each a different color. Like the Sufis who dance in white wool, we, too, are dressed in the white of all colors.

The Afterlife

Most of us believe we'll have one. We carry with us into the afterlife (wherever it is) much of what we value in this life. In other words, I don't think we'll be all that much different. Since our minds create, our afterlife minds will create what we expect to see in this new dimension — this new vibratory space. And when we're ready, we'll go on to learn and grow and enjoy even more colors.

Eben Alexander, a neurosurgeon, came out of a seven-day coma and described what he had experienced as a giant cosmic womb — an inky darkness that was brimming with light. A river of life and color. He writes of his newfound understanding of consciousness in *Proof of Heaven*.

Imagine we're fish swimming in a shallow pond. We're floating around there with the green lily pads thinking that this is the only world there is. Then it rains and the surface of our pool is suddenly rippled and we can see beyond our own little world into another dimension of light. What if, like string-theory scientists tell us, there are ten — or even twenty-six more dimensions in hyperspace? Or more? What a lot of ripples! Then scientists came up with the "M Theory" — the mysterious theory. A "multi-verse" theory. I like to think of it as the "Mother Theory." It combines all the other mathematical theories about our universe rolled into one. Harvard's Lisa Randall sees it as a floating membrane wrapped in a much larger universe. When I read her words, I imagine a gigantic uterine membrane ready to birth all that is loving, vibrant, and colorful. Is this the afterlife? Giant variegated soap bubbles we can blow into different dimensions?

Jesus, whom many believe to be God's incarnation on earth, once took three of his disciples up a mountain and they saw their friend shining like the sun with blindingly white clothing. They must have wondered if they'd all reached the "afterlife." The three men with Jesus heard and saw things that day that they had trouble articulating. They knew the story of Ezekiel, so they compared what they saw to what Ezekiel had seen, but they knew from all that colored light that Jesus was, indeed, God's beloved Son. We can read about the Hebrew priest Ezekiel's colorful encounter in Chapter 1 of his Biblical narrative. Fires flashed out of a bright cloud and something like gleaming yellow-orange amber approached. A four-faced being had wings and fire shot out of its body. Then Ezekiel saw a wheel gleaming like beryl — emerald and aquamarine. This flying engine of fire took him up, up to a domed place where there was a blue throne with orange colors shooting out all around. It was, Ezekiel reported, like a colorful rainbow. Some think a UFO came down and carried Ezekiel off. I tend to think it may have been his Larger Self, his colorful aura-filled rainbow body writ large, that fired him up and floated him off.

The writer of the final Biblical book, Revelation, describes much the same scene in Chapter 4. In his vision, a door to heaven opened and he could see that the being sitting on the throne was jasper (a rich quartz brown) and cornelian (a reddish-yellow) and around the throne was a rainbow-like green emerald. And around the throne were twenty-four more thrones with beings all in white with gold crowns on their heads, all flashing lightning at him.

Goethe wrote a similar dazzling other-world vision in Faust where life throbs, dew hangs like pearls on the flowers and blades of grass and "color stands out clear, in glad device, And all the region is my Paradise."[13]

After a great deal of research, Christopher Bache concludes the following six things about our present realm and all stages of the afterlife (and, may I add, the "forelife.")

1) That materialism in its many forms is false.

---

[13] Johann Wolfgang von Goethe, Faust, Part II (New York: Penguin Books, 1959), 25.

2) That mind is not reducible to the brain but retains the coherence and integrity without its biological substrate.

3) That our identity is more than our conscious (and unconscious) personality.

4) That there must be a domain other than space-time in which we exist in an organized fashion between death and birth. Hence, the cosmos is multidimensional and populated by more types of beings than we had previously imagined.

5) That death is an illusion, a trick of the senses.

6) That there may be a deeper logic to the existential predicaments that we find ourselves in.[14]

Robert Monroe was a VP of NBC and then at forty-two began a career in consciousness research and founded the Monroe Institute in Faber, Virginia. He wrote in one of his many books describing people's out-of-the-body and near-death experiences: "There is no beginning, there is no end. There is only change. There is no teacher, there is no student, there is only remembering."[15]

Emanuel Swedenborg,[16] the late-sixteenth-, early-seventeenth-century Swedish scientist and visionary believed the soul was red — like blood — corresponding to the heart and blood with love and its affection. "In the spiritual world," Swedenborg said, "there are all kinds of colors, of which red and white are the fundamental, the rest deriving their varieties from these and from their opposites... Red there corresponds to love, and white to wisdom... For this reason in the heavens where love to the Lord reigns the light is flame-colored and the angels there are clothed in purple garments..."[17] He described his visions in such vivid colors. Artists who came after him, as well as poet-artists such as William Blake, tried to capture these otherworldly colors with words and paint. The heavenly realms explode in color, he said. Swedenborg's rainbow visions

[14] Christopher M. Bache, *Dark Night, Early Dawn* (Albany, NY: State University of New York Press, 2000), 36.

[15] Robert Monroe, *Ultimate Journey* (New York: Doubleday, 1994).

[16] Speerstra, 271-273.

[17] Emanuel Swedenborg, *Angelic Wisdom Concerning the Divine Love and the Divine Wisdom* (Amsterdam, Latin, 1763; English Swedenborg Foundation, 1988), e-book edition, 380-381.

were reflections (like Hildegard's) of divine magnificence. Each color, he said, "prefigures" something that is celestial and spiritual. Colors come from heavenly light and therefore change as the spiritual intent changes.

Swedenborg read the book of Genesis with great interest and interpreted angels intermingling with the likes of Noah, Abraham, Sara, and Hagar as colorful indications that light and rainbows and colors are visible aspects — signs and signatures — here on earth of even more dazzling light and colors to come. There the atmosphere will sparkle like precious stones, great pearls and diamond-like gold and silver. "There are atmospheres of flowers of variegated hue...gardens presented with such life...more vividly than the sight of the eye perceives such things on earth."[18]

To Swedenborg colors went way beyond descriptions of where angels live and all those colorful gardens. They also indicate our own human colors — the colors of our spiritual selves. This mystic was also a scientist. He came to these colorful conclusions by meditating on the words of Genesis that speak of Noah's long watery journey ending in a colorful rainbow. Swedenborg saw that colorful covenant sign as our own promise of entry into a sphere presented by colors where the "brightness and resplendence immeasurably surpass the beauty of the colors seen on earth; and each color represents something celestial and spiritual. These colors are from the light of heaven and from the variegation of spiritual light... For angels live in light so great that the light of the world is nothing in comparison... it is noonday compared with candlelight, which is extinguished and becomes a nullity on the rising of the sun... In heaven there are both celestial light and spiritual light." Celestial light, he said, is like the light of the sun and spiritual light is like the light of the moon, but with every difference according to the state of the angel who receives the light.

Jacob Boehme believed colors aren't just appearances — they show the primordial qualities of divine beings. Angel lights! Then F. C. Oetinger took both Boehme and Swedenborg's words and said colors are "a representation of God's Eternal power, which is at work at all times."[19] In the astral world where

---

[18] Emanuel Swedenborg, *The Heavenly Arcana* Vol. 1 (Swedenborg Foundation, Inc., 1949) Par. 1622.

[19] Ernst Benz, "Die Farbe in Der Christlichen Vision," quoted in *The Realms of Color*, Adolf Portman and Rudolf Ritsema (Leiden: E.J. Brill, 1974), 324.

our souls go to dwell, colors float freely, like flames — rainbows; lines change. It's a world of beings who speak to us through color.[20]

What Dreams May Come, a 1998 film, starred Robin Williams as Chris, a doctor who was killed in a car accident. He discovers what the afterlife is like from Cuba Gooding Jr., his "guide" in Summerland, which he learns is just one of many possible afterlives. Annabella Sciorra plays Annie, Chris' wife, who commits suicide from despair after her husband died. *What Dreams May Come* shows a riot of color in Summerland as opposed to the depressing grays and browns in "one of many hells," where Annie ends up because she mistakenly believes she doesn't have a choice. The movie is based on a very well-researched novel by Richard Matheson. Summerland, he said, is where colors are as vivid as a rainbow though more iridescent. Each flower gives off a stream of "delicate force" and "harmonious sounds." There aren't any shadows there because there is light without a sun. Everything in Summerland emits a beneficial energy. Flowers stay fresh and colorful until you lose interest in them, Chris' guide tells him, for it is your mind that keeps them going. People get nourishment directly from the atmosphere — from light, air, color, and plants. And in this "land," one can see original pieces of art with colors glowing from reality. They're created by earth's master artists who envision them here first, so the masterpieces we know on earth are only duplicates of the originals that hang here, ablaze in luminous color.

Long before seeing that movie, I had a colorful dream of flying over rooftops in my own Summerland. I looked down and instead of tiles, each roof had, like Aaron's breastplate, perfectly set jewels and gemstones. They glimmered in the sun in such an array of colors I wanted to stay there forever, just to soak up all the colored light. But, of course, I woke up, longing for this lost richness.

As I finished this book, my dear friend Janet Field died. She had read portions of my earlier drafts and loved to think about color. When I visited her in her hospice bed for the last time, she said, "Karen, I see purple all around me now." Light flooded her slender body as she lay near her Vermont window. She was, indeed, wrapped in color and was at peace. Unfearful. Ready.

---

[20] Rudolph Steiner, "At the Gates of Spiritual Science" from fourteen lectures given in 1906 at Stuttgart (Anthroposophy Press, 1986), 20.

Fear cannot live in a body of light. So, to nourish our souls, we need to forgo fear and surround ourselves with real or envisioned color. As we've already discussed, chakra points in our bodies can benefit from "color baths." But we need not stick to the ROYGBIV sequence. We can use bright peach for the second chakra, if we wish. Or pink instead of green for the heart chakra — the color of love. A blue shield around us can help with the fear factor and offer peace and relaxation; white for purity; and greens and yellows for deep healing.

What colors can we expect to see after we die? Millions. Winston Churchill (an artist as well as a statesman, remember) once said he expected "orange and vermillion will be the darkest, dullest upon it, and beyond these will be a whole range of wonderful new colors which will delight the celestial eye."

Color and Mysticism

> *"Color must be thought filtered through the imagination.*
> *Without imagination beautiful colors are hard to construct."*
>
> Gail Sher, *The Intuitive Writer*

Mysticism pushes us beyond our three-dimensional world into other dimensions. The term comes from the Greek mystery cults — people who were initiated into secret knowledge of divine things. Under threats of severe punishment, they could not reveal those secrets to just anyone. You had to be ready. You had to be initiated — often with a three-day "death" experience in a dark place inside a pyramid or some other "grave." You had to die to yourself and be reborn. You had to let the part of yourself that feared death go and you became someone new. But does everyone have to go through this? I believe that's the question behind the question posed to Jesus: "Must a man be reborn to have eternal life?" Must we go through that three-day "dying experience" (as, by the way, some people believe Jesus had done, John the Baptist may have done, and Paul most certainly did)? No. And we no longer need the intense initiatory experience either. We've evolved. We're growing in our spiritual knowledge. Now, we can grow spiritually by using new tools like color!

The term "mystic" became associated with many esoteric doctrines and the Sufis (sometimes called God's spies) called mystics "friends of God." "The soul of the mystic feels itself identified in union with the Divine; it has passed from consciousness of self and is absorbed in the consciousness of God and it has become defied."[21]

Former nun and religious historian and author Karen Armstrong points out that mystics, who are found in all religious traditions, encounter a presence that transfigures their lives. They have real but often unexplainable experiences, revelations that transform them. These "knowings" or "showings" as Julian of Norwich described them, are their attempts to interpret their rich faith in new ways.[22] So we can't really equate any particular religion — or even that word — with "mysticism."

Canadian writer Robertson Davies said this about "being religious." He points out in an essay called "Jung and the Writer" that the word *religion* comes from the Latin word meaning to "take care, to pay heed, to give thought to something." To be attentive, careful. "And to look at life through eyes that are as clear as one can make them, and to bring conscientious scruple and a measure of intuition to whatever life presents to one's experience."[23] When we are attentive to color, we are, in Davies' words, being "religious." We're mystics. Or mystics in the making. Albert Einstein believed scientists were truly religious because they trained themselves to search out the truth. Searching out the "truths" of color will take a lifetime. But the journey is the goal.

Ken Wilber, a contemporary Coloradan philosopher who has developed what he calls "integral theory," says in one of his many books (*Sex, Ecology, Spirituality*) that mystical development takes place in four stages: the psychic, the subtle, the causal, and the nondual. He came to this understanding through reading about the mystic Teresa of Avila, whom he identifies with the "subtle" stage — an advanced stage of personal development.

---

[21] Margaret Smith, *The Way of the Mystics* (New York: Oxford University Press, 1978), 1, 8.

[22] Karen Armstrong, *Visions of God* (New York: Bantam Books, 1994), Introduction.

[23] Robertson Davies, *Happy Alchemy* (Toronto: McClelland & Stewart, Inc., 1997), 349.

This whole idea of our evolutionary development is mind-boggling. But I ran across a model, thanks to Peter Russell, that makes great sense to me. In his book *The White Hole in Time* he describes how we can understand our own development, along with our planet's, by imagining a tall building. (I've taken some liberties in the retelling, here, but the analogy, of course, is his.) Imagine how tall the World Trade towers were before the explosions. One hundred and eight stories. OK. So imagine a building that size. That's earth. You're on the ground floor. There's a plaque that says, "You are here — 4.6 billion years ago." You get in an elevator and exit on the twenty-fifth floor. The doors open and you see simple living cells. They don't look like much, so you go back into the elevator and punch the fiftieth floor to see what's there. Photosynthesis is happening here. Back in the elevator to the ninety-seventh floor where, when the doors open, you see fish. They'll crawl out of the sea on the ninety-seventh floor. Then the door opens onto the 104th floor and you see dinosaurs. They go all the way up to the 107th floor. Mammals appear in the penthouse and we humans appear a few inches from the uppermost ceiling of the uppermost 108th floor. First, the Neanderthals appear a quarter of an inch from the ceiling; Cro-Magnon humans — a bit later, and then us. Russell says we arrived when there is about the thickness of a layer of paint left on the ceiling.

We've been a long time in coming! And we've grown. A lot! When I view our planet and its inhabitants in this way, I am struck by not only our precious planet's tenacity and beauty, but also its vulnerability. Housed in a metaphorical New York skyscraper that we all watched go down in a matter of minutes, I look around and think, "This 'house-planet' could fall into its footprint nearly as quickly. How might we learn to love and value it even more while it stands?" We need our planet because we still have more to learn about how color stirs our souls. How colors relate to "religion" and "mysticism" is all intertwined with falling in love with our planet (and with each other) all over again.

The great works of art over the ages have been inspired, primarily, by mystical interpretations of how art feeds the soul. All we need do is look to Greek art, which they based on their mythology. Or at Christian sculptures — *David*,

The Pieta. Or all the colorful frescoes, mosaics, and paintings that artists have created that continue to say: Look how much God loves you!

We marvel at Muslim/Arabic/Turkish carpets, tiles, and illuminated miniatures inspired by the Sufis. When we look closely at the Tantric paintings of India created by obscure Hindu sects, we know there are deep, deep meanings attached. Statues of Buddha. Minoan art. Ephesian architecture. Shaker furniture. Navajo sand paintings. Japanese tea bowls. They're all created by people grounded in their own brand of mysticism and soul work.

In a nineteenth-century book written by a Persian sheikh, Karim-Khan Kermani, he claims we can't explain color — only descend into its archetypes. These deep ways of perceiving leave imprints on all earthly beings and things — and even beyond our earth. Like the mind is linked to the body, color is linked to this world and to others.

So, I've come to believe that like other mystical revelations designed to elevate our souls, a new awareness of color can wake us up and thrust us into fresh appreciation of our surroundings. After reading some draft chapters of this book, several of my friends said, "I'm looking at sunsets in a whole new way." And "I'm seeing colors now like I never have before." And, "You have increased my sensitivity to color in amazing ways... how orange the sunrise was on the Mississippi this morning and how it became such a light yellow in minutes." It's as if we've been imprisoned in grayness and now we're ready to break out as the Sufi mystic-poet Rumi encouraged us to do. He said, "Take an axe to your prison walls and escape... walk out like someone suddenly born into color."

Philipp Otto Runge, the young man we met in Chapter 3, believed color to be very mystical. Since light, to him, was goodness, black and white were, then, clear representations of good and evil. This color genius wanted his spherical mathematical figure to represent not just how colors related to one another but also how they related to our various philosophical reflections. Blue, he believed, is the Father in Christian Trinitarian teachings; red, like the sun, is Christ, the mediator between earth and heaven; yellow is the Holy Spirit, the consoler, (Sophia), like the moon. "The divine trinity is the symbol of the highest light, just as the three primary colors represent sunlight... When we understand the thousand refractions of the three primary colors, then we will be able to approach comprehension of the divine trinity that we feel in our souls."[24]

For centuries, people imagined the divine as an ancient mother who also was viewed as a trinity: mother, virgin, crone. Her colors were red, black, and white. Her stories were eventually encoded into songs, fairy tales, and folk legends. Baba Yaga, for instance, in Russia, was believed to appear in all colors. Indian traditions call her the Black Kali. Christians associate the Black Virgin with Mary. Often miracles are assigned to her. Black is associated in old traditions, with wisdom. "The symbol of the Black Virgin establishes a link between the heart of the believer and the divine presence using the symbolic charge inherent within the statue aligned to the telluric power of the site... Thus the Black Virgin is truly a symbol of a vibrant power, total and esoteric. It cannot be apprehended by the intellect, it is too simple, it has to be experienced and thus it can only be apprehended by those who listen with their hearts... She speaks a universal language."[25]

The Black Virgin, many of us think, originally stems from Black Isis holding the baby Horus in her lap. In Egypt she was known by many names. One was the "Initiate of Light." Artemis or Diana of the Ephesians, along with Cybele, were thought to be black. The Roms, also known as Gypsies, still call her St. Mary of the Egyptians. Her black statue made of pear wood was present at Chartres from very early times when the Druids had their university there. When Julius Caesar decided to conquer the Gauls and destroy the Druids' sacred groves, he arrived and found her statue already there with this inscription: "The Virgin About to Give Birth." The Black Feminine is the Sulamite in the Song of Songs. The Black Virgin shows up along the Camino Santiago route to protect pilgrims as they walk the eight hundred kilometers to the shrine of St. James at Compostela. "Bernard of Clairvaux as a young boy at Fontaine is said to have drunk three drops of milk from the breast of the Black Virgin at Châtillon."[26] Nine million people each year visit her icons at Czçstochowa at the Pauline Polish monastery of Jasna Gora, many walking for nine days from Warsaw.

[24] Runge's own words from *Letters and Writings* (E. P. Betthausen, 1872), 141 as quoted in Lynn Gamwell, *Exploring the Invisible* (Princeton, NJ: Princeton University Press, 2002), 67.
[25] Tim Wallace-Murphy, *Cracking the Symbol Code* (London: Watkins Publishing, 2005), 190.
[26] Ibid., 187.

Our Colorful Wisdom Mother (or Sophia, as I call her) appears in the obvious as well as the hidden places.

In her book *Colour and the Human Soul*, Gladys Mayer suggests "whereas in blue we abandon ourselves to the Universe, in yellow we experience the radiant force of our own being." This was quoted by René Huyghe who added, "A luminous center arises within us from which the rays of light radiate into the darkness constantly."[27]

It behooves us, then, to wear and surround ourselves with blues and yellows so we remember to send our light out into all the parts of our beleaguered planet and beyond.

Is there actually a spiritual being living within each color as Goethe thought? He believed that our souls live and expand through color. And he wasn't the only German philosopher who thought that way. So did Martin Heidegger, the famous philosopher most noted for exploring "the question of Being." Humans span the space on the earth and beneath the sky, he said. The blue radiance of the sky is not only sheer light but also "the darkness of its all-sheltering breadth." The dawn and the dusk of twilight.[28] This space between where numinous light dwells, Heidegger calls holy. This is the space that awakens, ensouls, and enlivens everything and it's specifically identified with the blue sky. "Blue is not an image to indicate the sense of the holy. Blueness itself is the holy, in virtue of its gathering depth which shines forth only as it veils itself."[29] Blue actually becomes one with the sky; blueness IS holiness.[30]

I like the idea that colors can enliven us. Especially colors opposite on the color wheel when they come together. They "do something" to our insides! Van Gogh said, "The nature we see and the nature we feel, the one out there and the one in here, both must permeate each other in order to last, to live." It is the soul that projects the complementary color into our internal vision. "Thus, the taking in of the sense world is always accompanied by a pouring out of the soul,

---

[27] René Huyghe, "Color and Interior Time," *Color Symbolism*, Eranos Yearbook (Spring Publications, Inc., 1972), 162.

[28] Martin Heidegger, *Poetry, Language, Thought* (New York: Harper Collins, 1975), 226.

[29] Martin Heidegger, *On the Way to Language* (New York: Harper One, 1982), 169-170.

[30] These ideas are explained more fully in Roberts Avens, *The New Gnosis* (New York: Spring Publications, Inc., 1984), Chapter IV, "Language, Poetry, Art."

for all the colors of the rainbow, the complementary colors are called out from within…For the mobile, yellow quality of soul, the blue quality of the world is required; the two together are needed to experience the soul of the world… Meditating on individual colors is thus a practice in strengthening the powers of soul needed to bring out the soul colors of things. Such mediation was one of the disciplines carried out in all of the centers of mystery wisdom…. In our time, this practice need not take place in mystery centers, but rather in the full presence of the everyday world…. Without the soul of things our soul is a play of shadows in a dark cave, a prison."[31]

In the Hadith, the collection of anecdotes about Muhammad and other founders of Islam, *The Cosmic Throne of Mercy* is described as having four colored light columns: white, yellow, red, and green. Each column is linked to four archangels: Seraphiel, Michael, Azrël, and Gabriel. This is all grounded earlier in the Iranian or Persian approach to fire and light.[32]

When light comes in through the stained glass, it splits into many colors. I stood under Chartres' western rose window, which is suspended directly above the labyrinth, and felt like even my consciousness was splitting apart. All I could think of was, "I must get home and research why I'm feeling like this — and what makes this place so special." That was my head, so enamored of Boston's libraries, speaking. But my heart just wanted me to stand there and soak it all in. Rudolph Steiner draws the analogy of that light splitting into many colors as similar to the single spiritual light, the Divine Force, flowing into the physical plane and being divided among the people. We all share it.

The Slovenian expert in geomancy, Marko Pogacnik, believes "evolutionary movement comes into being only at the level of the soul."[33] *Geomancy* is an old word that Pogacnik calls "sacred geography." It refers to invisible as well as visible dimensions of earth's landscapes. He has spent his life promoting a deeper and more responsible relationship toward our earth, the cosmos, and all beings. When he visited Chartres he had an unusual encounter. At one point, he stood under the famous lapis-lazuli blue window (page 231) where the Madonna's blue

[31] Robert Sardello, *Facing the World with Soul* (Hudson, NY: Lindesfarne Books, 1992), 130-132.

[32] Henry Corbin, "Les Couleurs en Cosmolgie Shi'ite" from *The Realms of Color*, Adolph Portmann and Rudolf Ritsema (Leiden: E.J. Brill, 1974), 176.

[33] Marko Pogacnik, *Sacred Geography* (Hudson, NY: Lindesfarne Books, 2007), 16.

is in stark contrast with the Christ Child's earthy brown clothing, so that, as he put it, they together represent the holy marriage of heaven and earth. There, he heard the words: "The cathedral is so constructed that it enables the Second Coming of Christ to occur at every moment — not as a future event, but now and always, when the principle of the eternal Soul joins with the principle of the eternal Earth."[34]

What does the metaphysics or "spirituality of color" mean to us today in a world so often depleted of color and surrounded by people in need of food, water, shelter, health care? We see the grays and graffiti of neglected neighborhoods and the dark entanglement of ruined structures after cataclysmic earth changes. We see sickening ash from fallouts, and we ask ourselves, "Where are the greens? What happened to the clear blues and the sunshine yellows?" Then I remember all the New Yorkers who plant daffodils and my heart soars.

Christian Icons

Don't expect Christian icons to be realistic images. For one thing, the people shown there have eyes that are much too big and mysterious. Their clothing seems trapped in the Byzantine era. They're not meant to be physical portraits, but spiritual ones. They're theology in line and color. Most icons are copied from earlier works onto thick gessoed wooden planks, reminiscent of how the first icon "writer" (icons are written, not painted), Luke, did it. He painted a portrait of Mary onto a table, legend tells us, which Jesus built. In some of the earliest icons discovered, Mary's robes are purple and dark blue with gold; she stands on a red carpet. St. Sophia Cathedral in Novgorod may be the oldest church building in Russia. It was built from 1045 to 1050. A famous icon of Sophia hangs there and visitors to Novgorod in 1200 described many lamps burning olive oil around the icons. Archbishop Anthony once counted eighty silver candlesticks in the dome of the church. Imagine this shimmering light flickering across so many holy faces!

Medieval icons were painted with scarlets and crimsons from small pregnant beetles found in oaks in Greece, North Africa, and Spain. After the beetles

---

[34] Marko Pogacnik, *Christ Power and the Earth Goddess: a Fifth Gospel* (Scotland: Findhorn Press, 1997), 189.

were steamed in vinegar, the colors were ready to use. Yellow pigments came from pulverized gall bladders of turtles or fish. Icon colors are predominantly reds and blues, and oranges, with some yellows and greens. Egg tempura is not gummy or oily, but clear and transcendent. They mixed egg yolk and rye beer and painted the darker colors first with lighter colors on top. The purples in Byzantine icons are a deep red-brown. And of course they use gold — the eternal Divine Light. If a medieval goldbeater had one ounce of gold, he could hammer seven hundred and fifty sheets of gold leaf, three-and-a-half inches square.[35] In Byzantine iconography they used twenty-three-karat gold leaf. When gold is added to an icon it's called an "assist."

I have a Sophia icon written by a Katriina Fyrlund of Varberg, Sweden, who studied with Russian monks. She covered my finished icon with linseed oil, crushed blackberry seeds, ox gall, and a secret combination of other ingredients known only to Russian icon writers, which, she claimed, will protect the surface for up to six hundred years. And she "assisted" it with gold. (Sophia Icon, page 232)

The Ecumenical Council of Nicaea in 325 officially defined the dogma behind the veneration of icons. Sacred icon colors take on mystical forms as the various images are created. The beliefs surrounding icons is that God is utterly transcendent and unknowable and yet God's transcendence has been bridged through Christ's incarnation and can be shown through the icon writer's eyes. Icons open up our inner senses. The Holy Spirit — Sophia — makes us very ordinary people capable of seeing in a new way. Icons unveil the dazzling brilliance of God's beauty inside everything. Or as the Syrian Saint Isaac put it, "they reveal the spirit within the flame of things." In Russian homes, I have learned, icons hang in the "red" or "beautiful corner" of the room.

Illuminated Sacred Texts

Christian Psalters and Gospel Books with jeweled covers, such as the famous Book of Kells, were created by early Celtic Druids who embraced Christianity without bloodshed. There may not be a better account of how

---

[35] Linette Martin, *Sacred Doorways* (Brewster, MA: Paraclete Press, 2002), 49.

they invented "green martyrdom" than Thomas Cahill's *How the Irish Saved Civilization*. These new monks left behind the comforts of home and retreated to nature, to islands, or up mountains to study scriptures and commune with God. They thought twelve men was about the right number for starting a new religious community and so they set out to seek insights from nature in their drive to turn darkness to light. They'd sit under trees and colorfully illuminate sheep and calfskin pages — each taller than wide. New manuscript sections usually began with large fanciful initial letters in their treasured Celtic style. Their intricate spirals and knot-work often created birds, cats and mice, otters and fish, and angels and humans all intricately intertwined. Letters were usually outlined in red dots, giving pages a rosy glow. Within a generation, they had mastered Latin, Greek, and some Hebrew so they could read and copy most anything. They translated important documents that would otherwise have been lost during Europe's dark ages.

The 370 folios (340 still exist) of the Book of Kells (page 230) may have been created on the Scottish island of Iona under St. Columba's management, and then taken to Kells to protect it from the Vikings. From there it went to Lindesfarne. It's a miracle it still exists since those wild Norsemen beached their *langskips* on that slender eastern peninsula finger of Christianity at least four times between 867 and 893. But they were looking for gold and silver, not painted calfskins. Then it was stolen in 1007 and wound up in a ditch, minus its jewels. It's now in Dublin. It's estimated that about two hundred calves gave their lives to create the vellum on which it's painted. Local red lead, chalk, and woad were used, plus imported pink (folium) and red (kermes). They also used red lead (minium), which later gave the name "miniature" to smaller illuminated books. Brilliant greens and shades of purples joined oranges and yellows when powdered gold or beaten gold leaf was not to be had.

Rich colors also appear in the tiny Christian books created in fifteenth-century Europe called "books of hours." They were known as "cathedrals in your hands" and portrayed Christian concepts and prayers in a high gothic style. Only the richest people could afford these jewel-like miniature paintings and elaborately decorated alphabets. Jean Duc de Berry, with his ten castles and fifteen hundred dogs, commissioned at least twenty different books of hours. The most famous, *Tres Riches Heures* ("The Abundant Hours"), was painstakingly created by three Flemish brothers named Limbourg. These artists used different shades of red from lead and kermes; blues from woad and ultramarine; verdigris, a green from copper acetate; light yellow from arsenic sulphide called orpiment. And, of course, burnished gold when budgets allowed.

Silver and copper oxides suspended in vinegar and fired onto an object gave a metallic yellow-copper color that reflected light. A "Blue Manuscript," so precious that its leaves were sold singly, was discovered in the twelfth century. It is said that the gold lettering on it was inspired by the stars in the dark-blue night sky. "The word of God is more precious than gold and lapis," according to the Qu'ran. Some art historians hold the theory that Islamic art is so completely filled with delicate imagery because they originated in the desert where people had a fear of empty spaces. It is said that before a master painter could be certified to paint these complex, intricate ornaments, he had to paint a design on a grain of rice by using a one-cat-hair brush.

In Geraldine Brooks' *People of the Book* she tells a story of a global journey following a book. It begins in Sarajevo during the spring of 1996. A Jewish Haggadah came to light there in 1894, which contained painted miniatures. Hannah, the main character who is brought by the UN to examine the book, says (as Geraldine Brooks obviously did in writing it): "By linking research and imagination sometimes I can think myself into the heads of the people who made the book..." The reader is then privy to how the book was created, which may be exactly how other illustrated codices were made. Gold leaf was beaten and folded into soft scoured calf intestines; lapis lazuli came from Afghanistan. Opaque white was made by a method discovered in Egypt — lead bars were covered with dregs of old wine and sealed in animal dung. The acid in the vinegary wine converted lead to acetate which in turn combined with carbon dioxide released from the dung to make white lead carbonate. Yellow came from saffron, each blossom containing only three tiny precious stigmas. Even though we can make yellows today, from carbon, hydrogen, and oxygen, they are not as beautiful. Greens from malachite, worm scarlet from insects crushed and boiled in lye until alchemists later learned to make red from sulfur and mercury.

A Haggadah is used in a home where children can learn "to tell" the story of the Hebrew Exodus. Being Australian, at one point Brooks speaks of Australia's art history: "Aboriginal people were making sophisticated art on the walls of their dwellings 30,000 years before the people in Lascaux chewed the end off their first paintbrush."[36] Noting red slashes across some figures, the reader learns that indicates that the spirit of the person depicted is killed. It's much the same way noses were broken off Greek statues — so they couldn't "breathe."

There is a Jewish legend that goes like this. God sent the Archangel Raphael down to Noah with a book of wisdom. In it was written all the secrets and mysteries of the world. Noah read it and that's how he knew that he was supposed to build the ark because a great flood was coming. He knew from Raphael's book that he was supposed to bring on board a pair of each animal. The book, made of sapphires, went onto the ark as well. And the most amazing part of this story is that it provided light for all the creatures on board during that dark and stormy time.

Moses was so pure he could gaze into even the hidden colors. "Therefore it is written: 'I appeared to Abraham, to Isaac, and to Jacob through *El Shaddai*, through the colors that can be seen... These are high colors, hidden and glowing." The colors of El Shaddai, we are told, are colors in a cosmic prism that can be seen. But Moses could see the hidden and invisible ones even without a prism.

Color and the Cabbala

I'm not Jewish, nor have I ever formally studied this complex esoteric system designed to capture a very old oral tradition. So I must rely on what others tell me about this mystical oral law Moses supposedly brought down from Mt. Sinai with him, along with the Ten Commandments. It literally means "to accept or receive." A Hassidic teaching tells us that Divine Light is in everything that exists. In the beginning, Light went through the universe and then it got stuck

---

[36] Geraldine Brooks, *People of the Book* (New York: Viking, 2008), 35.

in pieces of matter. Our task is to send it back to The Source. The Cabbala is one way of helping us do that.

The Cabbala was an oral tradition, sharing a common source with Zoroastrianism, until about the 1200s when it was first written down and when Cabbala schools were established in Europe. As far back as 763 C.E., a manuscript showing a wheel, rather than the more common "Tree of Life," captured portions of this ancient teaching. In the thirteenth century Moses of Leon wrote *The Book of Zohar*. In it, he describes ten "states of being" from The Source, on down. Each of these "four worlds" is so universal it can "unlock" any religious system. These "four worlds" can be described as archetypal, creative, formative, and active. Or looking at it another way, they are mystical, philosophical, allegorical, or literal.[37]

Many symbols and numbers including the ten circles on the Tree of Life portray what is called the *Sefirot*. This shows God's progression from infinite and unknowable to the active presence that created the universe. Each of the ten stages has a symbolic color attached — a color that symbolizes a person's relationship with God.

"Cabbalists speak of the Lightning Flash. Divine Energy that emanates from the Kether (the first Sephirach of the Tree of Life) and streaks through all the higher worlds to illuminate the earth."[38]

An Internet search will readily bring up many good illustrations of how the Tree of Life is laid out, with its ten circles and twenty-two lines and with the Kether, or crown, at its tip. But it would take decades to learn its intricacies. And even then, it's impossible to ever fully understand it all. God is not a "substance" to be known by us. However, light and color can help us come a bit closer to understanding.

The godhead, En-Sof (Sophia), is the light that withdraws and hides itself. It's a dark flame, neither white nor black, neither red nor green — nor any color. It's beyond metaphor and symbol. However, Cabbalists believe Creation to be an expression of the godhead's hidden life — so students of the Cabbala, from the thirteenth century onward, have attributed color to some creative powers of the Deity. A special role is attributed to white, red, green, and blue

---

[37] Edited by Roy MacLeod, *The Library of Alexandria* (London: I.B. Tauris, 2000), 147.

[38] David S. Rubin and Arlene Raven, *Reminders of Invisible Light: The Art of Beth Ames Swartz* (Easthampton, MA: Hudson Hills Press, 2002), 33.

(in contrast to black, which was the dark element/absence of color.) God's dynamic unity can be seen in the play of flame (Zohar). "In the change of this highest principle of form which breaks forth out of the darkness and out of the ether, ten forms and color patterns will arise which are reflected within each other, and multiply from ten to a hundred and, in the course of their increasing potency, will finally return to their original unity."[39]

The color green is important to the Cabbala. It portrays divine mercy. Two columns of the Sephiroth tree unite to form a third — bringing balance symbolized by green.

All powers are included in the Cabbala. It represents the presence, the immanence of God or as she is also called, Schechina or Shekina — the dark mirror in which the prophets revere God. Colors in the Cabbala form the background to the constructions that promote an understanding of the world as the expression of divine wisdom.

It's unrealistic to try to even begin to describe the Cabbala's complexity or the color codes within it. The interconnections between each separate Sepiroth are just too mysterious and diverse to pin down any one color at any one point. However, Cabbalists tell us that the sum of all colors can thus be synthesized in the colors of the rainbow (the basic colors as they describe them are white, green, and red). They devote great attention to the figure of the rainbow since it is the symbol of the pact between God and Creation.

Reading Our Soul Colors

"An abiding melody of color and sound echoes through the soul of each person. For some it is a haunting, lingering refrain experience as the clarity of purpose. For others, it is almost totally forgotten by the deafening noise of earth life. Nonetheless, there is an ancient melody of peace retained within the recesses of your god-mind and soul experience."

Ann Valentin *&* Virginia Essene, *Descent of the Dove*

---

[39] Gershom Scholem, "The Realms of Colour," *The Eranos Yearbook*, 1972 (Leiden: E.J. Brill, 1974).

If we could totally sink ourselves in a color, could we penetrate into its true nature? Would it bring us insights we may otherwise not have known?

In her book, *Hands of Light: A Guide to Healing*, Barbara Brennan suggests a way of reading the colors of the soul. "To read the colors of the soul level, clear your mind through deep meditation and then ask to be given the colors of the soul level. After some practice, these colors will appear on your mind-screen." She says all the colors of the rainbow are used in healing and each color "charges" the chakra that metabolizes that particular color. By becoming aware of the significance of colors — and by learning to use them to soothe, to heal, or to create places for action and rest — we can actually guide our present consciousness to harmonically attune itself to those higher levels we are constantly moving toward.

Colors, like our souls, have been with us from the very beginning. From Surah 35, Section 4:27, 28 of the Qu'ran we read of the marvelous colors of creation: "Allah sends down rain from the sky. With it we then bring out produce of various colors. And in the mountains are tracts white and red, of various shades of color, and black intense in hue." The footnotes to this text read: "These wonderful colors and shades of colors are to be found not only in vegetation but in rocks and mineral products. There are the white veins of marble and quartz or of chalk, the red laterite, the blue basaltic rocks, the ink-black flints, and all the variety, shade, and gradation of colors. Speaking of mountains, we think of their 'azure hue' from a distance, due to atmospheric effects and these atmospheric effects lead our thoughts to the glories of clouds, sunsets, the zodiacal lights, the aurora borealis, and all kinds of Nature's gorgeous pageantry."

But we won't see these colors if our souls are not ready to read them. "In the spiritual world that variation or gradation is even more subtle and more comprehensive. Who can truly understand it? Only Allah's servants who know, i.e., who have the inner knowledge which comes through their acquaintance with the spiritual world — it is such people who truly appreciate the inner world, and it is they who know that the fear of Allah is the beginning of wisdom.[40]

---

[40] Abdullah Yūsuf ʿAlī, *The Meaning of the Holy Qur'an* (Beltsville, MD: Amana Publications, 1999), 1109.

Viewed from space our earth is a blue ball swirling in silvery white. We look at it and know everything on that blue ball is connected to everything else. This is the only home we've got — we can't throw things away any longer because there is no *away*. This is it. We're it.

There is a special place in northern Vermont called the Green Mountain Monastery. On a visit there in April, I walked through the woods, past enormous Vermont boulders. It had been raining earlier so my feet, cushioned by the moss and wet leaves, made not a sound. I could hear a faint wind chime as the path opened out to a field. A mowed path led to a newly planted tree holding the little music-maker that called me here, a huge rock, an obvious grave, and a framed picture against the rock of a white-haired grandfatherly man. I had reached Thomas Berry's final resting place. I spent a few quiet moments with this eco-theologian whom scientists — and many of the rest of us — revere. He once said, "Never before has the human community been confronted with a situation that required such a sudden and total change in lifestyle under the threat of a comprehensive degradation of the planet."[41]

There are so many of us it seems we're squeezing every last drop out of our blue planet. "We are moving into a time of steel-gripped necessity — a time of intense, planetary compression," Dwayne Elgin said in *Awakening Earth*. He likens it to our falling into a pressure cooker of a super-heated planet. How do we maintain our colorful outlook? How do we keep from falling into the steely gray morass he predicts?

Lao Tzu, the Chinese philosopher born sometime around 600 B.C.E., once wrote of a vision he had in which he traveled to the world's very beginning. There, he saw Yin. Female energy. If I could have gripped his silk jacket and floated with him into that dark space, what would I have seen? Icy silver crystals hanging off every branch, perhaps. Lao Tzu said everywhere he looked, the world was filled with "motionless grandeur." Then he saw Yang — "rampant in its fiery vigor." As he put it, earth's quiet grandeur reached up to heaven's fire — maybe a blue moon kind of fire — and "the two penetrated one another,

---

[41] Bache, 236.

were inextricably blended and from their union the things of the world were born." As I walked I felt I was suspended inside that crystalline winter morning when the whole world was willed with white potential.

Llewellyn Vaughan-Lee says it's time now for feminine wisdom to be combined with masculine consciousness so that a new understanding of the wholeness of life can be used to help us to heal our world. Our souls, he says, are made of a quality of light that belongs to God and carries a knowing of its source. But, he cautions, bringing the light of the soul of the world into the collective consciousness of humanity requires perseverance and patience.[42]

I like the notion that we are building a new world for our grandchildren — indeed, as Christopher Bache puts it, a whole new species — *Homo spiritualis*.[43] By that, he means humans who have reached a true spiritual discernment — and I like to think that involves a new understanding of color as well — a spiritually awakened humanity.

One day I took a winter walk after I'd been reading the fourth book in Christopher Alexander's series called *The Nature of Order*. As a result, I was looking for living centers. I noticed that each shadow fell precisely where it is ordered to fall. Each tree stood in perfect living relationship to its neighbors and each branch was expertly placed one to another. The snow knows how to mold the rocks.

The sky took on a deep lapis-lazuli blue the likes of which I see only on crisp winter days. It was about three o'clock so the sun aimed its fiery path behind me toward the western mountains at a pretty fast clip. I faced a cloud-moon of light and dark, split exactly in half. It's strange to see the moon during the day. It's as if she's saying, "Whoops. I really don't belong here, but I wanted you to see me equally balanced like this. Later tonight I will be oh so bright against the white empty canvas of your yard, but right now I'm just a wispy-whispery thing sent to share a secret: it's important to be balanced... to keep extremes at bay."

---

[42] Llewellyn Vaughan-Lee, 11, 149.
[43] Ibid., 256.

I stopped to listen and could hear not one sound. Not a grinding snow machine. Not a bird. Not a dog. Not even the dropping of a twig. But wait. Between heartbeats, I noticed a trickle of water running under the ice. A tree groaned from the cold.

"Who," Alexander asks, "has not had the feeling, listening to Mozart's 40th Symphony or to Bach's B minor Mass that something significant is happening, that in some inner sense, the heavens are opening, and that this structure of sound somehow reaches in and hits the heart?" Who, indeed?

For that brief walk, the sun, the moon, the trees, and the snow all quietly chorused up to show me a universe of living beings. I realized then that I am embraced by nothing I can measure, certainly nothing mechanical, but definitely groupings of living centers that form an unbroken whole surrounding me.

Something significant IS happening and it continues to hammer at my heart. My prayer is that if you don't hear lapis-lazuli-azure-blue and all the other colors hammering your heart right now, you will. You will.

"In our life there is a single color,
as on an artist's palette,
which provides the meaning of life and art.
It is the color of love."

Marc Chagall

Colorful Voices

. . . . .

HILDEGARD OF BINGEN (1098–1179)

Hildegard became a Benedictine nun in the Rhineland area of Germany when she was about eighteen and an abbess while in her thirties. During her long and fruitful life, she authored ten books on such subjects as health and medicine, science, theology, cosmology, art, and politics. Her first book, Scivias, *(Know the Ways) contains thirty-six renditions of her images or visions and it took her ten years to write. She also wrote over seventy poems, seventy-five songs, Gregorian chants, the first Western opera, plus baskets of letters to popes, bishops, kings, queens. As one scholar put it: "She castigated a pope for his timidity and an emperor for moral blindness." She preached to clergy in all the large cathedrals and churches of her time. And for a time, she managed a monastery with monks and nuns before establishing her own monastery named after a Celtic monk, St. Rupert.*

She began seeing visions when she was three, but kept denying it until she became sick. She didn't recover until she began writing her visions down. She was the tenth in her family, and the one to be "tithed" to the church when she was only eight years old. They called her an oblate, a give-away, and as a result, she spent her growing-up years walled up inside a church with an anorexic nun named Jutta. Some of her original manuscripts were lost during World War II, but, fortunately for us, the nuns at Eibingen had copies. Matthew Fox, Barbara Newman, Barbara Lachman, Fiona Bowie, Sabina Flanagan, and many others en-sure that her words and paintings are still with us. For about seven hundred years her music and writings were virtually unknown outside of Germany. Even within Germany, she was not widely recognized, until recordings of her music began selling. Feather on the Breath of God *inspired many subsequent recordings.*

It's difficult to describe what I see... a stream of light washes over my face but I'm not asleep. I'm very awake. I use my inner ear to "hear" what I'm seeing and I make notes so later my dear friend and companion, Volmar, can elaborate on them. These dazzling flashes of light have been exploding around me all my life.

Once I saw a woman with crystal-clear brilliancy around her head and her body was bathed in red light. She looked like dawn. I think it was Sophia — Wisdom. I have seen her many times and red is usually her color. But once, next to her, I saw a little girl with black hair. I heard, "This will be a Mother — a rose blossom and a lily of the valleys. She will be mother to exalted children." It was the Blessed Virgin. Around her I saw a huge group of people, also brighter than the sun. Some were veiled in white with gold rings glittering around their heads. I heard the words: "These are the daughters of Zion." They were playing instruments and I was filled with joy from the colors and music. The light glittered in colors of purple and hyacinth and the woman in red seemed girded with fire. The colors were so vivid, I couldn't view them long before I fainted, trembling, unable to talk. I really can't describe this radiance, but it was so real, I felt I could touch it if I simply stretched out my hand.

Viriditas. Greening power. It's the exquisite greening of trees and grasses, and all that bears fruit. The Holy Spirit is greening power in motion. She makes all things grow, expand, and celebrate. I tried to portray this in the opening lines of my opera. I wrote: "In the beginning all creatures were green and vital; they flourished amidst the flowers. Later the green figure itself came down." The green figure is Jesus. He is the vine and we are the branches. Therefore, we, too, are green.

O, life-giving greenness of God's hand... the greenness of God's finger.... I sing the words and greenness becomes the light!

Our Lady Mary is the greenest branch of all. When she flowers, Christ appears to make all things green. The Holy Spirit — Sophia — is the cosmic force that floods the earth with greenness. When I wrote the play *Ordo Virtutum* I knew I had to open it with: "In the beginning all creation was full of greenness; flowers blossomed in the midst of it; later, greenness sank away."

Once in a vision I saw a great mountain. It was iron in color. Upon it was sitting a person of such very great brightness that I had to back away from looking at him. The mountain, and its strong gray color, I believe, shows the eternal Kingdom of God. All the wings I saw circling around offer gentle, soft protection. Eyes. Eyes. So many eyes. They appear all over bodies and they see with great clarity. The girl in this vision is clothed in a pale tunic with a white dress covering her feet. She is poor in spirit. A strong voice comes out of the mountain. "Wake up!" the mountain cries. Thus, I believe, does this iron mountain heal our souls.

There is only one light, one God. My paintings are attempts to capture this brilliant illumination — the universe surrounded by a firmament of fire. I saw a bright flame. There was an egg and it was lit by three torches at the top. The inner layer of the egg contains a gloomy fire so horrible that even I was unable to look at it. It shook the skin of the universe; but inside this gloomy fire lay the purest sky. Cosmic fire enters our human realm.

One vision showed me a light-filled person sitting on a throne with gold permeating everything. Another, a golden kite with little red balls, which are burning spheres or fireballs. The sun's energy of this fireball is the soul that possesses the heart of a child. The soul burns with the fire of deep understanding. The fireball is not flesh but comforts the heart of the woman who receives it. This soul-fireball pours through the limbs and greens the heart, the veins — all the organs as a tree gives sap and greenness to all the branches from its root. Like the fiery tongues that burn greenness and strength.

I use blue for compassion — it floods everything. I painted my own awakening with flames rising from my head. Reds. Oranges. Yellows. I show the egg of the universe with those colors. Sophia as Mother Wisdom holds everyone within her peach arms; her "mountainous" skirt and face are blue. Again, compassion. When I first saw this woman, she was transparent, like a crystal with brightness white as snow. How could I ever paint that? I wondered. Then I heard a voice say, "This is the mother and flower of roses and of lilies of the valley." In the center of her bosom stands a woman in red and all around her is a great tumult of persons brighter than the sun, all wonderfully decorated with gold and jewels. There is great joy and celebration. When I meditate, I hear celestial music and it is laced with gold and blue — and I see a very bright sky above celestial cities. Earthy active browns move me. Wheels and circles came to me in my visions and I feel compelled to bring out my most yellow yellows. I try to capture the red glint in fire. Rainbows come alive and in the center is a sapphire human being. Around this person is first a silver color and then a fiery red-gold. I see a rainbow within a rainbow within a... light circles.

I must share what I see, for I am God's mouthpiece. If God did not give us these divine sparks, how would the Divine Flame become visible? No creature lacks color and radiance. And wherever soul and body lie together in proper agreement, they attain the highest reward in mutual joy. *Gloria Patri et Fillio et Spiritui Sancto.*

· · · · ·

RUDOLF STEINER (1861–1925)

This Austrian, whom many believe to have been a genius in dozens of areas, called his spiritual philosophy "Anthroposophy," meaning "human wisdom." Before leaving to study in Vienna, he met an herb gatherer one day, Felix Koguzki, who taught him the "language" of plants, about healing and searching for knowledge. This older man told Steiner he had a task before him: "to show people how to reverse the plunge of Western thought and culture into materialism." At thirty-six Steiner moved to Berlin to became an editor, most notably of Goethe's writings. At forty he began to "see" and "hear" many amazing insights into our human spiritual development. Uncommonly prolific, between 1900 and 1925 he wrote three thousand books, only about two hundred of which have been translated into English, and gave six thousand lectures — often four, five, and six a day. From his spiritual investigations he provided suggestions for renewal: education (The Waldorf School), agriculture (biodynamic farming), medicine, economics, architecture, science, philosophy, religion, and esoteric Christianity as well the arts.

One of his books, Color, *was originally a series of pamphlets, and based as most of his books are, on a series of lectures. It was published in 1935 in London by Rudolf Steiner Publishing Co. and Anthroposophy Press of New York. It is in three parts: "The Nature of Color," "Color in Light and Darkness; Dimension, Number, Weight" and "The Creative World of Color." The preface is by his wife, Marie Steiner, and is, for anyone interested in color, a book well worth reading.*

> *"We become painters through a soul experience*
> *of the world of color, through learning to live with the colors,*
> *feeling what each individual color tries to convey."*

Rudolf Steiner, *The Arts and their Mission*

"Color is the soul element of nature and of the whole cosmos,
and we have a share in this soul element when we experience color."

Rudolf Steiner, *Color*

I try to anchor color into my daily life. Without my awareness of them, colors can float away. When we are really awake, and listen, deeply, to them, colors can speak to us in a celestial language. I can hear what each color is trying to say to me. I can, in a way, digest color. I internalize the color. Colors keep my soul soft. Lack of color hardens my soul.

Over time, I have realized that my eyes can grasp individual colors only one by one out of a complex of many colors, so I must concentrate on that particular color.

If the color is red, *I live the red.* I learn to pray into that color, and by *living in* the orange, for example, I can experience the desire for knowledge of the inner nature of things. Or if the surface is yellow I can feel myself transferred back in time.

Or I can identify with green and float over a green field. By shutting everything else out and concentrating on the green, I dive down into it. Then I can sense an inner strength. If I gaze on the surface of a colored sea, I can feel renewed inner health. I can feel this strength inside me and specifically for me!

And when I look at something with a blue surface, I feel the desire to surrender "myself." I feel as if I'm going through the world blessed with divine mercy. It's then that I know that the soft luminosity of blue is thus the luster of the soul.

But I must remember that colors never stand alone. Nowhere, for example, is the individual quality of red present all by itself. It is surrounded on all sides by other qualities, to which it belongs, and without which it could not exist. Nor do colors stand quietly. Suppose I have a blue surface and a yellow surface before me. Are these colors "real" or do I just think so? Everything vibrates — including colors. Everything moves and changes.

Color is something I see only in certain dimensions, but hues exist on the spiritual plane much finer than the colors we experience. When we let color speak to us in its true celestial language, we begin to communicate with angelic beings. A distinction must be made between the color of the object and the soul's inner experience of the color. I can look in all directions and feel the power of light and color, and then that can become a revelation of what lives in the spiritual world.

So I have learned to know the inner nature of color. The world comes alive in colors. Green is no longer lifeless. It lives! Peach actually forms my skin. When I think about peach, I see a vital, healthy tone that lies between white and green. Just as we can sense a dead image of life in green, so we can feel in the peach-blossom color a healthy living image of the soul. White becomes my psychic image of my spirit. Black can be lifeless. Light and darkness both live in the soul. I *live* in colors.

Black and white must be counted as colors. I have detected four colors with soul-character: black, green, peach blossom, and white. Red carries the luster of the living; violet is the soul being. White and black play into red and violet to create peach blossom. Colors are more than "objects" on some surface. Red, for instance, can attack. Red can make me want to run away. It pushes me back. Violet-blue runs away from me and gets darker and darker. In red-yellow, I CAN see streams of fear, and when I look at the blue-violet I feel that I'm looking into the seat of all courage and valor. The whole rainbow reveals something like a spiritual waltz.

I live suspended in light and color and the air around me is the shadow of light. Under certain circumstances, the air gives rise to deep shadow. If color is present, the air no longer reflects the color, but the color is real. Leonardo da Vinci understood this fluid, watery aspect of color and painted light and shadow as no one else had before.

Art, science, and religion were once inseparable. They can be again. To experience color in a painting, for instance, the soul is free to move about in the cosmos. Every color has a direct relationship with something spiritual.

Children know how to bring color into form. They paint out of their joy or their sadness. They feel the colors and paint what arises from their souls. This may be what Jesus meant when he suggested we become as little children. It's what the painters of the Renaissance, Raphael, Michelangelo, and even Leonardo, did. They really *lived* color. Artists don't bring the Divine down to earth by letting it flow into the world, but by raising the world up to the sphere of the Divine. That's the power of color.

I prefer to paint with plant colors rather than mineral colors because they are more alive. And I like to paint right out of the pot rather than mix my colors on a palette. When I paint with blue, I'm satisfied only when I paint it darker at the edge and lighter toward the center. When yellow speaks, it's stronger in the center and gradually fades toward the periphery.

When I study the masters, I see that color is usually the active ingredient. In Titian's *Ascension of Mary* I can hear greens, reds, and blues crying out. I can feel how Titian lived in the element of color and by using color, he really reacted to three worlds: lower, middle, and the heavenly heights. Mary's world in the intermediate realm where a dull darkness from below connects her feet and legs with the earth. Above her is the third and highest realm where her head radiates in dull light, lifting her whole body up. The formless angels could be clouds as if they're passing into wisdom. The Apostles stand down below in brown tones, in earth's gravity. Mary soars up through the colors.

Color is a spiritual reality. Colors correspond to the character of ideas. Because I am physical, psychic, and spiritual, color can never be "just" a physical experience, but also a psychic and spiritual reality. Ideas born from a purely sensual instinct have different colors than those serving noble beauty and eternal good. Ideas that help us ascend are bright yellow; ideas born of the sensual life carry shades of red; ideas springing from devoted love are a marvelous pink. Color helps us move beyond discord and dissonance and to "worlds" where conflict and contradictions simply don't exist.

Our senses have become so dulled that for many of us, colors no longer speak with integrity. But as we evolve, we will be able to see them with greater intensity. Intuition and observation are the sources of our knowledge. I have "foreseen" things. I have "seen" a time when light is woven and gleaming around ascended humans. All will abound there in an infinite fullness of life and color, where we will follow our hearts with wisdom.

. . . .

WASSILY KANDINSKY (1866–1944)

Kandinsky was born in Moscow, studied music, and lived in Odessa, where his businessman father ran a tea factory. He became a lawyer and taught law before moving to Germany in 1896. In 1901 he founded Phalanx, an art group, in Munich and started a school, in which he taught himself to paint. For four years Kandinsky had arranged twelve exhibitions of the painters who were Phalanx's members. During WWI he returned to Russia, but then was invited back to Germany to head the fresco shop and teach color theory and drawing at the Bauhaus from 1922 to 1933. He had already published his famous work, Concerning the Spiritual in Art, *in 1913. He had his students play with chromatic opposites and devised many color codes and systems. Between 1926 and 1933 Kandinsky painted 159 oils and 300 watercolors. Many of them, unfortunately, have been lost after Nazis declared Kandinsky's and many other artists' paintings to be "degenerate." He published* Point and Line to Plane *in 1926.*

His last decade was spent in Paris, where he turned to more nuanced colors, more biomorphic forms, and continued to believe that "abstract" art was really "concrete" art, connected to common laws of the cosmic world. His ten large-scale paintings entitled Compositions *were among his most ambitious works.*

Bright, juicy greens — I've loved them since I was three. I don't remember what objects the colors were on, but I do remember those amazing colors: carmine red, yellow, black. Ever since, I've found colors to be more important than forms. But I am fond of linking colors to geometric figures. A yellow triangle. A blue circle. A green square. Each has a unique spiritual value. Keen colors are suitable for sharp forms and soft, deep colors for rounded forms. I have grown to disdain yellow, but a cold light red is always pure.

Colors can speak, if we but listen. I learned as a child to hear colors. Wagner's *Lohengrin* has red trumpets, green violins, blue cellos, violet bassoons. It seems to me that flutes are a lighter blue than bass strings. Maybe it's because I play the cello, I can feel my whole body ringing when I'm near deep blue. I remember bits of the poem I once wrote about blue: "Blue is profound. Blue, blue got up and fell... Fat Brown got stuck — it seemed for all eternity... White leap after white leap... and another white leap... Then Crash!"

Colors are warm or cool and as a result, they either advance toward yellow or to blue. Orange is sometimes rung from a steeple; sleigh bells have a light raspberry color.

If you draw two circles and paint one yellow and the other blue, the yellow will spread out from the center toward you and the blue will recede, retreating like a snail into its shell. And gray is motionless.

Franz Marc and I loved horses — how we loved horses. So I guess *The Blue Rider* almost invented itself. We named it after that painting I finished in 1903 of a blue horseman. Too bad the journal only lasted four years, but we gave it our best. I feel more of a man around blue. I think Franz and I both did. We used to laugh. I like to think he's still laughing in spite of the sadness at Verdun and the bloody war.

Blue brings me to God. When blue deepens to black it's almost too sorrowful for me to look at. It's an organ tone, deep, mournful. The brighter it is, the more white I add, the less I can hear it. It's sad to think that one day my inner ears will be so dim I can't hear the colors singing.

Ever since I fell under the spell of Monet's *Haystack in the Sun* at a Moscow exhibition, I've known color is all-sufficient. Monet taught me the hidden power of the palette. But how can I explain to people how my soul vibrates with color? So many don't even believe they have a soul, much less one attuned to that quiet place inside. Sunrise and sunset links yellow, blue, and red together and ties it to my heart.

What are colors and form for, if not to affect one's very soul? There are three pairs of colors that create this soul-harmony: yellow-blue, red-green, and orange-violet. I admit, my ideas of color spring from my love of Russian and late Byzantine art. Earthly yellows, halos, icons, angels, celestial blues. We hang, balanced between yellows and blues. And in between, green can be madness or tranquility. What, I wonder, is the color of fear? How is it that one color can affect each spectator differently? Each color is precise, yet imprecise. We "think" we know what the color means. But do we?

Do colors always have to mean something? Does yellow mean "envy?" No. Colors aren't signs for something else. They are of themselves and speak directly to our emotions. Every form says something but we may not always get the message... likewise every color says something to us. We can hear them speak, if we are listening. Yellow, as an earthy color, has no real profound meaning. Vermillion, on the other hand, has a feeling of sharpness and orange is convinced of its own powers.

One of my young protégées, Robert Delaunay, wrote me about his discoveries in which he called color "the fruit of light." He's right. It's our foundation. Our language. Colors have four shades of appeal: warm and light or warm and dark, cold and light or cold and dark. Yellow is a keen color, best suited to sharp forms; soft, deeper colors like blue are more suited to rounded forms. The most movement is found among primary colors. Orange is red brought nearer to humanity by yellow; violet is red withdrawn from humanity by blue.

I do not necessarily believe, as Steiner taught, that yellow leads to "higher worlds." Nor do I concur with Goethe's understanding that blue has a more demonic character. Both earthly yellow and celestial blue have places in our lives. We live here *and* there. Likewise, black and white both are realities in our lives. In white is a great silence like pauses in music. It's not dead, but rather filled with possibility. Black, on the other hand, has an inner sound of nothingness, an eternal silence without hope. We move between the two on an ever-sliding scale of grays.

Abstract art is purely spiritual art. But art without a "what" is art without a soul. The artist must have something to say. The artist must recognize inner reality. Color can move the spectator's soul. We artists have to be concerned about the effects, the results, and the consequences of color. Color can titillate, like spicy food; color can calm or cool one, just as if you'd run your finger over ice. Those are the physical effects of color. But color also reaches the emotions of the beholder.

The inner character of color provokes a mood. The older I get, the more I know that color has a profound and direct effect upon my very soul. We don't know enough yet about how color can so affect our entire human bodies but its scent and its power are very real.

When is a painting done? People like to ask that question. It's done when it's internally fully alive. Art and color have purpose. We must never think it exists only for its own sake.

Color is the keyboard. The eye is the hammer. The soul is the piano, with its many strings. The artist is the hand that purposefully sets the soul vibrating by means of this or that key. Thus it is clear that the harmony of colors can only be based upon the principle of purposefully touching the human soul. Emotions, deep down, vibrate. It's an abstract vocabulary, but nevertheless real.

I believe colors can stimulate a spiritual vibration within the sensitive soul and artists are here to be spiritual leaders. Color provokes a psychic vibration. Color hides a power still unknown but real, which acts on every part of the human body. We're here to examine the inner world of the soul. Passionately. Intensely. We're here to revitalize people's spiritual selves. You might say art is faith and the artist is the priestly figure leading the way. But to do that, the artist must have something to say.

A MEDITATIVE PALETTE

"Craving color like a drug, we will rise at dawn,
or trek long distances to scenic lookout points,
just to drink color from the fountains of the sun."

Diane Ackerman, *Deep Play*

Immersing ourselves in colors in an intentional way deepens our connection to the world and helps us grow spiritually. In other words, color feeds our souls.

Next time you look at a rainbow, ask yourself what it is you're really seeing. Which colors are hidden? Which are obvious? What are they saying to you? Wash yourself in this heavenly spectrum. Think of it as a bridge taking you to a different dimension where colors will be brighter, even more varied — if that can seem possible — and in hues that sing.

Sufi mystics meditate on flowers. I have to believe it is the colors they are contemplating. They do it to experience the angelic nature of the flowers, believing that every material thing has an angelic or spiritual counterpart that can be accessed through interpretive reflection.[1]

Paul Klee said color is the place where our brain and the universe meet. In an attempt to join our brains, our senses, to the universal realm of color, I invited my friend, Boston-based watercolorist Julia Blackbourn, to create abstract paintings that would capture the essence of various "moving" hues, thereby providing, without using form or line, light or shadow, a new way to experience color. I chose fourteen colors, believing you could readily supply black and white. In standard English, we name only eleven in common usage: black, white, red, yellow, green, blue, brown, purple, pink, orange, and gray. I added peach, magenta, aqua/teal, violet, and indigo to that "standard" list.

---

[1] Suzanne Zuercher, *Enneagram Spirituality* (Notre Dame, IN: Ave Maria Press, 1992), 157.

Julia decided to meditate before she created the colored abstracts, and use the colors that "called" to her. Then I meditated on her work as I wrote the "Colors Speak" portion. Finally, you, as the reader, might choose to mediate on both the visual image and the written words. This would, in effect, create a trinity of possibilities — a three-way experience as you add your own personal insights evoked by each color. You will, in that way, build your own personal palette. One that you may return to again and again. Maybe you'll decide to create your own color wheels. Imagine, for instance, that you meditate and a particular color comes to you. Say, red. So you decide to create your own red color wheel using paints, crayons, cut-apart paper, or your own creative method. Or choose paint chips or fabric swatches. Perhaps you'll just write your color insights into a journal or put everything into your own color scrapbook.

An interesting exercise might be to think of a word: *circus, dusk, silence...* and then using only color, "paint or color" it, but without form. Which colors come to you that "mean" that particular concept or idea?

However you wish to record and build on the concept of what color means to you, it will be meaningful.

Choosing a Color

You can think of your color selection as a way to tap into your inner wisdom. Or gather your meditative thoughts. Colors will appear. As you play with your own color choices, you will find yourself drawn to some over others. Or you can close your eyes and choose one at random. Some people prefer using a dowsing technique like a pendulum to draw them to a specific color to concentrate on. You can determine "Is this the color I need right now?" by the direction of a "yes" or "no" spin.

Select any color. Trust that the color you choose is the color wishing to speak to you right now. Feel that color's deep connection to all the other colors — the opposites or complements, as well as the ones lying closest to it on the color wheel. Perhaps you'd like to make your own set of color cards so you can shuffle them and play with them in various ways. Or you can use Julia's watercolor abstracts in various ways.

You may find that you want to work through the colors in a "chakra" or rainbow sequence, moving from one to another up from your "root chakra" or red color.

As you clear your mind and concentrate, you may discover actual body sensations rising up from your intense focus on that particular color.

Additional insights to how colors may "speak" to us can be found in *Hunab Ku: 77 Sacred Symbols for Balancing Body and Spirit*.[2] My son, Joel, and I organized it by the seven chakra colors beginning with red and ending with violet. Light [and color] reminds you to give your imagination free rein; let it blossom. This is a time to birth your imaginings into reality by using your magician's power of illumination and transformation.

Interacting with Color

Imagination is a spiritual seeing and inspiration is a spiritual hearing. Color and light will "speak" to us if we quiet our minds, relax our bodies, pay attention to our breathing, and focus on a particular color. You may discover that reds, oranges, and yellows will likely fade way; greens, blues, and violets are perceived more clearly. But everything about that color will begin to feel as if it is alive and constantly in motion.

This will be an opportunity for you to use color and energy. Energy follows thought, so you will be using your mind and your body, particularly your hands, for they are quite sensitive. Rub them together for half a minute or so and bring your hands, palms together, out in front of you — but don't let them touch. Can you feel anything? A pull? Draw them slowly apart — feel anything? A pulsing or a building and receding pressure? Imagine an "energy ball" between your hands. Now choose a color and hold a ball of that color between your hands. Or pass your hand over one of Julia's color plates of the color you choose. Do you sense any change in "pull"? You may wish to close your eyes and place your dominant hand over the color. Now the other one. Is there a different feel? Soon you may be able to detect each color merely by touching it and feeling its energy.

---

[2] Karen Speerstra, Joel Speerstra, *Hunab Ku* (New York: Crossing Press, Random House, 2005).

Reiki practitioners learn to sense body energies with their hands even without touching a person's skin. If you are particularly sensitive you might be able to raise and lower the temperature in your hands by simply thinking about it. Visualize red and see if they get "hotter." Visualize blue and see if they cool down. You can, by breathing deeply and relaxing, apply coolness to someone's aching head, for instance, by visualizing a cool blue color.

I have a friend who was in a bad car accident. Her Reiki practitioner sensed areas of greatest pain and as he placed his hands over her knees, she went into a meditative state — first a chaos of images reflecting her physical state. A cacophony of images and colors filled her inner mind. At the end of the session she felt as if she were suspended in a clear, quiet blue.

Note how you're feeling as you gaze for a short period of time on a particular color. What emotions surface for you? Where in your body might you have been affected by what happened that day? Breathe the color in. Let it flow deeply into you. Continue this for awhile until you actually feel more balanced.

Meditate by "Color Breathing"

Meditating by color breathing can be done in various ways. Morton Walker suggests you breathe rhythmically from twelve to eighteen times a minute but not as the last exercise you do before falling asleep. It's too revitalizing and may keep you awake. He suggests that you first imagine white light entering your body from the cosmos, through your head and moving down to your extremities. Now draw from this spectrum of all light the colors you desire. Next visualize reds, oranges, and yellows coming up through your feet from the earth. Blues, violets, and indigoes arrive in your body through the atmosphere and enter vertically through your head. Now imagine green coming in from a horizontal plane. Finally, bathe your body in white light. "The color-breather is a deep breather who is conscious of the Universal Life-Spirit that is around him. The Universal Life-Spirit lends healing strength. With each deep inbreathing, the color healer draws in a portion of this power. He does this inhalation while consciously feeling the grandeur of being in harmony with the Infinite."[3]

---

[3] Morton Walker, *The Power of Color* (New York: Avery Publishing Group, 1989), 102-103.

Ken Cohen, on the other hand, suggests visualizing colored gems and his color sequences don't necessarily match the conventional chakra colors. He suggests inhaling five times five different colored lights into various parts of your body. These five colors carry with them strong archetypal primal forces. First, inhale white light into your lungs and when you exhale, the dark light leaves your lungs. Your lungs will become like a white pearl. Next focus on kidneys and inhale deep ocean-blue light. Exhale the toxins. With each breath, imagine your kidneys glowing with wonderful sapphire blue. Next become aware of your liver and inhale forest green until it glows like an emerald. Now breathe into your heart a healing red light and it will glow like a ruby. Finally inhale yellow light into your spleen and it will glow like a topaz. "Enjoy this image as long as you wish, then let them dissolve and disappear in simple awareness of the body. Notice if your internal organs feel different. How alive are you now, compared to the beginning of the meditation?"[4]

Gordon-Michael Scallion also suggests using colored stones and gems. Or large panels of poster board in the seven colors of the prismatic spectrum. He calls it spectral analysis. It's important that red, yellow, and blue are very true colors. Close your eyes, touch the colors, sense them without seeing them with physical eyes and note how they make you feel. Place colors near your bed to see if you sleep any differently. Be conscious of what colors you're wearing or carrying around with you.[5]

Breathe in through your nostrils and out through your mouth. That's one very good way to be revitalized. Hold the in-breath a few seconds before exhaling. After doing this for a while, try breathing in the seven rainbow colors, one at a time. Breathing a particular color in for a few minutes may give you a noticeably "different" feeling. Each color you try may energize or warm you in different ways. Each color can "speak" to a particular part of your body and for a specific purpose. If you wish, you can read the "Colors Speak" section for additional help in better tuning in to a specific color.

---

[4] Ken Cohen, *Colored Light Meditation*, (Louisville, CO: Sounds True), 168.
[5] Gordon-Michael Scallion, *Notes from the Cosmos* (Los Angeles: Matrix Institute, 1987), 93-95.

Try breathing color in through your fingertips. Feel them tingle with this wonderful hue, feel the swirls and values enter your hands and move through your bones. Imagine your bones being hollow like a bird's so the color bathes your marrow. Pretend the color is electric and you have become electricity, carrying this particular color to your every pore.

Now imagine a blue ball. Make it into earth as seen from space. Some people see it as a "blue pearl." Imagine the white clouds swirling over the expanse of blue; see the continents being held by blue. Now, invite blue to bring in powerful peaceful thoughts in order to touch every living being on that fragile blue ball. Every breathing being. Every plant and tree. Every rock and mountain. Every trickle of water, running down to join larger trickles to join larger streams, to join ever larger rivers, and finally to join the sea. Now let those blue waters enter your own bloodstream so you become one with the water. Bless it with your thoughts of plenty and purity. Clean it. Wash it with your love, for without this blue, blue water, nothing can live.

Trust your own knowing to be able to feel what each color is telling you.

Sense any heat moving up through your chakra points beginning at the root with red and ending with the crown as violet. Imagine the color going deeply there, spinning with pure clarity and with no muddiness or sootiness overlaying the pure color.

Let your green heart chakra meet the others, going down and going up. What is your heart telling you? Breathe deeply into every color you choose in order to access its story. Listen with your whole being to what it is saying about itself. Do you sense any blockages with a particular color? Was someone wearing that color once at a time deeply impressed on your memory? Why do you suppose your body is reacting this way? Does any color repel you and say, "Move on — you don't want to be here." Maybe there is a reason you need to explore further with someone qualified to help you dig a bit. We all need friends or professionals along the way to help us to see things we tend to overlook. Or if we don't feel completely safe doing it by ourselves.

However you decide to use the information here, rest assured, that color IS telling your soul something. And it's your job to figure it out. You are responsible for all colors! It's you who is seeing them. You choose certain colors to be around you, you tend and nurture them so you can "eat" them and grow from them. They feed you — each of them in its own way with its own nourishment.

As you reflect on a particular color here, you may wish to read one of the following "prose-poems" which I attempted to write in the color's "own" voice. It's my way of offering you an alternative and perhaps in some ways, a deeper way, to consider that color.

Color Speaks

. . . . .

WHITE

I can stand cold and clinical; or round, warm and soft. I am snow banked with blue and violet. Clouds over-washed with yellow and pink. Salt, clear-edged crystals of hard silver. Billowing sails, wedding veils, droplets of cream. Vanilla ice. Pure. Clear. Near. Dear. Divine.

Jesus, they say, threw seventy-two colors into a dyer's vat and I came out. Can legends be true? Why do Yorkshire fishermen fear me? Too death-masked to be a friend?

I am air. The quintessence of light. Innocent and pure. The soul-image of spirit. And I can be empty, bored, frightened, lonely. A polar bear on a sinking shelf. Emily Dickinson wrapped in gauzy muslin, white-framed in a lacy window. Moonlight in Vermont.

Albino. Albedo. Desdemona. White Buffalo Woman. Moby-Dick. Garlic and ginger, onions, potatoes, parsnips and banana peeled. Mushroom meat. Turnips to eat.

Silvery white birches in snowy moonlight. There is nothing so difficult, Renoir said, and at the same time so exciting, as to paint me — white on white. Snowdrops, daisies, paperwhites. Frost bites. Glassy snow globes. Ivory. Clergy collars. Pearly shells. Titanium. Zinc. Bubbles in the sink.

Rice cakes. Snowflakes. Chalk marks. Warrior caulks. White flags of surrender and the white dove of peace. I am maximum lightness, brightness. Simple. Reflective. Sublime. Porcelain dolls. Pale palls. Bitten lips. Ephemeral. May Sarton's white tulips turning brown at their tips.

· · · · ·

BLACK

Mysterious, restful, hidden. Maximum darkness. Subconscious. Prima Materia. Nigredo. Negative space. Outer space. Weighty. Solid. Strong. Sophisticated.

It's not fair. All too often I'm linked to death, rats, fleas, plague, hopelessness, despair, sleeplessness, depression, dark night of the soul. The inferno. Funeral colored. But I'm so much more. I'm life itself. Cave-Mothered. Black Virgins. Fertility. Womb-dark growth. Isis and Kali. Undersoil earthiness. Rooted. Rested. Relaxed. Regenerative. Replete and restored.

Pepper and ebony. Carbon and jet. Cats and night. Magnetite. Absence of light. Ravens and crows. Rubber tires tracking. Ink and coal. Lamp black, black on black, matte pottery glazing. Amazing. Black ball. Bowling ball. Black list. Black tie. Black eye. Black jack. Black magic. Blackmail. Black belt. Black velvet. Blacktop. Black market. Black holes. Black out. Georgia O'Keefe felt me, hidden away.

· · · · ·

RED (Page 217)

Look at me! See how strong I am. See my long wavelength, my passionate nature. I form your very root energy. Impulsive. Instinctive. Active. Hot. I conquer, courageously. I'm the color of martyrdom and revolution. Anger and danger. Scarlet fever. Mars and the Sun. I'm aggressive and assertive. Sharp. Glowing. I fly in flags and grab you in traffic. I make you stop. I don't distribute my vigor aimlessly. I'm always focused. I paint the town. I wake you up.

Call me a primordial paradox. Blood and war, blood and birth. Fight or flight. Splendid or menacing. Fertility... death and life. Devil and virgin. I'm crescent and cross, masculine and feminine, valentines and romance on the one hand and fighting and violence on the other. Brutal and heavy. Hunter's gear. Little Red Riding Hood wandering in the woods. Breasts of robins. Cardinals — the flying kind and the robed men. The brightest of maple leaves. Lava. Luck. Lust. Red Dye No. 2. Poppies. Pomegranates. Parades.

Adam carried my name from the color of the clay God used to formed him. And I'm also the apple. Who knows? Eve, like Mary Magdalene, may have worn my color in her hair. Cinnabar. Cochineal. Sacred ochre. Henna paste. Christ's blood. Dragon's blood. Bull's blood.

Babies see me first. When I'm on a page, I say, "Read me now!" "I'm special. Look at me." And when you hear me, you can't miss my low bell-tones. Dominant. Dynamic.

With yellow and orange, I'm fire. And sunsets. Call me strawberry. Cherry. Tomato. The Lancaster rose. Coca-Cola and holly berries to match Rudolph's nose. Dorothy's clicking ruby slippers. A fine wine. A radish. Vermillion. Crimson. Madder magic. Insects crushed. Rush, rush.

Red tape. Red carpet. Red alerts. Red necks. Red herrings. Scarlet letters. Scarlett O'Hara. Exploding star. Earth core and so much more.

· · · · ·

PINK (Page 218)

A "slow down" red, I think of myself as even more romantic than my more active scarlet sisters. I'm a young rosy lightness. Watery melon. A gentle, more feminine, spun sugar sweet candy. Coral. Blush-blood close to the skin. Flamingoes with angled legs. And there I am, bordered by beige inside a seashell. I'm in peach, and if they're feeling well, folks are in the pink. Pillow soft. But I can also be pink slips and pink elephants. Mostly, though, I'm raspberry rich with valentine vigor. Loving and kind, with romance on my mind.

· · · · ·

PEACH (Page 219)

I'm where all colors merge. I live where blue goes over to red and lodges in yellow. My blossoms, then, are where the spirit and the physical meet in a future cushion of fuzz. Peaches and cream. Peachy-keen. Like a light lilac, I tend to vanish into new forms. Fleshy soft and juicy... just the essence of your soul. I grow light and lighter and then disappear from hue, but remain the you of you.

· · · · ·

ORANGE (Page 220)

Dripping, sticky sweet. Not red, not yellow, but fragrant peels between deep warm layers of both. Peach gone bold. Marigolds and old gold.

Sometimes, I bring a warning: "Watch carefully. Take note." Emperor's clothes. Monk robes, mango lobes. Kumquats. Apricots. Honeycombs. Squash and yams. Pumpkins. Carrot and turmeric. Butterscotch caramel.

Tabby cats and ginger toms. Tiger lilies and the four-footed beasts for whom they're named. Fox brush. Citrus groves. Orangeries. Marmalade.

Solar disk and fired bricks. Terra-cotta rounds, loud autumn sounds. I'm warm, sunny, strong. Abundant. Confident. Self-sufficient. Lion's mane, my pride and joy. Ayers Rock at sunset. Catalan at noon. Amber agreeable and outgoing. Fruitful. Powerful. To be of good cheer, hold me near.

· · · · ·

BROWN (Page 221)

No one agrees where to put me; I'm left out of the spectrum. Some artists find me too humdrum. I nudge red-orange and slip into orangey-yellow. I'm tan-faced and desert-khaki clothed. Peanut butter. Chocolate, cocoa, coffee, whole wheat bread. Burnt toast. Burnt sienna. Burnt umber. Burnt ochre. Beef roast. Auburn. Copper. Mahogany. Warm russet, and rusty. Fawn and dark tea tawny. Monk dressed. Gravy blessed. Titian. Taupe. You see Mummy Brown? Rembrandt's in town.

Dependable, steady. Brazed bronze. Autumn's ease. Restful, warm though sometimes muddy. I'm chestnut, walnut and pecan. Polished wood. Beams. Planked floors. Grounded and earthy. Rooted and rich. Solid and stalwart. Tried and true.

. . . . .

YELLOW (Page 222)

Lemons and gold. Bananas, butter and cheese. Corn and coriander. Pine-apples to squeeze. Mustard-gild. Citron filled. Dandelions and daffodils. Waxy buttercups. Stripes on a bee. Sunflowers and saffron songs. Yellow brick roads. And, Aslan, of course, Narnia's noble beast. Krishna clothes. Spiritually radiant. Halo-sunny and rich, I strive and strengthen, embolden and lengthen. I'm proud to say, the brightest in the spectrum.

Airy as Libra yet solid as Taurus. Goldfish swift. Canary cheerful. Gen-tle. Sensual. But I signal danger — police tapes and adrenaline rates. Striped snakes. Jaundice. The "Other" triangle and star-marked. (You won't find me on airplane décor — I can make stomachs sore.)

With blue, I'm green. And am rarely mean. A wake-up color, chrome, cad-mium, with high energy and mental activity. (But bad luck in the theater.) I'm optimistic and cheery, sacred to many. Since I radiate in all directions, I'm hard to confine, but flaxen and fine. A luster like my blue and red sisters. Primary and Pure.

. . . . .

GREEN (Page 223)

Call me "in between." In between hot and cold. In between the joy of yellow and the serenity of blue. The offspring of Blue Hermes and Yellow Aphrodite. With that pedigree, I bring healing, harmony, and life. Cool growth, hope and the promise of spring. Verdant. Verdure. Verdigris. Grassy and ivy. Chlorophyll. You might say that plants own me. I'm malachite, emerald, and jade. Tree frogs and mossy bogs. The iridescence of a hummingbird. Flash of a dragonfly's wing. Cobalt. Celadon. The rare gleam in the setting sun. A flash. A brief bold band gone in an instant.

Tranquil and soothing. Sometimes jealous and moving. Vibrating and earthy. Fertile and steady. Lincoln green as Robin Hood's forests. Green Man.

Green Room. Green thumbs. Greenpeace. Surgery scrubs. Shamrocks, Ireland's most lucky. Machair green, Iona sea. Eternal gardens, Islam's most sacred. Mohammad's cloak. The gate of wonder.

Venus and love. Honest, reliable, stable. Evergreen pine. Elevated histamine. Pool tables, chalkboards. A magic fairy shade. Limes and grasshoppers. Leeks and lettuce. Absinth. Pickles, peppermint, parsley and peas. Broccoli and beans. Zucchini and kiwi. Spinach and sage. (Did you know Coca-Cola was green before it became brown?) Then, there is arsenic. And slime. Bold mold. Green with envy. Gangrene! Serpentine. The Green Lion... Vitriol. Corrosive.

I carry no undertones of grief — or joy. I'm neutral in my passions. Tolerant, wise, and steadfast. Wholeness. Harmony. I accept without judgment and offer you contentment.

. . . . .

AQUA-TURQUOISE-TEAL (Page 224)

Aquamarine. Tourmaline. Turquoise/Turquie/Turkish. Serious and cautious, I dance with small steps between all blues and greens. Like a magpie, I borrow everything from blueness and greenness and line my nest with both. Or like "Ch'ing" in Chinese: I'm the color of the sky and sprouting plants. Both. I'm more grounded than blue and less solid than green.

Named for Aztec gods, I'll protect you, like the gemstone around your neck. Or the color embedded into Egypt's scarabs. Old! As old as the blue-green algae off the Australian coast. So, I've been around for 356 billion years.

Gentle and cool, I am glacial green seas and wide and open calming Caribbean shores. Come, float with me. Relax. Open your arms and embrace all you see. That's me, welcoming all.

. . . . .

MAGENTA AND MAROON   (Page 225)

Bold and showy, I lean against red but bend toward blue. With pounding energy, I'm focused on achieving power. I'm ready to tackle anything that comes my way. I coil around Scorpio energy. Rigid? Perhaps. Willful, for sure. Hearts see me and beat a bit faster.

I'm dusty: a coal-tar discovery named for a northern Italian battle in 1859. (The French won.) Call me quinacridone. Or fuchsia. Ultra pink. Shocking. Psychedelic. Electric. Artistic, creative. Marooned. Self-sufficient. Rooted.

Mauve — a lighter, tamer, pinker me — inches toward purple.

I'm more hot than cold; more red than blue. Beets and plums. Hearty and hale. Leafy kale. Red grapes. Peruvian potatoes. Pomegranates. Eggplant. Aubergine. I'm meant to be seen.

. . . . .

BLUE   (Page 226)

Sapphire. Cyan. Cerulean. Chartres Mystery. Antwerp. Smalt. Lapis lazuli, the wine-dark sea. Powder. Wedgewood. Faience. Royal. Azure. Meek and profound. Once mixed by Mayans from clay and plants heated with resin. Or from Sar-e-sang, Afghanistan, the Place of (lapis lazuli) Stone.

Delphiniums. Lobelia. Blueberry sweet. Veined centers. Blue-white diamonds. Blue hands, blue eyes for good luck. Blue moons. Blue blood. Musical blues. True blue. The Blue Nile. Levi-denim blue. Out of the blue. Blue grottoes. The Civil War's Union Army. Airlines like me. I put people at ease. Cooks dislike me, preferring to be surrounded by yellow or green instead.

Once the Sistine Chapel ceiling was cleaned, there I am, a scarf around God! I'm Krishna-colored. Buddha lotus-blue. I make all other colors vibrate. I calm your heart. Open your throat chakra. Communicate with cobalt compassion, deep devotion. Seafarers read me in the sea. Elemental water and prophetic dreams.

What a hue! Welcome to my clear skies and somber seas. Aquarian cool color of truth. I stretch to infinity and to the sedate streets of celestial cities in the depths of heaven. It's a given, I'm the energy of the hottest, youngest stars. The brighter and whiter I become, the quieter, more serene. Tranquil. Cooling. Sedating. I connect you to your mystical self. Look inside. Meditate. Contemplate. Go to sleep. Deep. Deep.

· · · · ·

INDIGO (Page 227)

Indigofera — a short way to go to purple, yet woady-blue, tattoo. I'm a fighter. Woad against indigo. Old trade laws were passed and fines levied for how I was made and sold. I'm a priestly color, a royal blue, once worn only by the queen and nobility. In German, I am *gamüt*; I carry the sensitivity of feeling. Strong self-esteem.

I was made by ancient Harrapans in India four thousand years ago. I am deeper. Darker, even more mysterious than my lighter blue sisters. As I slip toward black, I can assume overtones of sorrow. Tranquil. Masculine. Sharp. Saturnine, Byzantine robes. Icon eyes. I'm darkness made visible in a Maxwell Parish sky.

Midnight blue.

I'm proud to be the first synthetic color — replacing rare ultramarine through chemistry. In the 1700s Diesbach was looking for red and found me instead. Accidentally Prussian! A mix of potash and animal blood, potassium ferrocyanide. Add iron sulfate and it's me. Affordable and brilliant. Then in Oregon in 2009 a new me was discovered. A grad student took some manganese oxides from a hot furnace and there I was resting on the tray.

"Mood Indigo." Indigo children. Sensitive. Aware. Connected to everyone. I assist with your dreams and your self-mastery. Antiseptic. Astringent. Intuitive. Third eye of the pineal gland. The seat of the soul. Insight I open to your spiritual awareness and offer eyes to the beyond. Heavenly grace.

· · · · ·

PURPLE (Page 228)

Transformative. Mystic. Active red; passive blue. Regal dignity. Sonorous. Livid, lofty, luscious. Mulberry. Blackberry. Orchids. Red cabbage. Deep plums. Wine and grapes. Shellfish dye-drops, Cleopatra's sails. Philosopher's colors. Emperor's robes. Majestic mountains. I'm rich, voluptuous, and ready to anchor your senses into a deep and very noble place.

· · · · ·

VIOLET (Page 229)

Gentians. Lavender. Violets. Pansies. Meditate under my presence. Your crown center — I am the consciousness color calling you to integrate all the others.

Call me the shortest wavelength. Then I become ultra and invisible. I'm amethyst points. Sharpening your passion for truth. Blissful. Dreamy. Wise. Wonderful. Willing to be silent, yet sharply awake.

· · · · ·

GRAY (Page 230)

Grey or gray? Neutral even in my spelling, I stay the middle course. Tread the neutral ground. I can be cold or warm, joyous or sad, dreary, empty and lonely. Tired and lackluster or brilliant with brainy matter. Salt and pepper. Like my brother, black, I am all colors.

Smoke and mice, elephants and eagles. Greyhounds and wolves. Doves and dapple grays. Grenadiers. Armor clad, iron sad. Cannon balls and muskets, greybeards, grizzled, frothy mouths muzzled.

Velvet shadows. Cloud-filled with monochrome mist. Foggy, fuzzed pussy-willow nubs and cobwebs glistening in the sun. The Burren coast of Ireland with its clints and grykes. The shale flats of Canada. A moon landscape. Granite and limestone cliffs. Humble stone stairs anywhere. Leaden battleships. Cool cement. Robes of Penitence. Moonlight silver. Rain-washed skies. Ash and mist. Pearly and powerful.

The hereness and the nowness of the dark gray stuff within each of us calls us to name it, to expose it, to change it. Face the shadows. Both/and. Old-bent, but wise and vital. Alive.

ANNOTATED LIST OF BOOKS ON COLOR

Alberts, Josef. *Interaction of Color* (Revised and Expanded Edition). New Haven, CT: Yale University Press, 2006.
> This book is by one of the most influential artist-educators of our time. Based on his Bauhaus experiences, Albers summarized here his experimental way of understanding color and their interactions. Practice for him comes before theory.

Alexander, Christopher. *The Nature of Order, Book Four: The Luminous Ground*. New York: Routledge, 2004.
> Chapter 7, "Color and Inner Light," is especially useful for anyone wishing a deeper look into the wholeness of color. The four volumes are a summary, as he puts it, "of what I have understood about the world in the sixty-third year of my life." He worked on these four volumes for twenty-seven years.

Babbitt, Edwin D. *The Principles of Light and Color*. 1878 first edition, Babbitt and Co., Science Hall, NY; edited and annotated edition by Faber Birren. New Hyde Park, NY: University Books, 1967.
> Babbitt, born in 1828, claimed he discovered the "form and constitution of atoms" and had surprisingly original views of how body, mind, and spirit work together—and how colors and light used in various ways can heal. He called them his practical applications, Chromo-Therapeutics. They are the "harmonic laws of the universe," he claimed. This is a combination of Babbitt's background as a scientist, mystic, physician, artist and essayist. Subsequent color writers relied on and quoted from his earlier wisdom. This edition has very helpful annotations by Faber Birren.

Ball, Philip. *Bright Earth: Art and the Invention of Color*. New York: Farrar, Straus and Giroux, 2001.
   With a background in chemistry and physics, Ball has written a comprehensive history of the materials of color. Besides covering, in depth, technologies associated with color and the tools of art, he presents a cultural history as well.

Barasch, Moshe. *Theories of Art, Volumes 1, 2, 3*. New York: Routledge, 2000.
   In this classic series, Moshe Barasch, Hebrew University, Jerusalem, surveys the history of art theory and traces hidden patterns, aesthetic developments and trends in art down through the ages.

Birren, Faber. *Color & Human Response*. New York: Van Nostrand, 1978.
   A brilliant combination of the practical as well as the more esoteric views of color as they relate to our physiological, visual, and psychological selves. It explores functional color from Birren's authoritative perspective — but much more. He draws from his extensive knowledge of biology and psychology, as well the metaphysical aspects of color.

Birren, Faber. *Color Psychology and Color Therapy*. New Hyde Park, NY: University Books, 1961.
   Comprehensive, as are all of Birren's books.

Bleicher, Steven. *Contemporary Color Theory & Use*. Australia: Thomson/Delmar Learning, 2005.
   Designed as a textbook, this lavishly illustrated book offers artists and students valuable insights into color theory, use, principles, and concepts.

Blühm, Andreas and Lippincott, Louise. *Light: The Industrial Age 1750-1900 Art & Science, Technology & Society*. New York: Thames and Hudson, 2000.
   This monumental collection telling the story of light, from many perspectives, captures the history of human perception and understanding with erudite prose and lavish illustrations.

Gage, John. *Colour and Culture: Practice and Meaning from Antiquity to Abstraction*. London: Thames and Hudson, 1993. Paperback ed. 1995.
   This lavishly illustrated (120 color illustrations alone) classic in fourteen chapters took him thirty years to assemble. Gage is a published authority on color, Turner, and Goethe. In this volume, he discusses the vocabulary of color, the materials that supply artists, and of course, the cultural aspects of color plus many color theories. It takes the reader from our art roots to Abstraction in erudite steps. It's been called a seminal book that has changed the perceptions of our generation.

Gage, John. *Color and Meaning: Art, Science and Symbolism*. Berkeley, CA: University of California Press, 1999.
   This book is a sequel to *Colour and Culture*, his massive earlier book. He's been called one of the best writers on art now alive and in this one, he explores many aspects of the meaning of color through the ages.

Gamwell, Lynn. *Exploring the Invisible: Art, Science, and the Spiritual*. Princeton, NJ: Princeton University Press, 2002.
   This large book undertakes the task of explaining modern art and modern science — the cosmos! She starts out with Romanticism and explores beauty in Western art, modern physics, and our inner ways of combining them. It's visually and intellectually stimulating.

Haftmann, J. Werner. *Painting in the 20th Century*. New York: Praeger, 1965.
   Strictly a painting book, but with some interesting insights into color.

Henri, Robert. *The Art Spirit*. New York: Basic Books, Perseus Book Group, 2007.
   Henri, an American artist and teacher, included here technical painting and drawing advice as well as inspiration based on his beliefs and theories. It's filled with quotations and short essay-vignettes about all aspects of art.

Jarman, Derek. *Chroma*. Minneapolis: University of Minnesota Press, 1995.
   A delightful romp through color by a controversial British filmmaker willing to blend philosophical ideas with edgy and often outrageous color images grounded in biography and poetic images that leap off the page.

Kandinsky, Wasily. *Concerning the Spiritual in Art*. New York: George Wittenborn, 1970.
   This was first published in 1914 under the title *The Art of Spiritual Harmony*.

Kuehni, Rolf G. *Color: An Introduction to Practice and Principles*. Hoboken, NJ: John Wiley & Sons, Inc., 2005.
   While more of an introductory primer on art principles, it is a concise overview of current research on color and presents it in fairly approachable ways, although there are many technical graphs and mathematical equations.

Leland, Nita. *Exploring Color*. Cincinnati: North Light Books, 1998.
   Although intended for artists, this book has a wealth of color information, both theoretical and technical, as well as poetic statements about color and insights into how various artists used color.

Livingstone, Margaret. *Vision and Art: The Biology of Seeing*. New York: Harry N. Abrams, 2002.

> Livingstone is a neurophysiologist who beautifully explains luminance and color as well as all aspects of light. She goes into great length about how we see and process color. Beautifully illustrated. This is a thorough representation of how we see color. One of the most interesting features are many of the photos rendered in color, juxtaposed with the black and white version.

Moholy-Nagy, L. *Vision in Motion*. Chicago: Paul Theobald and Co., 1965.

> While this book contains some good color information, it's primarily about educational approaches to art education and new approaches to design. I chose to include it because he was my first art-mentor (via his student, John Rogers, who taught me about the Bauhaus movement and introduced me to this Hungarian, along with teaching me the correct way to pronounce Moholy-Nagy. Hint: no "y" sound on Nagy.)

Malraux, André, translated by Stuart Gilbert. *The Voices of Silence*. New York: Doubleday & Company, Inc., 1956.

> An art history classic written in elegant prose. The section on "The Creative Process" is reason enough to read this one (again). His descriptions of "primitive" art and art of the antiquities expand our thinking. And his selective comparisons usher us into new ways of understanding what he calls "the museum without walls."

Maquet, Jacques. *The Aesthetic Experience: An Anthropologist Looks at the Visual Arts*. New Haven, CT: Yale University Press, 1986.

> A book that looks at the cross-cultural theory of aesthetics. It's filled with close observations of the human experiences of art.

O'Neill, Mary. *Hailstones and Halibut Bones: Adventures in Color.* New York: Doubleday Books for Young Readers; Reissue edition, 1989.

Why shouldn't a wonderful children's book find its way into this august company? Each color has its own story to tell and Mary O'Neill tells it like no one else I've discovered.

Ottmann, Klaus, editor. *Color Symbolism: Excerpts from the Eranos Yearbook,* 1972. Spring Publications, Inc.

This is a collection of six papers delivered at the Eranos Conference in Ascona, Switzerland, in August of 1972. The authors are: Adolf Portmann, Christopher Rowe, Dominique Zahan, Ernst Benz, René Huyghe and Toshihiko Izutsu. The theme of the conference was "The Experience of Color."

Portmann, Adolf; Ritsema, Rudolf; Eranos Conference Ascona. *Realms of Colour, The, Eranos Yearbook,* 1972. Leiden E.J. Brill, 1974.

The German chapters translated into English include: "Tradition and Innovation" by Peter Dronke, "Tradition and Innovation in Medieval Western Colour-Harmony," Christopher Rowe, "Conceptions of Colour and Colour Symbolism in the Ancient World" (see also in *Color Symbolism*), Dominique Zahan, "White, Red, and Black: Colour Symbolism in Black Africa" (see also in Color Symbolism), and Toshihiko Izutsu, "The Elimination of Color in Far Eastern Art and Philosophy" (see also in *Color Symbolism*.) For non-German readers, however, the English summaries at the ends of all the untranslated chapters are also of interest.

Riley II, Charles A. *Color Codes: Modern Theories of Color in Philosophy, Painting and Architecture, Literature, Music and Psychology.* Hanover, NH: University Press of New England, 1995.

After a decade of research, Riley, a professor of English at Baruch College, presents six interdisciplinary essays and draws parallels between them.

Sayre, Henry W. *A World of Art*. Upper Saddle River, NJ: Pearson Education, Prentice Hall, 2004.

> I read the revised fourth edition with Jim Sardonis' (a favorite Vermont sculptor of mine) gray whale tails waving up out of the snow on the cover. It's a comprehensive, classic text.

Shlain, Leonard. *Art & Physics: Parallel Visions in Space, Time and Light*. New York: William Morrow and Company, Inc., 1991.

> Shlain is a surgeon in California who writes erudite and compelling books. His twenty-seven pages of "color coverage" in this one furthers our understanding of the scientific aspects of "color."

Steiner, Rudolf. *Colour*. Hudson, NY: Anthroposophic Press, 1992.

> Color is significant in our human evolution. Steiner builds on Goethe's theory of colors and distinguishes between "image" and "luster" colors. He also offers insights into how color leads to creativity as well as health and well-being.

Steiner, Rudolf. *The Arts and Their Mission*. London: Rudolf Steiner Press, 1986.

> Steiner believed that art is stimulated and inspired by the spiritual realms.

Van Gogh, Vincent, Selected by W.H. Auden. *Van Gogh: A Self Portrait: Letters Revealing His Life as a Painter*. London: Marlowe and Co., 1994.

> A first-hand glimpse into the life of a complicated, talented Dutchman.

von Goethe, Johann Wolfgang. *Theory of Colours*. Santa Cruz: BLTC Press, 2009. Kindle download.

> Written in two volumes in 1810, Goethe's "doctrine of Colors" includes his scientific experiments and conclusions as well as a history of color theory, an examination of Newton's theory, and the third part is a history of science and color investigations. While parts are stand-alone essays, the whole, including his original plates, stands as a living testament to his genius.

Varley, Helen, editor. *Colour*. London: Marshall Editions, 1983.
    One of the most lavishly illustrated color books of all time! It brings
    together color consultants and specialists from across the spectrum (so
    to speak) and "celebrates the whole rich pageant" as Faber Birren says
    in the Foreword.

Walker, Morton. *The Power of Color*. Garden City Park, NY: Avery Publishing
Group, 1989.
    An older (and therefore more difficult to locate) yet excellent basic
    resource for information on full-spectrum healing including seventeen
    principles of advanced chromotherapy.

Ward, Mike. *The New Spirit of Watercolor*. Cincinnati: North Light Books,
1989.
    Ward is very knowledgeable about pigments.

ABOUT THE AUTHOR

Karen Speerstra is a veteran writer, editor, and author of seven books in print,
the latest being *Sophia: the Feminine Face of God.*
It is accompanied by a new ten-part audio guide available at
www.divineartsmedia.com.

Speerstra spent ten years freelance writing before entering the college text and
professional book publishing world. Her career and interest in travel have
taken her to many sacred sites in Europe as well as in the U.S. and the Yucatan.
She blogs on several sites including her own,
www.sophiaserve.com, and www.divineartsmedia.com.

Karen continues to aid others in their desire to write and to be published.
A mother of two grown sons, Karen lives with her husband, John,
in central Vermont, surrounded by her labyrinth and gardens.

INDEX

HERE ARE OTHER **DIVINE ARTS** BOOKS YOU MAY ENJOY

THE SACRED SITES OF THE DALAI LAMAS
Glenn H. Mullin   2013 Nautilus Silver Medalist

"As this most beautiful book reveals, the Dalai Lamas continue to teach us that there are, indeed, other ways of thinking, other ways of being, other ways of orienting ourselves in social, spiritual, and ecological space.."
— Wade Davis, Explorer-in-Residence, National Geographic Society

THE SHAMAN & AYAHUASCA: *Journeys to Sacred Realms*
Don José Campos   2013 Nautilus Silver Medalist

"This remarkable and beautiful book suggests a path back to understanding the profound healing and spiritual powers that are here for us in the plant world. This extraordinary book shows a way toward reawakening our respect for the natural world, and thus for ourselves."
— John Robbins, author, *The Food Revolution* and *Diet for a New America*

A HEART BLOWN OPEN: *The Life & Practice of Zen Master Jun Po Denis Kelly Roshi*
Keith Martin-Smith   2013 Nautilus Silver Medalist

"This is the story of our time... an absolute must-read for anyone with even a passing interest in human evolution..."
— Ken Wilber, author, *Integral Spirituality*

"This is the legendary story of an inspiring teacher that mirrors the journey of many contemporary Western seekers."
— Alex Grey, artist and author of *Transfigurations*

SOPHIA—THE FEMININE FACE OF GOD: *Nine Heart Paths to Healing and Abundance*
Karen Speerstra   2013 Nautilus Gold Medalist

"Karen Speerstra shows us most compellingly that when we open our hearts, we discover the wisdom of the Feminine all around us. A totally refreshing exploration, and beautifully researched read."
— Michael Cecil, author, *Living at the Heart of Creation*

NEW BELIEFS NEW BRAIN: *Free Yourself from Stress and Fear*
Lisa Wimberger

"Lisa Wimberger has earned the right, through trial by fire, to be regarded as a rising star among meditation teachers. No matter where you are in your journey, New Beliefs, New Brain *will shine a light on your path."*
— Marianne Williamson, author, *A Return to Love* and *Everyday Grace*

ENERGY WARRIORS: *Overcoming Cancer and Crisis with the Power of Qigong*
Bob Ellal and Lawrence Tan

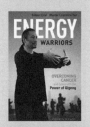

"The combination of Ellal's extraordinary true story and Master Tan's depth of knowledge about the relationship between martial arts and wellness makes for a unique and important contribution to the growing body of literature about holistic thinking and living."
— Jean Benedict Raffa, author, *Healing the Sacred Divide* and *The Bridge to Wholeness*

A FULLER VIEW: *Buckminster Fuller's Vision of Hope and Abundance for All*
L. Steven Sieden

"This book elucidates Buckminster Fuller's thinking, honors his spirit, and creates an enthusiasm for continuing his work."
— Marianne Williamson, author, *Return To Love* and *Healing the Soul of America*

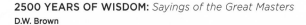

2500 YEARS OF WISDOM: *Sayings of the Great Masters*
D.W. Brown

The wisdom of the greatest minds on earth. All in one place.
This book of carefully selected and arranged quotations represents the greatest philosophical thoughts mankind has produced in its attempt to come to a deeper understanding of the human condition.

WRITING FROM THE INSIDE OUT: *The Practice of Freeform Writing*
Stephen Lloyd Webber

"I urge others to write from the heart to find their true artistic voice. Here is a book that profoundly helps one explore that mysterious personal journey. A navigation guide to our inner creative magic."
— Pen Densham, screenwriter, *Robin Hood: Prince of Thieves* and *Moll Flanders*

CHANGE YOUR STORY, CHANGE YOUR LIFE: *A Path to Success*
Jen Grisanti

"It turns out you can actually get a handle on your life problems by approaching them as an ongoing story that you can rewrite and direct for a better effect."
— Christopher Vogler, author, *The Writer's Journey*

HEAL YOUR SELF WITH WRITING
Catherine Ann Jones

"An elixir for the soul"
— *Psychology Today*

"This is so much more than a book on writing. It is a guide to the soul's journey, with Catherine Ann Jones as a compassionate teacher and wise companion along the way."
— Dr. Betty Sue Flowers, Series Consultant/Editor, *Joseph Campbell and the Power of Myth*

Divine Arts sprang to life fully formed as an intention to bring spiritual practice into daily life.

Human beings are far more than the one–dimensional creatures perceived by most of humanity and held static in consensus reality. There is a deep and vast body of knowledge — both ancient and emerging — that informs and gives us the understanding, through direct experience, that we are magnificent creatures occupying many dimensions with untold powers and connectedness to all that is.

Divine Arts books and films explore these realms, powers, and teachings through inspiring, informative, and empowering works by pioneers, artists, and great teachers from all the wisdom traditions. We invite your participation and look forward to learning how we may serve you.

Onward and upward,
Michael Wiese, Publisher